The Mass Media and Modern Democracy

RAND McNALLY PUBLIC AFFAIRS SERIES

The Mass Media

BY

ROBERT D. NOVAK
GEORGE E. REEDY
PETER B. CLARK
PAUL H. WEAVER
WALTER BERNS
A. STEPHEN BOYAN, JR.
GEORGE ANASTAPLO

and Modern Democracy

EDITED BY
HARRY M. CLOR

RAND McNALLY COLLEGE PUBLISHING COMPANY • CHICAGO

The essays in this volume were prepared as part of the program of the Public Affairs Conference Center at Kenyon College, Gambier, Ohio

RAND McNALLY PUBLIC AFFAIRS SERIES
Robert A. Goldwin, Series Editor

Edited by Robert A. Goldwin
- America Armed: Essays on United States Military Policy
- A Nation of States: Essays on the American Federal System
- Why Foreign Aid?
- Political Parties, U.S.A.
- Left, Right and Center: Essays on Liberalism and Conservatism in the United States
- Higher Education and Modern Democracy: The Crisis of the Few and the Many
- A Nation of Cities: Essays on America's Urban Problems
- Representation and Misrepresentation: Legislative Reapportionment in Theory and Practice
- On Civil Disobedience: American Essays Old and New
- How Democratic Is America? Responses to the New Left Challenge

Edited by Harry M. Clor
- Censorship and Freedom of Expression: Essays on Obscenity and the Law
- Civil Disorder and Violence: Essays on Causes and Cures
- The Mass Media and Modern Democracy

PRINTED IN U.S.A.
LIBRARY OF CONGRESS CATALOGUE NUMBER 73-21349

PREFACE

●

Recently intensified conflict between the news media and the government has stimulated a far-reaching debate between critics and defenders of the mass media in the United States. This volume of essays explores the basic issues in that debate, particularly issues concerning the character of contemporary political journalism and its relation to our democratic society. The essays are both analytic and controversial; they are systematic arguments representing different points of view.

One controversy is between those who assert and those who deny that ideological biases in the journalistic profession regularly result in distortion of the news. But behind this current conflict are broader questions about the nature of "news" and the functions of news reporting and commentary in a democratic society. Another set of controversies arises from considerations of freedom of the press —its scope and possible limits. Some of the authors in this book insist upon virtually unlimited freedom of the press to determine what it shall publish; others argue that some legal restraints are necessary to promote a responsible press. The contexts of this conflict over freedom of the press include foreign policy and national security matters, the right of individuals to privacy as against the right to publish information about individuals, and the propriety of requiring newsmen to testify and divulge confidential information in criminal cases. What is a responsible press? How is it best promoted? And what kinds of information do the American people need to have? Finally, there is discussion in this book about the effects of the mass media, particularly television, upon public morality, public opinion, and cultural values.

While these essays deal with matters currently in dispute, the underlying questions they address are questions likely to be with us for a long time. The questions concern the strengths and weaknesses of modern political journalism and the mass media in general, and their effects upon the health of our constitutional democracy. How do they contribute to the education or miseducation of American citizens? What kind of performance can we expect, and what should we expect, from the mass media?

This book, like all the volumes in the Rand McNally Public Affairs series, is the outgrowth of a conference held under the auspices of the Public Affairs Conference Center of Kenyon College. The work of the Center since its inception has been supported in part by the Ford Foundation.

The editing of this book follows the design of the other volumes in the series. The authors represent not only a variety of viewpoints on the subject under discussion but also a variety of professions and experiences. Some of the authors are practicing journalists, some are scholars who have devoted themselves to an important aspect of the subject, and some have combined both journalistic and academic endeavors. They were all invited to address themselves to long-range and theoretical concerns as well as current and practical ones. The premise of this educational endeavor is that these concerns can be brought together and that the combination contributes to political and civic education.

HARRY M. CLOR

Gambier, Ohio
January 1973

CONTENTS

THE EDITOR AND THE AUTHORS

•

HARRY M. CLOR

is Professor of Political Science, Kenyon College. His special fields of study include constitutional law and modern political philosophy. He is the author of *Obscenity and Public Morality,* 1969; "Woodrow Wilson" in *American Political Thought,* 1971; and "American Democracy and the Challenge of Radical Democracy" in *How Democratic Is America?,* 1971. He is the editor of *Censorship and Freedom of Expression,* 1971, and *Civil Disorder and Violence: Essays on Causes and Cures,* 1972.

ROBERT NOVAK

is coauthor of "Inside Report," a nationally syndicated political column. He also appears frequently on television as a commentator and panelist. His writings, both alone and in collaboration with Rowland Evans, have appeared in the *Saturday Evening Post, Esquire, New Republic, Harper's, National Observer, Atlantic Monthly,* and other publications. He is the author of *The Agony of the G.O.P., 1964,* 1965, and coauthor (with Rowland Evans) of *Lyndon B. Johnson: The Exercise of Power,* 1966, and *Nixon in the White House: The Frustration of Power,* 1971.

GEORGE E. REEDY

is Dean and Nieman Professor, College of Journalism, Marquette University. He was Special Consultant to the President of the United States in 1968; Press Secretary and Special Assistant to the President, 1964–1966; and Special Assistant to the President, 1963–1964. He has been Executive Director of the Senate Democratic Policy Committee, and United Press correspondent for the Senate and the House of Representatives.

His writings include *Who Will Do Our Fighting for Us?*, 1969, and *The Twilight of the Presidency,* 1970.

PETER CLARK
is President of the Evening News Association (the *Detroit News,* Detroit; WWJ-TV, WWJ-AM, WWJ-FM, Detroit; KOLD-TV, Tucson; WALA-TV, Mobile), and director of the American Newspaper Publishers Association. Mr. Clark's essays have appeared in *Nieman Reports, The Quill, Newspaper Controller,* and *The Congressional Record.*

PAUL H. WEAVER
is Assistant Professor of Government at Harvard University and Associate Editor of *The Public Interest* magazine. He is the author of several articles on the news media and a book tentatively titled *The Bias of News: The Form, Governance and Political Consequences of Daily Journalism in America,* to be published in 1973.

WALTER BERNS
is Professor of Political Science, University of Toronto. He is the author of *Freedom, Virtue, and the First Amendment,* 1957; joint author of *Essays on the Scientific Study of Politics,* 1962; editor of *Constitutional Cases in American Government,* 1963; and author of several articles in the Public Affairs Series, the most recent being "Beyond the (Garbage) Pale, or Democracy, Censorship, and the Arts," in *Censorship and Freedom of Expression,* 1971. He has written numerous articles for legal and political science journals.

A. STEPHEN BOYAN, JR.
is Assistant Professor of Political Science at the University of Maryland, Baltimore County. One of his major professional interests has been the study of First Amendment freedoms. He has published in the *University of Pennsylvania Law Review* on this subject; has authored articles in various journals of opinion; and has been a chapter president and state board member of the American Civil Liberties Union of Pennsylvania.

GEORGE ANASTAPLO

is Lecturer in the Liberal Arts, University of Chicago, and Professor of Political Science and of Philosophy, Rosary College. He also teaches regularly at The Clearing, Ellison Bay, Wisconsin. His fields of study include constitutional law, jurisprudence, classical tragedy, political philosophy, French-Canadian separatism, American government, and the contemporary Greek tyranny. He is the author of *The Constitutionalist: Notes on the First Amendment,* 1971.

ROBERT D. NOVAK

THE NEW JOURNALISM

I

On July 14, 1964, at the Republican National Convention in San Francisco, General Dwight D. Eisenhower roused the drowsy delegates when he read this line from the speech written for him: "Let us . . . scorn the divisive efforts of those outside our family, including sensation-seeking columnists and commentators, who couldn't care less about the good of our party." Neither General Eisenhower nor the thousands of journalists covering the convention were quite prepared for the reaction. Delegates rose in their seats with an angry roar, shaking their fists at the glass-enclosed booths containing Huntley and Brinkley, Walter Cronkite, and the other famous television journalists. In the tumult, it seemed as though the delegates, who a few nights later would nominate Barry Goldwater for President, were about to storm the broadcast booths.

The incident revealed dramatically an animosity toward journalism by conservatives which had been building for years. Time and again in that 1964 campaign and in the years to come, press buses following candidates would encounter jeers and shaking fists. The most intense reaction came from active conservative political workers but was by no means limited to them. Across the land the journalist, and particularly the television journalist, was distrusted and disliked by the ordinary citizen, who may or may not have considered himself a conservative but surely did not embrace the programs and policies of the liberal establishment.

This deepening change in mass attitudes toward the communications media reflected a gradual transformation in the media themselves through the 1960s and into the 1970s. The change was not dramatic transformation but an acceleration of trends begun some twenty-five years earlier. It consisted basically of two developments. First, the journalists working for the television networks, the big news magazines, and the important metropolitan press had now become part of the liberal establishment, both in their manner of living and in their ideological commitment. Second, in a later and less fully developed trend, these journalists were increasingly advocating causes of the moment rather than functioning as neutral observers. Taken together, the developments widened the gap between the mass media and the great mass of citizens, a gap that can result only in diminished credibility of the media, and therefore the inadequate fulfillment of the necessary function of the press in a democratic society.

II

In *Commentary* of March, 1971, Daniel P. Moynihan wrote:

> One's impression is that twenty years and more ago, the preponderance of the "working press" (as it liked to call itself) was surprisingly close in origins and attitudes to working people generally. They were not Ivy Leaguers. They now are or soon will be. Journalism has become, if not an elite profession, a profession attractive to elites. This is noticeably so in Washington, where the upper reaches of journalism constitute one of the most important enduring *social* elites of the city, with all the accoutrements one associates with a leisured class. (The Washington press corps is not leisured at all, but the style is that of men and women who *choose* to work.)

Moynihan's article generated a storm of angry rebuttal from Washington journalists. In fact, Moynihan had missed the mark in the details of his formulation. As Martin F. Nolan pointed out in the *Boston Globe,* the press corps contained more alumni of Boston College and the University of Illinois than of Harvard and Yale. Only a tiny fraction of them moves easily in the upper social circles of Washington. Even a tinier fraction possesses independent financial means. These people work because they *must,* not because they *choose* to.

But having pointed out these misperceptions, we must admit that Moynihan is basically on the track. The Washington press corps *has* changed. The employees of the networks, news magazines, and important daily newspapers do now have a more prestigious position in society, higher than that of their counterparts in any other Western capital. After years of shamefully poor pay scales, they are now receiving salaries at least commensurate with those paid by the federal government.

Partly because of this and partly separate from it, the press corps has been ideologized into a part of the liberal establishment. More and more, the members of the Washington press share in total the world view taken by the dominant liberals who control the Democratic party. More and more they share axioms that profoundly influence their coverage of day-to-day events in the worlds of politics and government.

Here is a list, by no means complete, of axioms shared by the Washington press corps of 1973:

Axiom 1: The Vietnam war was a shameful, immoral episode in American history, which blackens the good name of this republic. Consequently, the policy of anticommunism that led to involvement in Vietnam should be subdued and ultimately abandoned.

Axiom 2: The military-industrial complex is a sinister conspiracy, robbing the nation of its wealth and imperiling its future. To cut defense spending, therefore, is a laudable goal, no matter what the international realities.

Axiom 3: Severe measures must be taken to prevent the despoiling of the nation's natural resources by pollution, industrial and otherwise. If these measures result in unemployment, that will be unfortunate; but protection of the environment must take precedence.

Axiom 4: White racism, as defined by the Kerner Commission report in 1968, is a cancer that must be removed from the American body. That goal must take precedence over any personal inconveniences caused by such devices as forced busing for the racial integration of schools.

Axiom 5: The forces of repression in modern America threaten our liberties, a neofascist danger becoming a sinister reality under President Nixon.

Axiom 6: A reordering of priorities is essential and past due so that great quantities of federal funds can be funneled into the cities for social rebuilding purposes. That a substantial increase in government spending would result in at least some improvement is scarcely debatable.

Axiom 7: A redistribution of wealth in the country is similarly overdue through a realignment of the tax system and a general overhaul in fiscal policy.

The list of axioms is flexible. A year or two earlier, it surely would have included a belief in the transcendent wisdom of youth, now undermined by the present quiescence on the campus. Whatever the list contains, it is a considerable amount of ideological baggage for a journalist to be carrying. In short, he is approaching the political and governmental developments he is covering with a set of axiomatic beliefs identical to those held by some political figures and wholly antithetical to others.

These axioms exert a pervasive influence over journalistic coverage. Senator Henry M. Jackson violates so many axioms—the Vietnam war, the military-industrial complex, white racism, ecology—that no matter what his competence or his own professions of liberalism may be, he can scarcely be taken seriously. Mayor John V. Lindsay, on the other hand, conforms so closely to these axioms that he must be taken seriously, notwithstanding suspicions about his depth or administrative efficiency.

On a broader basis, issues are viewed by the press corps in relation to these axioms. Inasmuch as President Nixon did not write off the Vietnam war as shameful and immoral, his Vietnamization policy was indefensible. In any controversy between environmentalists and industrialists, the environmentalists must be given every benefit of the doubt. The specter of white racism casts its shadow on a vast number of public questions, granting the indisputable benefit of any doubt to spending programs for the cities or any scheme of racial integration.

To be sure, there are many journalists on the Washington scene who do not share these axiomatic beliefs. But increasingly a rigid conformity has emerged among the Washington press corps, which reflects in part conformity in the colleges producing the new journalists. But beyond this, the young journalist who violates these axioms can scarcely expect a rapid rise up the ladder of advancement. A young television network correspondent whose reporting reveals a lack of sympathy for environmental protection or racial integration or a reordering of priorities will soon find himself in some professional difficulty with his superiors.

Moreover, the Washington press corps, like any other group, exerts peer group pressure. When Washington journalists gather among themselves socially, as they often do, there is a startling consensus on the basic perceptions. There may be a difference of opinion on the relative merits of politicians or programs, but there is seldom any debate about goals or broad principles.

The result is a gap of widening proportions between the national journalist and the mass of Americans, paralleling a gap between liberal politicians and the masses, specifically the white workingman. Whereas the national journalist feels the Indochina conflict is immoral and shameful, the white workingman is angered by the failure to win it militarily. Whereas the national journalist condemns President Nixon's efforts to restrict school busing as demagogic, the white workingman feels a sense of outrage and futility over the whole busing process. Whereas the national journalist is basically convinced that the solution of our national problems lies in the area of governmental spending, the white workingman is disillusioned with the effectiveness of government.

There is, further, a vast difference in the instinctive reaction of the journalist and the white workingman. An example: On March 14, 1972, badly beaten by Governor George Wallace in the Florida presidential primary, Senator Edmund Muskie went on national television to denounce Wallace and those who had voted for him. Walter Cronkite, on CBS, immediately commented on the courage and eloquence of Muskie's statement. But polling data showed that a vast majority felt Muskie's statement was graceless and ill-tempered, an attack on the wisdom of the voters of Florida.

The gap between the national journalists and the mass of voters is so basic in its reaction toward life that it can scarcely be bridged. Furthermore, it transcends questions of the journalist's individual background. It really makes no difference whether his school is Ivy League or land grant college, whether his family background is first family or immigrant, whether he comes from Manhattan or Main Street. The national media have become a melting pot where the journalists, regardless of background, are welded into a homogeneous ideological mold joined to the liberal establishment and alienated from the masses of the country.

III

Advocacy is by no means a new element in American journalism. The early nineteenth-century newspapers were open advocates of a political party, with no pretense of objectivity. The muckrakers of the progressive era were practitioners of advocacy journalism. Until recently, the great conservative dailies of the Midwest followed the example of the *Chicago Tribune* in brazenly espousing, in news columns and editorial columns alike, an undiluted prairie conservatism.

But until the early 1960s, objectivity was at least the goal, if not always achieved, of journalism and journalists. The concept of the journalist openly advocating one point of view or another was abhorrent, at least in theory, throughout the profession. Even today, many journalists who fully subscribe to the axioms outlined above at least give lip service to the concept that these beliefs should not intrude upon the way they report the news.

The new advocacy journalism became evident in the early 1960s and has been rising steeply since 1970. It is centered among a new generation of journalists who view objectivity quite differently from their senior colleagues and are themselves a reflection of the turbulent 1960s on college campuses.

Sharing the campus consensus, they see the American system as basically corrupt, in need of drastic and immediate revision. It must be changed root and branch; simple reform alone will not do at all. To accomplish this, the young graduate has several options. He may seek a post somewhere in government. He may seek to enter directly into the political process as a campaign worker. He may join one of the new activist organizations, such as Common Cause or Nader's Raiders. He may join a public interest law firm or a law firm that permits its employees to take time off for public interest work. If wholly despairing of the system, he may seek to promote the revolution as a demonstrator or through an underground organization, though these courses have now become less fashionable.

Or he may become a journalist. The rise in social status and remuneration of journalism described earlier makes this a more attractive option than would have been the case even a decade ago. But the young activist fresh from the campus enters journalism not solely to seek fame, fortune, and adventure, as did his predecessors, but to redress the ills of the republic.

The journalist as advocate makes no pretense at objectivity. He is the avowed enemy of the industrial polluters, and his writing is intended to flay them, not merely to describe and analyze. In any coverage of the Nixon administration's prosecution and persecution of dissenters, the journalist advocate intends to help actively the cause of the dissenter and stay the repressive hand of the administration. An advocate-correspondent covering the Pentagon must as his first priority seek out the waste and inefficiency that will discredit the military-industrial complex.

The middle-aged news executives encountering these advocates are appalled by their lack of concern with objectivity, and they resist it. But they may well be fighting a losing battle. In the nationally important media of communications, the shared axioms between the executives and the new advocate journalists make the argument strictly one of objectivity or nonobjectivity. Furthermore, the new journalist is fresh from the turmoil of the campus, knowledgeable in skills of organization for dissent. In the newsrooms of the great metropolitan newspapers, the executives are encountering young journalists organizing and mobilizing to influence the editorial policies of the newspaper. Far less certain of themselves, the executives can scarcely resist the temptation to retreat.

The full impact of the new generation of journalists is yet to be experienced. But even now, advocacy journalism can be detected in newspapers of national importance. For example, the *Washington Post's* thorough coverage of the hunger controversy in 1969–1970 did not disguise the reporter's obvious belief that Senator McGovern was correct and his opponents incorrect in their assessment of the seriousness of the problem. The *Post*'s accounts left no doubt as to its sympathies in the question; in the news stories, it was implicitly advocating greater expenditures for food distribution to the poor. Again, the accounts in both the *Washington Post* and the *New York Times* of the recurrent difficulties of the Nixon administration in dealing with school desegregation in the South have made no pretense at neutrality. Advocacy for vigorous school desegregation and against any compromise is undisguised.

Advocacy journalism also has accelerated in the abbreviated news reports of network television, reaching an audience many times larger than that of the newspapers and news magazines. The coverage by CBS of social welfare legislation during the Nixon administration, reflecting superb reportage, is unmistakably on the side of vigorous racial integration in the schools, a considerably larger federal stipend to welfare recipients, and a substantial federal role generally in the solution of social problems. The widely supposed fear cast in the hearts of the network executives by Vice-President Agnew's invective had no apparent effect on this brand of advocacy journalism.

All three networks have played the role of advocate in their reporting of the school busing controversy. By implication, busing is defended as necessary, however unpleasant it might be, whereas the foes of busing are interested wholly in political advantage and catering to popular passions. After President Nixon addressed the nation with new antibusing proposals, the immediate analysis over CBS was revealing. One correspondent, not a lawyer and with no access to expert legal opinion at that moment, asserted flatly that the President's proposal was unconstitutional by resorting to the old separate-but-equal doctrine, which had been declared unconstitutional by the Supreme Court in 1954. Disapproval of what Nixon had done was imprinted in his and his colleagues' brief remarks.

All these examples of advocacy journalism, implicit and indirect, involve mature journalists raised in a tradition of objectivity and balance. Their advocacy quite probably is not a conscious design, but rather an intrusion on their intentions of objectivity caused by the depth of their adherence to the axioms listed earlier. The sea change in journalism will come if and when the new generation of avowed advocates is ascendant, unencumbered by any obsolete notions of objectivity and balance.

Why not? That is the question posed by the young journalists. Why should they be hindered in their efforts to right the wrongs of a corrupt and failed society? And in such a society, what is wrong with advocacy? Indeed, is it not the older generation of journalists, who failed to condemn the evils in our land, that should be condemned?

Certainly there is no dishonor in being an advocate. He is welcomed in many fields: politics, government, the law, social work, education. Advocacy is an integral part of journalism as well. The editorial writer, the columnist, the writer for journals of opinion all must be advocates by definition.

It is the reporter of news, in either the electronic or printed media, who is subject to heated controversy over advocacy journalism. It is in the news columns and on the news broadcasts that the new journalists want to carry on their advocacy.

But to do so subverts the function of the press in informing the citizenry of a democratic society. If the evening news telecast and the morning newspaper are advocating positions and policies, how can they be relied upon to report the news accurately? The problem is aggravated significantly if the advocacy is based on axiomatic beliefs foreign to the mass of citizens. If the vast majority of citizens is clearly opposed to school busing and the national communications media are advocates of school busing, the credibility of the media on this and other questions is eroded, and with it the media's ability to fulfill their vital function.

IV

On March 31, 1972, regular North Vietnamese divisions poured across the Demilitarized Zone into South Vietnam to begin a long-awaited offensive that broke over three years of relative quiescence in the endless Indochinese war. The reaction by the most prestigious national communications media was remarkably in keeping with the coverage of the war that had developed over the years.

On April 4 the banner headline of the *New York Times* declared: "U.S. SAYS HANOI 'INVADED' SOUTH, KEEPS REPRISALS OPTIONS OPEN." The quotations around "invaded" derived from the lead paragraph of a Washington dispatch: "The United States accused Hanoi today of launching an 'invasion' of South Vietnam and said Washington was leaving open all retaliatory options—including renewed American bombing of North Vietnam." Implicitly, the "invasion" was a figment of the imagination of the U.S. government, not the description of massive artillery bombardment actually preceding columns of armor and infantry pouring down across the border.

That same morning, in the *Washington Post,* a dispatch from Danang began: "Hanoi's offensive in the northermost section of South Vietnam means that the Saigon government's stumbling pacification program in that bloody battleground has taken a bad fall." Pacification in Vietnam generally was measured in terms of government control in heavily populated areas, and by April 3 the North Vietnamese offensive had occupied mostly wilderness with a relatively small outflow of refugees. On the basis of that small amount of evidence, the dispatch implied a major defeat in the critical struggle for the countryside. The headline: "A Setback for the Pacification Program."

That evening the three national television networks painted a picture of impending doom in the northern provinces of South Vietnam, with the South Vietnamese Army in full retreat as it ran from the enemy legions. Flashed on the screen were pictures of hapless South Vietnamese soldiers who, having lost or thrown away their weapons, joined the stream of refugees fleeing from the front line. The televised reports gave the unmistakable impression that the end was near, military collapse at hand. From watching them, no television viewer could have guessed that in a few more days the northern front would be stabilized at a point not much farther south than the line of April 4.

These accounts of the early days of the 1972 Communist offensive reflect dominant themes in coverage of the war by the national media which first appeared years before: a disinclination to put the North Vietnamese clearly in the aggressor's role (as in the use of quotation marks around "invaded"); a quick trigger in proclaiming the failure of American-managed programs in Vietnam, such as pacification; an inclination to assume the worst in any military confrontation between North Vietnamese and South Vietnamese.

These dominant themes are part of a general pattern of reportage on Vietnam by the national media, encapsulating more than any other single issue the trends discussed earlier. The view of the Indochina war given the American public by the national media is shaped by the axiom on Indochina commonly held by the vast majority of the news correspondents who cover or have covered the scene.

There are practical reasons for much of this. The young journalists who won a name for themselves by critical reporting of the Vietnam war a decade ago—David Halberstam, Neil Sheehan, and Malcolm Browne—pointed the way to the young men subsequently assigned there; surely the Pulitzer Prize does not await him who is positive in reporting the war.

Beyond the practical lies the ideological. Both the correspondents in Saigon and their editors back in Washington and New York share, in overwhelming numbers, axiomatic beliefs about the war. The correspondent, consciously or not, tends to look at the worst side of things. The editor, consciously or not, tends to select news that is negative.

An example occurred in the autumn of 1971 when a CBS correspondent, an excellent reporter with previous Vietnamese experience, visited Binh Dinh province, the worst hotbed of Communist insurgency in South Vietnam. In absolute terms, the situation in Binh Dinh was dreadful; in relative terms, however, it was much better than it had been only six months past, thanks to an accelerated pacification campaign. The treatment given by the CBS correspondent was that, despite the new campaign, pacification was far off in Binh Dinh. He described the glass of water as half empty rather than half full. Furthermore, the introduction to his account by the network anchor man was to the effect that nothing ever changed for the better in Vietnam.

Both the correspondent and the anchor man in question are known critics of the present Far Eastern policy, a view that may well have cast a long shadow on their treatment of the Binh Dinh story. But there is another dimension to the problem. Assume the correspondent, inhibiting his own beliefs, approached the story from the standpoint of limited progress in Binh Dinh. There is serious doubt that this would have made the evening network news, ostensibly on the grounds that the story lacked bite and viewer interest. Here too, however, the beliefs of the editors come into play, though perhaps subconsciously.

The problem can be framed in this pattern, which fits the

experience of several young correspondents assigned to Indochina. Arriving from the United States, the neophyte is prejudiced against U.S. policy and looking for the worst. But as he digs into the problem, he discovers new elements of hope and accomplishment that surprise him and, he believes, deserve to be reported. The dispatches he writes on these subjects are then relegated to the back pages of a back section of his newspaper. It is the stories of despair and failure that receive front-page treatment. This is in the ancient journalistic tradition that "man bites dog" is news whereas "dog bites man" is not. But it also conforms to deeply felt beliefs about Indochina within the media. The fact that the negative stories also conform to the correspondent's personal beliefs about the war makes it easier for him to write the negative stories that please his superiors and win him advancement.

All of this more or less subconsciously tailors Indochinese reportage to antiwar beliefs. There is, in addition, *conscious* emphasis on the negative by correspondents who believe in advocacy journalism and practice it, either clandestinely or openly. Most of these are free-lancers, but some correspondents for national media view their mission as one of undermining U.S. policy in Indochina.

To them, this is the highest form of patriotism. Many are not many years away from the college campus, where U.S. intervention in the Vietnam war was universally perceived as an abominable moral outrage. To be assigned to Vietnam is for them to be given a rare opportunity at advocacy. This is the highest form of patriotism; to retreat to obsolete standards of objectivity would be unthinkable.

The most famous of the journalist-advocates in Vietnam has been Seymour Hersh, winner of the Pulitzer Prize for his exposure of the My Lai massacre. In interviews, Hersh made no secret of the fact that his avowed purpose in Vietnam was to discredit the U.S. effort there. Obviously, to balance the atrocity at My Lai against Communist atrocities at Hué and elsewhere in the 1968 *Tet* offensive would not be to his purpose. Just how many correspondents in Indochina share Hersh's goals but are less candid about it is impossible to say.

On the surface, it would seem that the new journalism has profoundly affected public opinion on Vietnam. Widespread support for the war in 1965 gradually changed to widespread opposition. Seldom has the public change in viewpoint been so complete on a major issue in so short a period of time. It would seem that, on this issue at least, the mass media and the masses are together.

But how much the media really converted the masses on Vietnam is debatable. The national media's position on U.S. policy in Vietnam, mirroring the attitudes of the peace movement, was that it was ineffective, unwise, and immoral; the masses accepted only that it was ineffective. The national journalists argued that it was indecent of the United States to have been in Vietnam; the masses have come to the conclusion that our one and only sin was *not winning militarily*. The gap between the masses and the media over the underlying moral basis of Vietnam persists.

It may be said that the media played a major role in pushing the masses to the conclusion that the war was unwinnable. That judgment was surely formed by years of televised news from Vietnam, putting the military situation in the blackest of terms. Certainly the great turning point in American public opinion on the war was the great Communist *Tet* offensive of 1968, when the national media failed badly in reporting the magnitude of the Communist military defeat.

At this writing, a national inquest into who is to blame for Vietnam seems unlikely. But in any such inquest, the media would be sharply attacked for their role, and a demagogic politician, following Vice-President Agnew's success, might well whip up an uproar of public hysteria. The potential exists because of the gap between the mass and the media on Vietnam and the lack of restraint by the media in either consciously or subconsciously shaping the news of the war to fit their own axioms.

On most controversial events of the last decade, the gap between the mass media and the masses has been even more obvious than in the case of Vietnam. On no point was the gap more noticeable than in the coverage of the disturbances at the 1968 Democratic National Convention in Chicago by the national journalists, particularly the television networks.

The televised accounts gave the unmistakable picture of a police riot against unresisting young protesters. But polling data show a wholly different picture perceived by the masses, who felt the networks were distorting an antipolice provocation by organized radicals. So intense was the disbelief by the masses that even indisputable excesses by the police visually portrayed on television were doubted by viewers. Though the truth of the situation rested somewhere between the version of the media and the perception of the masses, and probably closer to the media version, the consensus of disbelief showed a rugged resistance by the television viewer against being forced into new patterns of belief.

On a less violent level is the gap on the school busing question. Television coverage that tends to defend busing has had no effect whatever in diminishing mass abhorrence against the practice. The public believes that busing is irrational, ineffective, and against its interests. Television commentators cannot convince it otherwise.

But even if the impact of the national media is limited in transforming public opinion, the effort is not without significance. As the gap widens between the public and the media, so does the media's credibility decline. The media must play a role as watchdog critic in a free society, but they scarcely can do so effectively if they lack credibility. If separated from the masses and disbelieved by them, the media are constantly vulnerable to political attack, which could ultimately result in a shrinking of freedom.

An easy corrective is not at hand. Any governmental or quasi-governmental agency to police the press is unconstitutional and unthinkable, the corrective being worse than the malady. Self-policing by press boards probably would reflect existing views of the media, which constitute the heart of the problem. Informal watchdogs over the press, such as the journalism reviews around the country, are so dominated by advocates of advocacy journalism that they even denigrate examples of objectivity and balance.

The return of the media to a goal of objectivity, balance, and nonadvocacy, though difficult to blueprint, is nevertheless essential. Without progress toward this end, the communications media cannot be free from growing fears and dangers in the years to come.

GEORGE E. REEDY

•

WHY DOES NOBODY LOVE THE PRESS?

As a second-generation newspaperman, I have spent a lifetime listening to or participating in discussions of the press. For me, they began when I was a very small boy with very big ears drinking in the rich, and usually profane, denunciations of editors and publishers by my father and other reporters of the *Front Page* Chicago of the twenties. They took on new dimensions when college life introduced me to the endless delights of academic dialogue. They became a matter of personal, rather than notional, concern when I became a journalist myself. And they assumed the character of a free fire zone when, as a government information officer, I found myself caught between politicians who did not understand newspapermen and newspapermen who did not understand politicians.

In retrospect, it does not seem to me that any of those discussions ever resulted in useful or intellectually satisfying conclusions. They were always heated, and I cannot recall any participant who changed his basic views. Agreements were, at best, always peripheral. The recommendations that emerged were very few and always on narrow, legal issues or produced by groups that were selected in the first place for their similarity of attitude. The most discouraging aspect of the debates, however, was their remarkable circularity. The issues changed but the substance of the argument always went back to the same fundamentals that I had heard as a child.

Gradually the thought emerged that this is one area of human endeavor in which reality is very difficult to discern because it depends so very much upon individual perception. The critics of the press rarely questioned the factual material that was presented through the media. Instead, they based their case on the assertion that the media were adding up the facts to present a picture that did not accord with their view of the universe. Most human beings confuse their own views with the "truth" and other views with "distortion." As individual views vary so widely and as the press cannot alter its tone for each individual recipient, it is hardly remarkable that journalism is a target for critics from every side.

The problem is compounded by the inability of any of us to see the press as a whole. Even those with the broadest interests read only a few newspapers and periodicals and view telecasts sporadically. This does not prevent us from generalizing our limited personal experiences into universal truths. More insidious is the human propensity to see what we want to see and to ignore anything that does not fit our preconceptions. From this flows the propensity to denounce the media generally for sins of which they are guilty only individually.

Sometimes the thoughts of moderate men and women can be illuminated by examining the positions of those with extreme views. Perhaps some light can be shed on the character of debates about the press by that kind of examination.

Of all the recurring themes, the one that has been the most persistent is what I regard as the "Perfidious Albion" theory. It acquired that name for me through an Irish teacher in the fourth grade who spent at least ten minutes out of every school day explaining to the class that the people of Chicago were deprived of the "real truth" of what was happening in the world "because Chicago newspapers are controlled by King George" of Great Britain. He was unquestionably a busy monarch, as, according to the good lady, he also produced all of our textbooks.

I was very fond of her. She was warm and motherly, and my Irish name had assured me favored treatment. But even so, it seemed to me that there was a flaw in her argument. The publisher of the *Chicago Tribune* shared her Anglophobia and expressed his feelings in simple, lucid English on the front page of his paper every day. After the third lecture, I made the mistake of raising the point and drew from her the only flash of anger she directed at me during the term.

"My fine Irish boy," she replied, "you are just too young and innocent to understand the full iniquity of the Sassenachs in Perfidious Albion.[1] They are trying to confuse you. King George has told the *Tribune* that Thompson must be defeated at all costs even if it means that the newspaper must pretend to be against England to disguise the real reasons for its opposition."

The answer did little to dispel my skepticism. As the son of a newspaperman, I was well aware of Big Bill Thompson's mayoralty campaign, which was based on a promise to take the first boat to England after the inauguration and "punch King George on the snoot." I also knew that the *Chicago Tribune,* my father's employer, was anti-Thompson. But the concept of the newspaper's publisher, Colonel Robert McCormick, who was a very strong-willed man, taking orders from His Britannic Majesty strained my credulity beyond limits. It simply didn't make sense.

Even at the tender age of eight, however, I recognized the strength of her position and held my peace. By attributing everything she did not like to King George, she was basing her view of the universe on the bedrock of human deviousness. Her logic was unassailable, whatever might be said of her premises, because she could explain any facts that ran contrary to her thesis by ascribing them to conspiratorial intrigue. Those to whom she was addressing herself could believe or disbelieve, but they could not refute.

There was a simple charm to her Perfidious Albion theory. To this day, I savor the mental picture of broad-bottomed dukes and viscounts reporting daily to a suite in Buckingham Palace to pore over items about the Chicago City Council. I have often wondered how they reacted to such aldermanic characters as Hinky Dink Kenna and Bathhouse John Coughlin, and what censorship policies governed the treatment of stories on Chicago's Sanitary District. They could not have been a very effective group of propagandists, as Big Bill Thompson won the election that fall quite handily. However, it is possible that he too was finally subverted by King George. He did not make the promised boat trip, and I do not recall any significant change in the character of the textbooks available to the public school system.

[1] For the benefit of those unfamiliar with Irish nationalism, Sassenach is Gaelic for Saxon. Perfidious Albion, of course, is England. It is not a Gaelic phrase. I have never heard anyone but my schoolteacher use it, even though it is common in literature.

Of course, however enchanting the concept, it was far too simplistic to be accepted anywhere unless the atmosphere was supercharged with ethnic tensions—which it was in the Chicago of that period. My teacher was a direct, forthright woman, unfamiliar with the intricacies of dialectic and the syllogism and unaware of the euphemisms of the behavioral sciences. To her, it was a simple matter of an evil person controlling the thoughts of innocent "right-minded" people. She did not know the tactical advantages that accrue to a debater who dehumanizes his devils and transforms them into a class. This I did not encounter until a later stage of my life.

I did not recognize the Perfidious Albion theory the next time I met it. It was during my college days, when I had become a Socialist and the editor of a magazine called *Soapbox,* which took its title from a statement by William Randolph Hearst: "Red radicalism has planted a soapbox on every campus in America." The term was the only thing we accepted cheerfully from the Establishment (a word not then in use) press. Every issue had at least three pages lambasting American newspapers as deceivers of the toiling masses. It was a highly intellectual organ that attracted every would-be author on the campus, one of whom later became a major American writer, and, even though I could not foresee this development, I was quite smugly satisfied with what I regarded as a landmark in my intellectual growth.

Actually, I had not grown beyond my fourth-grade teacher at all. I had picked up some intellectual baggage (dialectical materialism, the labor theory of value, the class struggle, and so on) which had served only to blunt the healthy sense of skepticism I had as a child. For Perfidious Albion I had substituted capitalism, for Sassenachs I had substituted the bourgeoisie. And every time the American press produced a story with which I agreed, I explained it as a clever effort to confuse the proletariat as to the "true nature" of their troubles. I knew I was right about such things because I had mastered a body of knowledge known as "scientific socialism," and surely this was superior to the superstitions of those who had not seen the light.

It took me quite a few years to recover my sense of humor. It happened because I became a newspaperman who had to listen to all sorts and conditions of people, most of whom subscribed to the theory of Perifidious Albion but few of whom could agree on its location. For New Dealers it was in the Union League Club; for Republicans it was in the Democratic National Committee. For Populists it was in the eastern banks; for industrialists it was in CIO headquarters. For the German-American Bund it was in the offices of the Anti-Defamation League; for interventionists it was in the directorate of the America First Committee. All of these groups were united on one principle only: wherever and whatever it was, Albion controlled the American press.

The theory has not lost its vigor with the passage of time. More than fifteen years ago, Adlai Stevenson deplored "the one-party press" (by which he meant a Republican press), and today his thoughts, though not his words, are echoed by Spiro Agnew, who scorns "the impudent snobs" (by which he means a liberal Democratic press). The most appealing form that the concept has assumed, however, comes to us in the characterization of "elitism," first set forth by Daniel P. Moynihan in 1971[2] and elaborated and improved by Robert D. Novak in 1972.[3]

Although Mr. Moynihan and Mr. Novak differ considerably in detail, their basic concept is the same. It is that the American press is dominated by a "liberal" elite that has so warped the reporting of the news that it no longer accords with the perceptions of the American people as a whole. Therefore, there are increasing resentments that, over a period of time, threaten the continued existence of a "free press."

The force of this restatement should not be underestimated. In the first place, it comes to us from first-class minds who might be right or might be wrong but whose integrity is not open to serious question. In the second place, it is couched in the liturgical language of the behavioral sciences, which has a tendency to overawe all opposition. In the third place, it identifies the Sassenachs as a group against which the overwhelming majority of people can unite. Few—liberal or conservative—will own up to being elite.

Furthermore, the argument that is advanced is based on certain contentions that are demonstrably valid. For example, there is an

[2] Daniel P. Moynihan, "The Presidency and the Press," *Commentary,* March 1971.

[3] Robert D. Novak, "The New Journalism," in this volume.

elite in the Washington press corps, and it is readily identifiable. Its members lunch at such places as the Sans Souci and the Federal City Club; are favored with embassy invitations; and frequently slip in the side door of the White House for private interviews with the director of the National Security Council Staff, or possibly even someone higher. Like all elites, they have a tendency to pomposity and an overly developed self-esteem, but, generally speaking, it seems to me that most of them have traveled a much more difficult road in arriving at their present status than have their counterparts in law and government. I can get bored with them myself, but I am not going to blame human beings for acting like human beings, and there are not many of us who can resist the impulse to strut.

A person who travels in such circles can easily conclude, as Mr. Novak has done, that the members of this elite group dominate the American press simply because they are commanding figures in the periphery of the Washington governmental community. They are quoted on the floors of Congress; federal officials react to them as though they were foreign plenipotentiaries; they are on the standard invitation lists for all of the more important social gatherings in this highly protocol-conscious city. A President, Vice President, or Cabinet officer may damn them or praise them, but he will certainly take them into account as an important factor in his political problems.

The key words in the preceding paragraph, however, are "the Washington governmental community." It is a long step from being part of a community elite to dominating the communications of a nation. And Mr. Novak's theory cannot stand unless he can demonstrate that this elite dominates a substantial part of the Washington press corps, which produces the bulk of the news that reaches the people of the United States. I do not believe that this demonstration is possible.

At the outset, it must be conceded that the elitist theory, like all other Perfidious Albion concepts, is impossible to refute conclusively because most of it rests solely upon assertion. In his entire paper, Mr. Novak names only two specific elitists, Walter Cronkite and Seymour Hersh, neither of whom had played any part in the daily life of Washington at the time Mr. Novak prepared his article. He lists only two newspapers, the *New York Times* and the *Wash-*

ington Post, which put together are hardly a drop in the bucket of daily newspaper circulation. Of course, he mentions the three major television networks, and one must infer that he includes the two largest news magazines.

These are mighty slim pickings when it comes to the identification of the "elite" unless we assume that a job with a television network or a news magazine automatically carries membership in the exclusive club—an assumption that would be gratifying but also surprising to quite a few people of my acquaintance. Perhaps, however, identification can be worked out on the basis of characteristics. To this end, Mr. Novak offers seven axioms, which, he says, were "shared by the Washington press corps of 1972." Here I encounter trouble immediately. These are not seven principles to which a group of men have subscribed. Rather they are characterizations by Mr. Novak of the attitudes of others whom he does not specify. As such, they may be valid or they may be invalid, but they cannot be accepted as axiomatic any more than could a Democratic National Committee characterization of the Republican party platform. They are simply arguments, not statements of fact.

I would argue that no newspaperman in Washington would accept all seven axioms—certainly not in the form in which they are written—let alone a substantial number. If they were placed in neutral language, it might be possible to get a sizable group to sign some such statement. But I doubt that it would cause much comment without the pejorative words. Many newspapermen believe that the war in Vietnam was a mistake; that we have spent too much money on weapons systems; that we ought to clean up our air and water; that slavery and segregation are not particularly glowing chapters of American history; and that we should do something about the problems of our cities. I do know of some, with very substantial audiences, who believe we should have gone into Vietnam harder and earlier; who think we have not spent enough on armaments; that the discussion of the environment is just a passing fad; and that our cities can take care of themselves. Admittedly, I know of only a few who I suspect favor segregation and I have heard none advocate slavery.

Naturally, the identity of the elite is far less important than its impact. If it can be established that the flow of news to the American people is badly warped, it will always be possible to trace the process backward to its source. Therefore, the vital task is to examine the evidence that is offered and to determine what it indicates. Once again, when I turn to the evidence, I find mighty slim pickings. The hard fact is that there is very little into which a man can sink his teeth. The case for the elitist theory rests primarily upon assertion.

Mr. Novak, to be sure, lists ten specific instances of alleged liberal bias. But when they are examined with care, it develops that there are only three that can stand by themselves as statements of fact, and of those three, two are prima facie open to other interpretations. The third I have not looked into and do not intend to simply because it is too trivial to make a case. The three are:

1. Walter Cronkite "commented on the courage and eloquence" of Senator Muskie's statement denouncing the voters who supported George Wallace in the Florida primary.

2. The *New York Times* put the word "invaded" in quotation marks when reporting the North Vietnamese offensive, thus evidencing "a disinclination to put the North Vietnamese clearly in the aggressor's role...."

3. At the beginning of the same invasion, the three television networks

> flashed on the screen... pictures of hapless South Vietnamese soldiers who, having lost or thrown away their weapons, joined the stream of refugees fleeing from the front line.... From watching them, no television viewer could have guessed that in a few more days the northern front would be stabilized at a point not much farther south than the line of April 4.

I have no idea of what Walter Cronkite said because Mr. Novak does not quote him directly. But even assuming the paraphrase is valid, this is hardly sufficient evidence upon which to erect a theoretical structure. The other two examples do not even require much examination.

It seems to me that the editor of the *New York Times* was justified in putting the word "invaded" in quotation marks simply because President Nixon himself had been so careful to characterize extraterritorial activities of the South Vietnamese armies as "incursions." Obviously, the United States government regarded an invasion as something different from an incursion, and there is nothing unusual in calling attention to such a distinction. To argue this one is simply hairsplitting—what Jewish intellectuals would call *pilpul.*

The third example leaves me completely baffled. During the first few days of the North Vietnamese invasion, what pictures could be taken other than those Mr. Novak describes? They simply fitted the facts of what was happening. I have heard no one dispute the reality that the invasion caught the South Vietnamese by surprise and they fell back in disorder. The fact that the television viewer could not guess that the line would be stabilized a few days later is hardly remarkable. I doubt whether anyone in Vietnam could have made such a guess at that point. When the line did stabilize, it was duly reported, and I would like to suggest that this is all a newsman can do. He is not equipped with a crystal ball even if he himself believes there is one in his suitcase.

The other seven examples cited by Mr. Novak actually sound more impressive than the preceding three, but when they are examined carefully they do not give enough hard facts for even a snap judgment. They depend upon his characterization entirely.

For example, the *Washington Post* "left no doubt as to its sympathies... in the news stories" on Senator McGovern's hunger hearings. The *Washington Post* and the *New York Times* "have made no pretense at neutrality" in dealing with President Nixon's school desegregation policies. CBS coverage of social welfare legislation is "unmistakably on the side of" ultraliberal proposals. All three networks have "played the role of advocate" in the antibusing controversy. An unidentified CBS correspondent employed questionable legal logic in commenting on President Nixon's antibusing proposals and "disapproval of what Nixon had done was imprinted in his and his colleagues' brief remarks." A *Washington Post* dispatch "implied a major defeat" in the Vietnamese pacification program on the basis of a "small amount of evidence." The televised accounts of the demonstrations at the Democratic National Convention in 1968 "gave the unmistakable picture of a police riot against unresisting young protesters." (The use of the word "unmistakable" leads one to wonder why most viewers got the opposite impression.)

Admittedly I have not covered all of Mr. Novak's examples,

but the fact remains that the others are in the same category. With a few exceptions—too isolated to serve as a characterization of something as complex as the communications industry—the whole concept of elitism depends entirely on individual perception. It is not one that can be established on the basis of factual data that will convince a reasonable group of diverse men and women. These are matters that can only be "known"—not proven.

There is no point in telling me that "I know" that liberal elitists have taken over the press. I have spent too much of my life being told by radical students that "I know" the United States entered Vietnam to make profits for the oil industry; by John Birch Texans that "I know" that Sam Rayburn was a tool of Nikita Khrushchev; by McCarthyites (Joe, not Gene) that "I know" the government was riddled with communist spies; by isolationists that "I know" that Franklin D. Roosevelt deliberately provoked the war with Germany, Italy, and Japan; by anti-Semites that "I know" that banks are controlled by Jews; by black leaders that "I know" that whites are determined that the color line shall be unbroken. I do *not* know those things, and I do not believe them and will not believe them on the basis of isolated examples.

However, a theory is not disproven any more than it is proven by lack of facts. I have known many occasions when people who could not cite a shred of evidence turned out to be intuitively correct in the final analysis. I cannot dismiss Mr. Novak's perceptions in any final and conclusive sense. What I can do is to advance my own perceptions as a counterweight, and let people make their choice.

Let us begin with a description of the Washington press that the American people read and hear rather than the press that is discussed by political leaders and forums. The distinction is usually overlooked—probably because it would eliminate about 75 percent of the discussions—but it is vital to any real understanding of the problem.

From the standpoint of warm bodies, the Washington press corps consists of about 2,500 correspondents, newscasters, and cameramen, with the bulk of them—some 1,800—producing accounts that will be printed in some form before they reach the ultimate consumer. Despite the rapid growth of electronics and specialized trade journals over the past two decades, the largest contingent—1,200—is still writing for the daily press.

Naturally, these correspondents do not rank equally in prestige, influence, or size of audience. A tiny handful, most of them columnists of opinion, have fabulous incomes and can afford Georgetown mansions. A somewhat larger group, mostly newscasters and correspondents for the more prestigious (in Washington) papers, receive salaries roughly equal to those of their counterparts in government, but that number is probably small (newspapermen are even more reticent about their incomes than other professionals). The bulk of them have incomes that are modest even by Washington standards, and a surprisingly large number are not very far above the subsistence level, eking out not much more than a bare living by "stringing" (part-time correspondence) for groups of small newspapers or radio stations.

These estimates of income do not represent an examination of specific figures, and I have yet to see any statistics that will bear examination. But I am reasonably confident of my assertions because I have been—and still am—in a position to hire newsmen into allied professions, and I know the market price with a high degree of accuracy. I am not going to embarrass anyone, but the averages are not even close to those of the federal government for comparable responsibilities.

In terms of social cohesion, these correspondents are just about like any other similar group of professionals. They are clannish, clique-ridden, jealous of each other, and usually in total ignorance of other segments of the press with which they are not in contact. In thirty-four years in Washington I have never felt that I was communing with the whole press, even though I have dealt with it on the broadest possible scale. The only safe characterization of the philosophy and social environment of Washington journalists is that no one can place them in any single category broader than the term "newsman."

Mr. Novak comments on the "startling consensus" found among Washington correspondents at their own social gatherings. There is nothing startling about the consensus at all. The answer is simply that these are gatherings of newsmen who agree with each other.

There are very few functions that bring the bulk of the correspondents together, and most of them, when they are relaxing, split into small cliques. It would be quite possible to construct a theory of a Washington press corps composed of Archie Bunkers merely by attending the right parties.

In terms of prestige *in Washington,* Mr. Novak is unquestionably correct in his contention that there is an elite. But most of them are columnists hired to write their opinions, not to produce "hard news." A few of them, of course, are switch-hitters who alternate between editorial and news pages, but, generally speaking, I find their hard news copy to be produced by the same professional standards used by other newsmen. As for his two newspapers, they are dominant in Washington discussions simply because they are edited to address themselves to the federal bureaucracy.

The first problem with Mr. Novak's theory, however, is that he must make some startling deletions from his "elitist" list if the rest of his theoretical structure is to stand. By any reasonable definition of the word, Joseph and Stewart Alsop are elitists, William White is an elitist, and so on, for that matter, is Mr. Novak himself. Government officials react to them just as sharply as they do to Scotty Reston or Joe Kraft; they are on the standard social invitation lists; and they have even better access to White House and Cabinet officials.

The factor that is truly "startling" when the "elite" is examined calmly is the relatively small size of the newspaper audience for their product. The combined circulation of the *New York Times* and the *Washington Post* amounts to less than 1 percent of the American population, and it is a concentrated 1 percent of like-minded people. Even in their home cities, the two journals are more than balanced by others with a different point of view.

It is quite a commentary on human psychology that the audiences that rise to their feet with loud roars of approval when Spiro T. Agnew attacks the two newspapers are composed of men and women who quite obviously have never seen a copy of either publication. This would be true, although to a lesser extent, even in New York, where readers of the *News* (which has about three times the circulation of the *Times*) seldom look at the rival paper.

Both the *Post* and the *Times* have syndicates that distribute some of the stories produced by their newsmen. But generally speaking, these are the opinion columns, openly labeled as such and generally printed on editorial pages along with the output of other columnists who have as much prestige in the cities where they appear as do the lords of Washington. Newspapers that take Tom Wicker are quite likely to subscribe to Joseph Alsop and to give them roughly equal billing.

In this connection, it is an interesting aside to note that the two newspapers most criticized for "liberal elitism" are the two that give their readers the widest variety of opinion. On the editorial pages of the *Washington Post,* Joe Kraft alternates with Joe Alsop; Tom Braden with Evans and Novak; and Garry Wills with John Roche. The *New York Times* "op ed" page is as likely to have essays by Senator Barry Goldwater as by Senator George McGovern. Naturally, in both journals the editorials produced by their own staffs are consistent, but it is difficult to argue with the right of a liberal newspaper to be liberal or a conservative newspaper to be conservative.

The same thing is true of *Newsweek,* which regularly carries such columnists as Stewart Alsop and Milton Friedman. I am still unclear as to the precise nature of Mr. Novak's definition of liberalism, but I know that neither of those two writers fits the description. As for *Time* magazine, it always seemed somewhat conservative to me, but there is no way of really making a determination. This is a question to be resolved by the perception of the individual reader.

The television networks are a somewhat different problem. To Mr. Novak, the news shows reflect liberal elitism; to college radicals who have argued with me in classes they reflect frantic efforts of the "establishment" to rescue a "reactionary system." My own perception is that they are characterless, a disjointed and almost incoherent collection of headlines, sports bulletins, and weather information, which I view only because the afternoon newspapers no longer put out late editions that tell me what has happened in the world since lunch. I cannot agree with Mr. Agnew that eyebrow waggling or voice inflection has political significance. I wish the commentators would waggle a few more eyebrows and squeak occasionally in order to put some life into an otherwise lackluster performance.

The content of the news shows is, in my judgment, sterile—too lacking in red meat to be either instructive or biased. When the cameras happen to be on the scene of a dramatic event—such as the shooting of Lee Harvey Oswald or the attempted assassination of George Wallace—they are capable of presenting news in dimensions denied to the printed word. When able telecasters have some time to put a documentary together, what comes out is invariably fascinating, although naturally it has a point of view that creates controversy. But these are not ordinary news shows, which usually are rescued from utter boredom only by the personality of the commentator.

There is no way of proving or disproving the case, but I simply do not believe that a group of reasonable, though diverse, men listening to network newscasts over a period of time can come to a consensus on bias. The verdict is more likely to be banality; and perhaps it is this very quality of presentation emptiness that convinces Mr. Novak that the telecasters are liberal and convinces radical college students that the same telecasters are conservative. Anything can be read into them because there is so little there to read, and for some reason I have never been able to fathom, human beings are more likely to project their fears and dislikes into a void than their hopes and their desires.

There is no doubt that the network newscasters reach a far larger audience than any part of the printed press, or perhaps even than the printed press as a whole. There is a considerable doubt in my mind, however, as to how much of that audience is really listening. I still find that in any political discussion in the United States, participants are much more likely to quote a newspaper, a magazine, or even a newsletter than ABC, CBS, or NBC. There are studies that purport to prove that people are more responsive to television than to the printed word, but all the studies ever proved to me is that people turn their television sets on. That does not mean that they necessarily watch or think or even react to what is on the screen.

The fact remains that the bulk of Washington news does not come to the American people through the "elite." It is produced by correspondents who are quite anonymous in Washington—who do *not* eat at the Sans Souci; who are *not* on standard invitation lists; who do *not* slip in the side door of the White House; and who do *not* figure on the society pages. Many of them regard their lives in Washington as a camping-out experience, and they maintain tight enclaves in the capital—a form of extraterritoriality for the South, Southwest, Midwest, and West Coast.

The largest audience remains, as it has for decades, with the Associated Press and United Press International—about 170 editorial employees who are not elitist by any definition other than competence. Neither are they liberal nor conservative. The *New York Times* and the *Washington Post* may dominate academic and governmental discussion, but the stories that move people in the mass usually bear the logotypes AP and UPI. Furthermore, the impact of the two wire services is far greater than the quality of the stories they write and distribute. In a very direct manner, they are more responsible than any other organization or group for establishing the *pattern* of daily news coverage not only for newspapers but for the television industry.

I do not want to set up another Perfidious Albion theory, so I hasten to add that the two wire services do not dominate news coverage by other organizations nor do they determine the content of stories written outside their own shops. But they do provide a form of cohesion without which any systematic form of national or international coverage would be impossible. This happens because they are the only institutions that have the necessary resources to put what is happening on a global basis into some kind of coherence.

No experienced reporter has any difficulty covering a story once he knows of its existence. His problem is knowing that the story exists in the first place. If he has a daily beat that is not outsize, he can resolve this difficulty by constantly checking the key people in his area. But no out-of-town newspaper—not even the *New York Times*—has the economic resources to establish a bureau in Washington with a staff sufficiently large to divide the government into small enough beats for the purpose. This is left to the wire services.

In Washington, both the AP and UPI have city news tickers that are distributed at key points, one of the most important being the National Press Club. Very few correspondents, cameramen, or telecasters go through the day without checking those tickers several times—not to let the wire services do their work, but in order to determine whether they should be in some other part of town. The most important thing they check is an item that opens both wires every morning: the so-called news budget, which lists the major stories the services are anticipating for the day. There is literally no other institution that performs this function of integrating the news in advance.

This influence is not confined just to Washington correspondents. The two services open their wires to client newspapers with the same news budget. It is the first thing that most news editors, whether print or electronics, look at when they reach their desks. The problems of putting together a newspaper or a television news show are staggering under the best of circumstances. They would be impossible to surmount without some capsulized view of what will happen made available early enough to permit some planning of the relative amount of space to be assigned to local, national, and international developments. Furthermore, some knowledge of what is likely to happen is absolutely essential to a TV news editor. Electronics equipment is heavy and awkward to handle. The costs of its use are high. Television crews do not just roam the streets looking for news. They go where they think it will take place.

In short, it is not possible, in my judgment, to make any sense out of the formal communications structure without studying the wire services. They have worldwide networks that intermesh at certain key points with press services of other nations. They are on duty twenty-four hours a day, seven days a week. Their role is so significant that, should they disappear, the communications industry would be compelled to devise a substitute. The "elite" provides material for an interesting study of human psychology. But the wire services provide the pattern that makes up the news.

This brings us to the really important issue. Just how good is the product that is supplied to the American people? It is almost heretical to make such a statement, but it seems to me that in the overall context in which the media operate, it is astonishingly good. Certainly, it is far superior to the product available to people in other parts of the world. The press of the United States has mastered an art that is virtually nonexistent elsewhere. It tells its readers what has happened in language that is both direct and lucid.

When an American newspaper states that something happened,

the reader can be certain that, within the limits of human fallibility, it happened. He or she may not like the adjectives used by the reporter; may quibble with the emphasis placed on this fact or that; may conclude that the whole story was not told. But when hard facts are cited, they *are* hard facts, and the audience, quite rightly, accepts them as facts.

This may not seem like a remarkable achievement when the press is contrasted with idealized models of what it should be. Neither is it a reason to stop prodding the press to do a better job. But the prodding will be useless if it is not based upon a recognition of realities, and one of those realities is that the American press is very strong indeed from the standpoint of presenting the facts.

English is a notoriously imprecise language that becomes even more so in the course of a debate. Therefore, it is not generally noticed that few, if any, critics challenge the press in this respect. Mr. Novak does not do so. He does not believe that Mr. Cronkite should have congratulated Senator Muskie, but he does not charge that Walter Cronkite distorted either the facts of the Florida election or the facts of the statement. Mr. Novak states that CBS was "unmistakably on the side of vigorous racial integration" in its coverage of social welfare legislation, but in the same sentence he describes the coverage as "superb reportage." Nowhere does he cite the existence of "nonfacts." He only alleges treatments with which he does not agree.

The reputation of the American media for reporting facts is, indeed, so good that the few occasions of blatant misrepresentation send shock waves through our society. This does happen, of course, simply because there is a streak of carelessness and laziness in all human beings. One of the most recent examples was the exaggerated number of Black Panther deaths at the hands of police which was carried in so many newspapers. When someone finally made a count, there were some very red faces and some very quick retractions and a sense of dismay that would not have occurred if such misrepresentation were habitual.

As a general rule, the person who says that the press tells lies is actually disagreeing with a selection of facts, a use of adjectives, or a placement of an article in a more or less prominent spot. Rarely is an unmistakable lie cited.

George E. Reedy

I have been in many parts of the world where misrepresentation is a regular occurrence and where newspapers are accurate only in reflecting the viewpoints of the government or the political parties they represent. There are newspapers in Europe, Asia, and Latin America where journalism is indistinguishable from fiction, except for the citations of names that are attached to real people and places that actually exist. The interesting point is that in most of these countries—and they are not all dictatorships—there is very little passionate discussion of the press. The newspapers and television stations are regarded as propaganda arms for a political point of view, and no one considers this a remarkable state of affairs.

I have a feeling that the American press arouses such heated controversy *because* of its high quality and *because* it is not dominated by consistent ideological viewpoints. This is not a statement that is subject to ultimate proof or disproof because it cannot be quantified or reduced to syllogistic terms. But it is suggestive that the strongest attacks upon the press invariably come from people with strong ideological or at least partisan views. For example, even Spiro T. Agnew would be unlikely to describe himself as impartial.

Mr. Novak was deeply impressed by the bitter animosity that delegates to the 1964 Republican convention displayed toward the press. At least, he thought enough of it to use the incident as an introduction to his article. Personally, I find it difficult to follow the logic in this instance. The 1964 convention was the one that nominated Senator Goldwater for the presidency, and whatever the merits of Goldwater's views may have been, his followers were certainly ideological and, as the following election disclosed, representative of *a distinct minority of the American people.* A press that satisfied those delegates would have been totally out of step with the majority of Americans.

The more important aspect of the convention's conduct, however, is that the delegates were merely reacting to the press in the same way that strongly ideological groups have reacted throughout my lifetime and probably throughout the history of the free press. My own experience began with some of the more extreme isolationist organizations that were constantly storming the capitol in the years that preceded World War II. Many of them were convinced that newsmen were in the pay of "the Zionist conspiracy," and just walking into the Senate or House building in the morning was not without its hazards.

I have vivid memories of the Wallace convention (Henry, not George) of 1948. As I and my journalistic colleagues moved through the delegations, we were met with such phrases as "Here they come. The jackals of the kept capitalist press." I was quite grateful for the presence of the Philadelphia police when a threatening group surrounded me on the floor because I was trying to learn the name of a Vermont delegate who had offered a platform amendment that had opened up the only important controversy in the entire meeting.

The isolationists of the 1940s, the Wallace delegates of 1948, and the Goldwater delegates of 1964 were certainly different in background, social views, and politics, but they had three qualities in common: they were intensely ideological, they were minority political groups, and they were convinced that the press was controlled by an adversary source. It would be an interesting experiment to try to devise a newspaper or a series of telecasts that would make them all happy and still be comprehensible to a majority of the American people.

This, of course, goes to the heart of the problem that confronts the American press. Our newspapers and television newscasts seek to be organs of general circulation. But the audience to which they address themselves is composed of people *all* of whom are ideological partisans to some degree and on some issues. The only kind of story that can please all or even a small part of the readers is one that involves a subject in which no one is interested. Newspapers are not going to serve any purpose—or last very long—if they confine themselves to such subjects.

The classic response is that newspapers should present the facts and leave the conclusions to the reader. I can agree with this statement and so can anyone else who thinks it through—including highly ideological partisans who quote it more than others. The only problem is that it provides absolutely no guide as to what facts should be presented and which assertions are facts. These are the real problems that confront newsmen. They do not have to choose between being partisan and being objective; they have already made that choice and most of them would want to be objective, if they could find a workable definition of the word. They *do* have to choose daily between facts of varying degrees of significance and words of varying degrees of validity. When the problems are considered, it has never ceased to amaze me that they do as well as they do.

More than any other profession, journalism is constantly confronted with the excruciatingly elusive quality of language. Even without a conscious effort to change them, words refuse to stand still. But they have the morals of a prostitute when attempts are made to manipulate them. When partisanship is involved, there are legions of men and women who are all too willing to attempt the manipulation.

An appeal to "law and order" can be an effort either to calm tensions or to incite a lynch mob. A ringing defense of "states' rights" can spring from genuine fear of the encroachments of big government or from fear that the federal government intends to guarantee some human rights. Pacification can mean mediation or suppression, just as peace can mean freedom or slavery. I can even recall speakers for whom "internationalism" meant a Jewish plot to enslave gentiles and whose audiences had no difficulty in decoding the key word.

Washington reporters face such Aesopian language every day, and it comes from liberals, moderates, and conservatives alike. The character of the administration in office makes little difference. All government statements are written defensively and are intended to conceal as much as they reveal. The world of government is a political world, which in turn means an adversary, partisan world. In this milieu, words are weapons, and no leader is going to give away points to his opponents. Many newsmen go too far in regarding all political leaders as liars. But any one of them should be fired if he or she persists in taking official statements at face value.

Somehow, the newsman has been able to circumvent the barriers and present an overall picture of the world which I believe comes rather close to the truth. But this accomplishment necessarily has its price. It cannot be done without, at some time or other, stepping on the toes of every part of the audience. The universe in which we live does not go along with our desires and our perceptions all of the time. In fact, it goes along with our individual desires and perceptions only a very limited part of the time. It is not at all surprising that the press is unpopular. What is surprising is that it survives despite its reporting of so much that people do not like to read.

As one who has a deep commitment to the value of a free press, I have always found myself in a minority. There are very few people who want the press to be free in any meaningful fashion. What these people want is a press free to tell the people what they believe the people should be told. They want a "responsible" press—meaning a press that withholds socially disturbing facts; they want a "truthful" press—meaning a press that reports *their* truths; they want a "reliable" press—meaning a press that can be relied upon to present the picture of the world that they see.

Mr. Novak finds that the heavy criticism directed at the press is evidence that it has become dominated by "elitism." He also believes that this criticism must be quieted if the press is to remain free. I read the signs differently. The fact that the press is criticized from every side is evidence to me that it is *not* dominated by any one group. And should the criticism die down, it would be evidence to me of the end not only of freedom of the press but of freedom in society, because both the press and the critics would have to be suppressed before this stage could be reached.

Unfortunately, what keeps the press free is not so much a deep commitment to the principle in our society as it is the inability of the critics to agree on the identity of their Albion. I doubt whether journalistic freedom could survive if enough people ever got together on a simple analysis of the universe.

The free press is a fragile structure that has existed only two hundred years or so. It was a product of the eighteenth-century Enlightment, when for the first time people began to toy seriously with the concept that ultimate truth may be unknowable. It flourished in this nation only because we began on a frontier where it was physically impossible for a small group of people to extend their domination over large population masses and where individual idiosyncrasy was buttressed by geographical isolation.

In reality, the free press has never been very popular as an actuality, whatever lip service may have been paid to it as a symbol. Groups entrenched in power have always looked upon it as subversive to good order; dissident groups have always looked upon it as a handmaiden to oppression. The language used today when people gather to discuss the media is no less violent than it was in the last century. It has merely taken on a more sophisticated tone.

Generally, discussions of freedom of the press do not get down to the basic issue. Only too often they turn on matters that are quite irrelevant, such as the "usefulness" of a free press or the "educational value" of a free press. Such arguments are quite dangerous, as they require the press to prove that it has qualities that exist only in the eye of the beholder, and if the proof is not forthcoming, then presumably infringement of press freedom is a legitimate objective.

The fundamental point is that freedom of the press is inextricably bound to freedom of individual expression. If the press can be required to withhold publication of some facts or to express some facts in a style determined by an outside agency, the same requirement can be exacted of every man and woman who is reachable by the law. The real issue is not whether the press should be free but whether American citizens should be free.

Ultimately, these are questions of value judgments. Those who value freedom as an absolute will also value the free and diverse press we have today. Those who look to what they regard as higher values will take a different approach. But if freedom is ever lost, it will be because enough people are convinced that at last they have found Albion, and when they place controls on the press, they will find that the controls will be exercised on themselves as well.

PETER B. CLARK

THE OPINION MACHINE: INTELLECTUALS, THE MASS MEDIA, AND AMERICAN GOVERNMENT

American public opinion has been radically transformed in a decade. Attitudes have changed about the goals of the society, the functions of the economy, and the role and reliability of government. Even more radically changed are attitudes toward America's place in the world and the way we should achieve it.

The changes were neither the inevitable workings of history nor totally an informed people's logical responses to events. The changes were largely the cumulative consequences of thousands of newspaper, television, and magazine stories. That is, they were the consequences of reports of events, not directly of the events themselves. Many of the reports interpreted events in the same way. Their consistent messages criticized public men, national policies, and American institutions.

This barrage of critical interpretation was in one sense an outcome of a rich society's extraordinary expansion of higher education. At a more concrete level of analysis, it was the product of a relatively small part of the total industry that supplies the nation with its news.

Over the past decade, the influence of this small part of the media has increased. Whether consciously or not, it took its policy guidance (that is, it was morally and philosophically informed about goals and courses of action) from a large part of the intellectual community, specifically that part which can be described as liberal.

This essay was written before the presidential nominating conventions of the summer of 1972, and the author's argument has not changed subsequently.

Peter B. Clark

Powerful new communications systems (especially network television news) conveyed new messages (mostly distortions of the opinions of intellectuals) about old facts to very large attentive publics. Public opinion about those facts changed.

In domestic matters, some of the consequences may be seen in the decade of rapidly shifting values and changing standards of conduct, erosion of public confidence in traditional processes of political, legal, and economic decision-making, and a general unease and restlessness.

In foreign affairs, the American policy of twenty-five years has been changed or reversed because public opinion changed. It changed largely because, for more than a decade, the most influential news organizations unrelentingly challenged the direct exercise of American power overseas and the motives for that exercise of power.

The influence of these few organizations did not result from a conspiracy. For the most part, their owners or managers did not set out to change public opinion. Many of their writers did. Many writers, for example, openly supported the same political candidates. But this essay will argue that the writers' efforts to change opinion, and their relative successes, should be explained not so much by their concrete political affiliations as by such more basic social facts as the expansion of higher education, the penetration of the unique biases of intellectuals into popular journalism, practical constraints within the news organizations themselves, and some recent historical events.

One's judgment of the most influential media performance in respect to government should not depend upon one's political *party* preference. This statement contrasts with the appearances of the past four years, during which Republican politicians regularly attacked the media while some Democratic politicians showed wry pleasure in defending the media. But President Lyndon Johnson's 1968 decision not to run again for the presidency relieved him of the need to continue his unsuccessful struggle with the same media organizations later so boisterously attacked by Vice-President Spiro Agnew. Although the memory of President John Kennedy played a part in creating the conditions to be described in this essay, while he was President he encountered many of the same difficulties with the powerful intellectual wing of the mass media which vexed his two successors.

There is, of course, some tendency for the party out of power to get along with the media better than the party in power, for both then occupy the role of critic. There is also a tendency, which will be discussed, for more media writers to be Democrats than Republicans. And as young intellectuals gain increasing importance in both the media and the Democratic party, similarities in the viewpoint of the two institutions increase. But the similarities of viewpoint to be discussed in this essay are prior to party and are based upon professions, life-styles, responsibilities, and other factors of experience. The point of this essay is that a connection exists between a particular kind of view of the world which has a philosophical and even a political content—the intellectual's view—and certain mass media. The intellectual's view is not the same as the officeholder's. The major question becomes: Is the increasingly powerful expression of the intellectual's view consistent with the officeholder's ability to govern properly and effectively?[1]

This essay is not about the strains that must exist between all American officeholders and all American journalists who do their jobs. It is about a new kind of journalism in a new kind of situation. The essay is informed by the belief that the disproportionate influence of a very few media organizations, and the effects of that influence, have so far been mostly bad. The essays argues a blunt thesis about an extremely complex array of fact and behavior. This risks, at the least, the error of oversimplification. The

[1] This essay relies upon many conversations with writers, editors, and executives of the mass media, with professors and with public officials.

I define an intellectual as a person whose income is derived from the written or spoken word (or directly from other symbols), in contrast, for example, with the artisan, whose income is derived from the work of his hands; the professional, whose income is derived from a codified body of shared knowledge; or the executive, whose income is derived from the maintenance of an organization, etc. This definition is based upon an activity rather than upon a status or a trait. This may somewhat reduce the tendency to equate intellectuals with intelligence, and intelligence in turn with good. Intelligence is a biological fact. The intellectual is a cultural fact. That is, he is a combination of traits, skills, and attitudes created by a particular role, at a particular time, in a particular society.

risk is taken consciously. The seriousness of the problem discussed may justify it.

The changes in opinion to be considered here may become clearer if the reader will consider two important contrasts. First, the reader should recall the public values, rhetoric, and mood of an earlier time; for example, the 1950s. This may help to place present attitudes in more vivid contrast.

Second, the reader should reflect upon the very real differences between the perceptions of the contemporary intellectual and those of the rest of us. It will be argued that intellectuals exercise increasing influence over some American perceptions. If this is true, then the perceptual differences between the intellectual and the rest of us are becoming increasingly difficult for us to detect. They will be especially difficult for those close to intellectual life, or the campus, to detect. The differences are very real, nonetheless. To see them more clearly, try to move away from the (academic) atmosphere of comfortably shared premises, inquiry for its own sake, and abstract debate. Instead, adopt for the moment the attitudes of members of other social groupings: mechanics, housewives, junior executives, black politicians, businessmen engaged in manufacturing, firemen, clerks, farm workers, professional soldiers, trade union executives, members of the southern white middle class, or members of any number of other American groups whose viewpoints may be distinct from those of the campus.

Both contrasts highlight the differences between traditional values and intellectual values. The traditional values include patriotism, national pride, respect for law and properly constituted authority, concern for one's family, and a substantial interest in material success. Traditional loyalties are more likely to be to specific individuals (family, friends, organizations) than to abstract ideas. The more complex and subtle intellectual perceptions and values will be developed in later pages.

I

There are about 1,700 daily newspapers and more than 800 television stations of all types in this country. The managements and news staffs of most of these believe in and live by some version of the traditional values. For the most part, traditional values inform their coverage of local news. For the most part, they would prefer to apply the traditional values to national and international news. But a small number of people who work for a very small number of news organizations exercise very great influence over the news of national and international affairs received by all Americans.

This small number of people consists of the managements, editors, and news-gathering and news-writing staffs of the *New York Times,* CBS Television News, NBC Television News, the *Washington Post, Newsweek,* and *Time.* They are highly intelligent and cosmopolitan, they take themselves and their responsibilities with great seriousness, and—until the last decade—they enjoyed almost universal reputations for journalistic excellence. In this essay they will be called the media elite.[2]

Given the income, status, or role of the *Times* and *Post* readership and that of the news magazines, the direct influence they exercise over the opinions of a select audience is not surprising.

Direct media influence results from a fact of psychology. The better the reputation and the higher the status of an information source, the more the information it conveys will be believed. The generally favorable reputations enjoyed, for example, by the *New York Times* and the *Washington Post* resulted, in the first instance, from their managements' evident interest in news and the large resources they invested in gathering and writing the news. These reputations were transmitted by journalists and others who were favorably impressed by both the interest and the investment. All reputations (good and bad) feed upon and reinforce themselves.

Less often discussed, but far more important, is indirect influence. The most influential media lead other media. Through indirect influence, the viewpoints expressed in the *New York Times,* for example, are passed on by local newspapers and local stations

[2] Some have argued that they do not constitute an elite in certain senses of the word, but since they constitute a highly select group that exercises great influence, the term may be useful. It is not implied that all of these organizations reach the same policy conclusions at the same time. In respect to many issues of the 1960s, the *New York Times* established a policy first and CBS, NBC, the *Washington Post, Newsweek,* and *Time* adopted much the same policy later, but not necessarily in that order.

throughout the country.[3] The process of indirect influence is especially important because it reduces the likelihood that viewpoints different from the urban orthodoxy will be widely expressed in the American hinterland. The major media viewpoint sometimes overwhelms the smaller media viewpoint.

Indirect media influence results from the basic nature of the news business. In it, at least two resources are always scarce and are thus precious. They are available staff talent and available printed space (or broadcast time) for news.

Almost by definition, no news organization ever has enough staff talent, space, or time to meet its deadlines and cover all subjects to its editors' satisfaction. Thus all news organizations are susceptible to the human temptation to compensate for these shortcomings by drawing upon the work of others.

Much of the *New York Times*'s indirect influence is based upon this fact. The *Times* employs the largest news-gathering and news-writing staff of any newspaper in the United States. It devotes more columns to news and editorial matters than almost any other American daily.[4] Each day the *Times* is found in newspaper and television newsrooms across the country. Second only to whoever may be the hometown competitor, the *Times* is the newspaper that exercises the greatest single influence upon most local American daily newspapers.

Because the local paper lacks the time and talent to form its

[3] The *Times*'s national influence is out of all proportion to its direct influence upon the mass population of New York. The *Times* ranks only twenty-first in the percentage of occupied housing units it reaches daily among the twenty-four daily newspapers in the ten largest metropolitan areas; the *New York Daily News* ranks third (*Detroit News* memorandum, May 5, 1972). But the *Times* is read in 11,141 cities and towns (*Interesting Facts About the New York Times, New York Times,* April 1972; see also Gay Talese, *The Kingdom and the Power* [New York: World Publishing Co., 1969], p. 72). Few other daily newspapers are distributed widely beyond their own communities. The *Times*'s wide readership by college and university faculty and students is also a major factor in its influence.

[4] The *Times*'s news, Sunday, and editorial staff (910 people) is almost twice the size of the second largest comparable newspaper staff. The total daily and Sunday space the *Times* devotes to news and editorial matters ranked fourth among daily newspapers in 1970 (*Interesting Facts About the New York Times, New York Times,* April 1972, and *Detroit News* memorandum, May 24, 1972).

own judgments independently on every subject, it defers to the *Times*'s judgment, both explicitly and implicitly. Story play, story size, location in the paper, and other marks of a story's relative importance to some extent follow the *Times*. More importantly, the nuances of the *Times*'s story set off continuing ripples. The *Times* establishes a national moral tone on a story by getting it first and in greatest detail.

Every news and feature story contains implicit moral judgments. Any given event can be described in many different ways. The way selected depends heavily upon the competence and art of the writer. But it also depends—overwhelmingly—upon the writer's moral values. The selection of themes, the choice of descriptive adjectives, the degree of sympathy or animosity that is implied toward the story's subjects, all reflect values. The most important expression of the writer's values is in the implicit major questions his story attempts to answer. (In the riot story: What were the riot's "underlying social causes"? Or why did the police fail to stop the riot earlier? Or what short-run and long-run damage did the riot do? In the war story: What injuries did napalm cause in the battle? Or why was the battle lost? Or what was the battle's place in the strategic context? Or what was the battle's place in the total diplomatic situation? A good story will, of course, answer all of these questions and more. But if the same kind of question consistently leads all the stories on a given subject, that question, over time, gains great force.)

Naturally, the local editor is free to ignore the *Times*'s tone on any given story. But he does so at a certain peril. The *Times*'s tone will be locally copied somewhere. The questions it asks probably will have to be answered locally. The local editor may either follow the *Times*'s tone or try to refute it. But the latter course takes much time and reportorial effort. Either way, the *Times*'s philosophy is felt.

Newsmen sometimes describe the closest possible approach to story objectivity as "playing it down the middle." But very large news-gathering resources may be required to offset the weight of reportage marshaled early on one side or another of a controversial story. The resources are often locally unavailable. Some questions are never raised. Others, when raised, are most difficult to answer by deadline time.

The major news medium that first develops any given story usually defines the key questions that persist in future coverage of that story. In other words, the first major medium to treat a subject often defines the universe of discourse and establishes the moral tone on that subject.

What if some regional paper develops a story before the *Times*? By definition, the local paper is usually not a major medium and is often ignored nationally. If the *Times*, the *Washington Post*, the Associated Press, United Press International, or the broadcast networks do not pick it up, the local paper's interpretation may simply never appear on the national scene. Or the local facts may appear but be interpreted differently.[5]

It should have been a major contribution to the diversity of viewpoints that another national newspaper with large resources sprang up to compete with the *New York Times*. The *Washington Post*, by the volume of its coverage of the federal government, has risen to very great influence. But on major national matters, the moral tone expressed in the *Post* is not unlike that of the *Times*.

The *Post* has artfully attuned the philosophy of its news coverage to its local readers—that huge mass of middle-level federal officials who do things in Washington. This policy has succeeded in attracting advertising. This, in turn, has permitted continuing increases in local staff size and in the space devoted to Washington matters. These produce substantial influence over the rest of the news industry on news centering in Washington. News services operated by the *Times* and the *Post*, which are sold to hundreds of papers around the country, directly reinforce their influence.

What of the Associated Press and the United Press International? These are supposed to be the basic sources of national news in the hinterland. The wire services do provide the accurate-in-detail, sometimes exhaustive, gray accounts that fill most of the

[5] In the classic story of the alleged "government conspiracy to murder twenty-eight Black Panthers," several local newspapers across the country almost immediately challenged the fashionable but incorrect version. But this fact was not noted in the New York or Washington papers for a very substantial time. See Paul Poorman, "Criticism of the Press," *Seminar*, September 1971, p. 3.

national news columns of most papers. They are influential (and a certain bias may also sometimes creep into their accounts). But merely by virtue of the fact that they are wire services and not newspapers, the AP and UPI cannot begin to approach the philosophical influence of the *Times* or the *Post*. AP and UPI are in business to serve everyone. They must not state viewpoints too strongly (on the one hand this, on the other hand that). They must not anger buyers of the services.

Ethical neutrality in the wire services, as in any form of communication, gives the moral advantage to the man or organization with a strong conviction and the will to speak it. Hence the philosophical influence of the *Times* and the *Post*. One should not expect the AP or UPI to counterbalance the *Times* and *Post*. They cannot. Only another newspaper with comparable staff size and bulk, but with a quite different moral philosophy, could begin to counterbalance them.

The television networks exercise enormous direct and indirect influence. There may be little need to argue the force of a communications system that can raise obscure men to sudden notoriety, simultaneously convey the same phrases, jokes, and modes of speech to millions of Americans, and transmit changed habits and popular fashions within months. Regional differences in taste and culture are disappearing under the homogenizing influence of the national networks' simultaneous showing of the same pictures in every part of the land.

As traditional institutions (the family, the church, the neighborhood, the primary and secondary schools) decline in moral influence, it may be that television is filling the vacuum. In what some believe to be an increasingly impersonal society, the face on the television screen may have assumed an increasingly "personal" character. The national television personality may have replaced the priest, minister, teacher, father, or big brother.

The television networks are intensely competitive with each other and with other kinds of news media. In their pursuit of the maximum possible audience they may tend to edit network television news for dramatic pictures rather than for the ideas in a story. Television is entertainment. Perhaps one would not expect it to carry a heavy burden of balanced or carefully qualified ideas. The logic of a TV news show is often the logic of the pictures that happen to be available instead of the words that accompany them.

But editing for pictures has produced a great emotional impact upon viewers. The viewer believes what he *sees,* even if the impression conveyed is wrong. The fact that the viewer sees films of startling events leads him to the sometimes erroneous conclusion that what the accompanying voice says about those films is true—or that what is said, with the particular pictures shown, represents a balanced account of the total event. But what about the pictures that for some reason were never taken or could never be taken? What about the pictures that were "left on the cutting room floor"? Can other pictures offset the first impressions conveyed by dramatic pictures? If so, can such countervailing pictures often be obtained? If not, can television news place complicated events in balanced perspective, whatever may be the intentions of its practitioners?[6]

Television newsman Roger Mudd has said, "The inherent limitations of our medium make it a powerful means of communication but also a crude one which tends to strike at the emotions rather than at the intellect."[7]

Television tapped a new audience for news—the huge audience that had little interest in newspaper reading but found the passive sport of television watching hypnotic. Millions of Americans became interested in some aspect of politics because of television. During the past decade many of them became active in politics for the first time.

But the social groupings that seem to be the most susceptible to television influence are the middle classes and upper middle classes who have some college education. Survey data can be construed as showing that those whose opinions have actually been changed by television are not those defined as poverty-striken, or those in the hourly labor force. Walter DeVries and Lance Tarrance suggest, for

[6] Television's visual emphasis may give it other opportunities for influence. The voices accompanying dramatic news pictures may repeat unproven (and unprovable) assertions. This is a technique of influence well known to professional propagandists and not much tolerated in American journalism before television.

[7] Roger Mudd, Washington and Lee University, December 7, 1970; quoted by Clark Mollenhoff, *Detroit News,* May 16, 1971, p. 2E.

example, that political ticket-splitting is most likely to occur in the upper middle class as a result of media influence.[8] And "other recent research confirms the argument of DeVries and Tarrance: the moderately well-educated are the ones most likely to change their minds when the media models of reality change."[9]

Television network news has influenced local newspaper journalism across the country perhaps as much as the *Times* or the *Post* and has in this way also exercised a significant indirect influence upon opinion. There is no way to measure how many newspaper headlines have been written or how many front pages have been made up with a keen consciousness of last night's network television news treatment of a national or international matter. But there can be little doubt that many newspapermen felt deeply influenced by last night's TV news programs, because that was what people talked about during the 1960s. Some newspapers may even have imitated TV's news selection and relative emphasis. Even if he wanted to, a newspaper editor could not easily downplay a riot, for example, if news films of it had been TV's prime story.

Those individuals whom network television made into heroes became the popular heroes of the 1960s. Then many local newspapers followed and ratified them as national heroes. Those whom network TV converted into villains became the country's villains. The newspapers largely followed.

By overreacting to television news, as if Cronkite or Brinkley or Huntley (or actually the anonymous producers and writers behind them) were the editors in chief of the entire national news industry, local newspapers failed to compete properly with television. Worse, local newspapers submerged their own special newspaper-based talents, insights, and special journalistic competence. Newspapers abdicated judgments to a medium that was derived more from movies, radio, and show business than from the disciplines of traditional journalism.

[8] Walter DeVries and Lance Tarrance, Jr., *The Ticket-Splitter: A New Force in American Politics* (Grand Rapids: Eerdmans, 1972).

[9] Andrew M. Greeley, *Commentary,* April 1972, p. 92. See James D. Wright, "Life, Time, and the Fortunes of War," *Trans-action,* January 1972, for a detailed analysis of opinion shifts on the Vietnam war which comes to a similar conclusion.

Newspapers themselves helped to condition people to accept TV's credibility by following its news leads. Many people formed their first impression of a news event from TV. Then they later read a newspaper account of the same event which closely followed not only TV's selection of facts, but the TV mood, emphasis, and moral tone. (Worse still, newspapers made an occasional factual error and people could say, "I *saw* what *really* happened.") Why should people not conclude that TV was credible?[10]

Because the resources of local television stations are relatively scarce, television networks provide almost all of the national and international news coverage that is broadcast by all local television stations. Few local stations even have a Washington bureau to supplement the news programs and news films fed to them by the networks.

Because the *New York Times,* CBS Television News, NBC Television News, the *Washington Post, Newsweek,* and *Time* exercise such inordinate direct and indirect influence over opinion, it is especially significant that they tend to convey the same general viewpoint. We should consider why they do.

II

Following World War II, all American news media became increasingly subject to the influence of intellectuals.[11] The most in-

[10] The Roper polls show that, when asked to identify the medium from which "you usually get most of your news about what's going on in the world today," the proportion of people who reply, "Television" appears to be slowly growing. When asked which medium would be believed "if you got conflicting or different reports of the same news story," a growing proportion of people replied, "Television" ("An Extended View of Public Attitudes Toward Television and Other Mass Media, 1959–1971," a report by the Roper Organization, Inc., Television Information Office, 1971). Note that this question was *not* "Where do you usually get most of your news about what's going on in *town* today?"

[11] The growing influence of intellectuals upon media has often been noted in recent years. See, for example, Nathan Glazer, "The Role of the Intellectuals," *Commentary,* February 1971, p. 55; A. James Reichley, "Our Critical Shortage of Leadership," *Fortune,* September 1971, p. 89; Peter B. Clark, "Scholars, Journalists, and American Foreign Actions," November 10, 1965, unpublished manuscript; Clark, "Will Success Spoil American Civilization?," *Congressional Record,* October 16, 1967, H13447–51; Clark, "The Vietnam War and American Attitudes," *Washington Report,* January 1968; Clark, "The Reporter and the Power Structure," *Nieman Reports,* March

fluential news organizations—those mentioned above—became the most susceptible to their influence.

Consider first the reasons for the increasing influence of intellectuals over all media. Newsmen share characteristics that have made them, as a group, highly subject to whatever may be the fashion of the day. If the "unusual event" defines today's news for the newsman, the currently fashionable trends affect what they take to be the "usual" or "unusual." Newsmen share perceptions of these trends among themselves. Over the past decade, the most fashionable trend-setters have come to be intellectuals.

It has been said that newsmen have a "herd instinct." Intense job pressures and personal preferences tend to keep them together socially. Basic similarities of opinions develop among people who share the same specific assignments; for example, members of the Washington press corps. A consensus on many matters develops. The reporter who does not share the consensus may feel quite uncomfortable. (Allen Drury and Clark Mollenhoff are among the relatively few recent Washington correspondents who allegedly did not share the Washington press corps consensus.)

It is understandable that the person who works with letters in the university should have some general impact upon the person who works with letters in the newspaper, or even in the television studio. The intellectual shares with the popular journalist the guardianship over the society's semantic usage. The intellectual's writings sometimes define the society's values or, if not the values themselves, its most valued symbols.

A few journalists have long been fascinated by the kindred but distant world of scholarship. For some of them, the most remote but highest goals repose in the university: the Pulitzer Prize is admin-

---

1969, p. 8; Clark, "The Press and Its Critics," January 5, 1971, unpublished manuscript; Clark, "Newspapers: Out of the Frying Pan into the 'Seventies," *Newspaper Controller,* January 1972.

Perhaps the most interesting question, which remains unexplored here, is how the specific policy preferences of some intellectuals and not others attract the attention of media elite writers and managers. A very small number of people and a very small number of journals probably play a crucial part. On this subject, the essay by Dennis H. Wrong, "The Case of the 'New York Review,' " *Commentary,* November 1970, p. 49, may be instructive.

istered by Columbia University; the Nieman Fellowship is operated by Harvard University.

But since World War II, the magnetism of the intellectual milieu has become more direct and more powerful: it symbolizes a kind of social status. During the war, the intellectual attained a public notice and moral authority he had never before achieved in America. The astounding postwar expansion of college and university faculties, while it may have diluted those faculties, certainly amplified the intellectual's voice. Continuing prosperity expanded the market for his products.[12]

After the war, higher education came to be almost equated with status. Thus, by one of those basic processes that retrospectively can be seen to have channeled history, the *policy views* of those people who enjoyed high status—that is, those engaged in higher education—came to signify social status. If a journalist wanted to enhance his own status, he occasionally learned to attach his by-line to the policy views of the intellectual. A symbiosis developed. The intellectual lent status to the newsman; the newsman lent exposure to the intellectual. This practical relationship did not imply that the newsman necessarily believed in the intellectual's ideas. But he transmitted them effectively.

Also, for reasons that date at least from the three-cornered relationship of journalists, intellectuals, and Democratic party politicians of the New Deal, a larger number of newspaper reporters and writers were disposed to be "liberal" than conservative in personal politics. In recent years, even editorial writers, who by convention more directly reflect the views of the supposedly conservative publishers, identify themselves more with the Democratic party than with the Republican party.[13] This maintains contacts between journalists and intellectuals which are more than random.

[12] College and university enrollments increased from about 1.5 million in 1940 to about 8 million in 1972. Total faculty size increased from 147,000 in 1940 to about 930,000 in 1971.

[13] "Nearly twice as many editorial writers for daily newspapers say they are Democrats as the number who say they are Republicans, according to a survey by the Indiana University Journalism Department.

"The study of 341 editorial writers from all geographic areas of the United States was conducted by Dr. Cleveland Wilhoit, specialist in research for the department. It was released Thursday.

"Mr. Wilhoit found that editorial writers 'are about evenly divided

Finally, a great part of the most influential media management and editorial talent is centered in New York City. So too are several journals of varying degrees of significance in the broader intellectual community (for example, *Commentary, New York Review of Books, Partisan Review, Dissent, The New Yorker, New York,* and many others). While some observers have exaggerated the point, some interaction and mutual influence do occur there.

The fact that newspapers and broadcast operations now recruit much of their talent from campuses substantially increases the intellectual's access to media (and simultaneously insulates him from media criticism). Compare the origins of the American newsman of the 1920s or 1930s with those of today. The *Front Page* reporter was likely to have been a street-hardened, practical man who looked with skepticism upon those who had learned only from books. Today the influential newsroom staffer is likely to be a "bright young" college graduate who has specialized in the humanities or some social science, and who carries with him, with greater or lesser fidelity, impressions, values, and questions from the campus.

During the great journalistic talent hunt of the booming 1960s, a few editors acted as if they were following a series of persuasive (but incorrect) syllogisms that went something like this: News media need talented writers. Talented people are found in colleges and universities. The most talented are to be found in the most famous or largest universities. College writers are often found on campus newspapers or engaged in campus politics. Therefore (some rea-

---

between those who say they are independent in political leanings and 31 percent who are Democrats and 17 percent who are Republicans.'

"Dan Drew, a graduate student and former Washington newsman who helped in the study, said: 'There are fewer Republicans than Democrats among the young writers, but with age, the proportion of both independents and Republicans goes up.'

"The study found that editorial writers were slightly younger, happier in their jobs and better educated than they were a decade ago.

" 'One of the significant findings is that most editorial writers say they are rarely or never asked to take editorial stands with which they don't agree,' Dr. Wilhoit said. 'That will surprise a lot of people' " (*New York Times,* August 8, 1971, p. 44).

Some data on the attitudes of culture critics and editors are provided in "Critics and Criticism in the Mass Media," United Church of Christ study by Louis Harris and Associates, Inc., 1969.

soned) we should recruit our young people from among the writers and campus politicians of the Ivy League or the largest state universities.

Some newspapers, news magazines, and television networks did. The explosive results have been apparent. There have been a few staff "revolutions" and a large number of "journalism reviews" intended to tell editors how to do right. Many advocates of a "new journalism" have appeared. They inform us that "objectivity is impossible" and "balance is selling out." They hint that good and bad reporting must be judged by which side of the issues the reporter is on.

These are mere symptoms of the very general influence upon American journalism that resulted from hiring many intense, energetic, politically active young writers directly from the campus, during a decade when the campus was fairly boiling with political fervor. If the news industry had been consciously trying to, it could not have found a recruiting ground more filled with zealous young people eager to change values and institutions. Some even seemed to feel put upon when they were asked merely to report events accurately so that *other* citizens might make informed policy decisions.

Perhaps some editorial executives assumed that the apprentices they were hiring in the 1960s had gone through the same diverse lives and difficult job experiences they themselves had known. But this was seldom the case. A large number of young people were hired with what seemed to have been excellent scholarly records but little or no intervening practical experience.

Some news organizations believed a few of the more extreme young people were representative of all young people and hired them for this reason. Those organizations took the "youth movement" or the "adversary culture" so seriously that they lent their pages to its spokesmen. By doing this, they lent not just exposure but credibility and a symbolic legitimacy.

The college graduate who was recruited during the 1960s also provided some reinforcement for media staff liberals of an earlier generation. He joined news organizations that were already less likely to be hierarchical than staff-run. The American newsman's mood has always been antiauthoritarian, especially in regard to the administration of his own news department. He resisted direction or guidance in general, and especially in regard to the substance of his writing. The news unions sometimes reinforced his resistance, although the newest recruits seldom found the unions fully satisfying.

In a period of great prosperity, when each journalist was virtually assured a job, the new recruit from the campus was generally quite free to pursue his own personal policy interests. The unwillingness and inability of editors to guide staffs during the 1960s combined with the general staff restlessness. The resulting vacuum of policy direction allowed, often encouraged, younger journalists to draw upon the ideas that came most naturally to them. In contrast to an earlier time, these were the ideas of campus intellectuals, or occasionally of books and journals of advanced intellectual opinion.

The top business managers of some of the most influential news organizations rationalized their acceptance of this infusion of policy ideas from the campus with a salute to "idealistic youth, the best hope for the future." Managements sometimes tolerated these trends for a commercial motive also. Advertising pressures were leftward, not rightward—to the extent that they had any policy effect. The search was always for the largest possible market. During the 1960s advertisers ardently sought the "youth market." "Young demographics" sold advertising space and air time. How better to do this, some managements may have reasoned, than to pay close attention to the campus mood?

The campus mood during the 1960s was highly political. The prevailing although not overwhelming campus attitude was a bland liberalism. The strong minority position was radicalism. President John Kennedy's explicit appeals to youth; the civil rights movement; the shock of Kennedy's assassination; the successful campus rebellions and the abdication of authority by some university administrations; the early, strongly negative reactions to the Vietnam war of some faculty and students; the government's failure to cope with this early response; the partially successful influences of young people upon national politics—all stimulated a widening interest in politics among students. All gave them some sense of competence and effectiveness. This was in marked contrast to the prior decade.

Faculty members encouraged student political interest and activity. They did so partly for educational reasons, but partly to support their own national (and sometimes campus) politics.

The unique university personnel system, by which committees of faculty members hire and promote their own colleagues, worked to produce an overwhelming preponderance of liberals in the academic specialties dealing with human behavior. For example, in recent surveys, 74 percent of political scientists identified themselves as Democrats, as did 78 percent of sociologists and 70 percent of psychologists.[14] The personal political preferences of faculty members made some mark upon the content of the education they provided.

Liberal senior professors trained like-minded students in their own image and hired them as professors. Liberal, like-minded men in turn recruited more liberals. Seymour Martin Lipset, a careful scholar of academic affairs, has written: "The values of the cosmopolitan liberal scholars continue to dominate academe because new recruits to the profession are socialized in the graduate schools. Those who most resemble their professors are most likely to be recommended for the best jobs, to be defined as the most promising."[15]

The dynamics of campus life mutually reinforced the inherent liberal and radical tendencies among faculty and students but inhibited or silenced the campus moderates and conservatives. The victories went to the most demonstrative, energetic, and forceful. Many faculty members fully understood and responded to their major constituencies—their own colleagues and their students. Stu-

[14] Everett Carll Ladd, Jr., and Seymour Martin Lipset, "The Politics of American Political Scientists," *PS*, Spring 1971, p. 135; Charles B. Spaulding and Henry A. Turner, "Political Orientation and Field of Specialization Among College Professors," *Sociology of Education*, 47 (Summer 1968): 253; Robert Yee, "Faculty Participation in the 1960 Presidential Election," *Western Political Quarterly*, 16 (March 1963): 213–20; D. Stanley Eitzen and Gary M. Maranell, "The Political Affiliations of College Professors," *Social Forces*, 47 (December 1968): 145–53.

[15] Seymour Martin Lipset, "The Politics of Academia," in *Perspectives on Campus Tensions: Papers Prepared for the Special Committee on Campus Tensions*, ed. David C. Nichols (Washington, D.C.: American Council on Education, 1970). That it is at least possible for this system to work in the philosophically opposite direction is demonstrated by the handful of departments that are described as "conservative."

dents tended to associate their own status with the political attitudes that enjoyed the greatest apparent campus currency.

Thus it came to be that most of the ablest students graduated as liberals or radicals during the 1960s. Although they were not necessarily intellectuals themselves (real intellectuals might actually bore them), they had cut themselves adrift from traditional values. Partly by default, as a substitute for the traditional values they had rejected or never accepted, they found congenial the only other values they had experienced, those of the intellectual.

The most politically interested young journalists from the campus, who thought of themselves as the agents of social change, sought jobs with the most politically influential news organizations, for they wished to extend their own influence over events. In their turn, the media elite organizations were the most likely to hire the politically intense young people, for they were often the most talented and energetic young writers around. Thus the media elite organizations themselves came to be the most influenced by writers who brought some version of campus values with them.

The administration of President John Kennedy recruited many intellectuals into responsible governmental positions. It gave other intellectuals (and some reporters) the feeling that they were participating in the making of history. Kennedy's assassination suddenly changed this. While President Lyndon Johnson retained intellectuals in office, their actual influence over important matters declined. Many of them suddenly forgot the differences they had had with the living John Kennedy. They questioned motives and decisions they had accepted before. They wanted to believe that President Johnson was basically changing his predecessor's policies. Intellectuals, especially in the academic community, became much more politically self-conscious and, perhaps for the first time, a highly effective political constituency.[16]

The intellectuals consulted by President Richard Nixon repre-

[16] One of the more perceptive accounts of the way intellectuals remembered John Kennedy is Tom Wicker's "Lyndon Johnson vs. The Ghost of Jack Kennedy," *Esquire,* November 1965, p. 87. An excellent analysis of the growing political consciousness among some intellectuals, written while it was growing, is Irving Kristol's "American Intellectuals and Foreign Policy," *Foreign Affairs,* July 1967, pp. 594–609.

sented a different viewpoint from the prevailing American intellectual fashion. The combined result was that, once having tasted power and having lost it, intellectuals redoubled their efforts to affect important events. They attacked government actions that, had Kennedy lived, they might not have treated with the same knowing and casual contempt.

During the 1960s the intellectuals overwhelmed traditional values by sheer force of intelligence, energy, newly found status, added material resources, available time, and the intense will to which the experiences of 1961–1963 and their shocking end contributed. Young journalists were increasingly exposed to political intellectuals during the 1960s and the intellectuals worked hard to enlist them in their cause. Factional politics within the Democratic party had played a part.

Because the newsman was different in the 1960s, his major sources were different. The reporter was likely to have as sympathetic and helpful sources people who had had training and experiences similar to his own.

Like most people, the newsman seeks to associate with others whose tastes and interests are similar to his. He likes people who help him. This means that he tends to like people who provide him with information, new ideas, or news. He likes people who talk well and are willing to talk at length. Thus he may not only prefer to see words rather than physical activity employed in practical matters, but he may feel more at home with men distinguished by exceptional verbal skills than with men who display exceptional action or executive skills.

Everyone is to some extent more likely to criticize strangers than friends. The current generation of college-trained journalists is more likely to have professors, government employees, or other newsmen as close personal friends than, for example, corporation presidents, labor leaders, generals, or police chiefs. The latter are more likely than the former to be targets of implied journalistic criticism.

The younger journalists are the captives of a consensus characteristic of their age group and similar to that of intellectuals. Many of them share a point of view—an unstated similarity of attitudes—about what is good and what is bad, about the way people are likely to behave, about the way public problems should be defined, and about the best way to solve them. This consensus is urban-bred, college-trained, confident of "progress," urbane, mildly idealistic, slightly optimistic, and somewhat bland.

Described in regional terms, the consensus is somewhat more the attitude of the East and North than of the West and South. It is more abstract than practical. It is surely more a reformist middle-class or philanthropic upper-class viewpoint than a skeptical working-class perception.

The consensus seems to assume that America can solve its problems with good intentions, education, university-trained expertise, rational analysis, earnest conversation, peaceful efforts, and sophisticated compromise. The consensus makes younger journalists more receptive than many other Americans to the values and policy preferences of intellectuals.

III

What are these values and policy preferences? What is the moral tone that has prevailed among intellectuals in recent years?

Seymour Martin Lipset has observed that "although important segments of right-wing intellectual criticism remain, it is clear that since the 1920's in the United States and increasingly in other Western countries as well, intellectual politics have become left-wing politics."[17]

Even among intellectuals themselves, it has become commonplace to label American intellectuals as "liberal" or "left-wing." But this provides only partial guidance for analysis, given the semantic wanderings of the idea of liberalism and the variety of left-wing factions.

An examination of certain character traits perhaps shared by most American intellectuals may shed some light upon the kinds of policies they advocate and their reasons for advocating them. The traits seem to follow from the kinds of personalities that choose to become intellectuals, from their training and work experiences, or from both.

Besides intelligence, originality, curiosity, and detachment, these traits might include an extraordinary interest in words, ideas, and

[17] Lipset, "The Politics of Academia," and see Lipset and Richard E. Dobson, "The Intellectual as Critic and Rebel: With Special Reference to the United States and the Soviet Union," *Daedalus,* 101 (Summer 1972).

theory; a disposition to be critical; a tendency to challenge or resist the authority of organizations (including nation-states); and, in policy recommendations for complex social, political, or economic situations, a tendency to maximize only a single value or goal.

The intellectual's work centers around words and ideas. Words are his tools and he molds his product with them. Like the newsman, he greatly enjoys informed conversation and intense debate. The disciplines of his craft, and of the American academic culture, impel an interest in theory (words constrained by formal logic). He seeks philosophical consistency. He is interested in general, as distinct from particular, philosophical consistency. He is interested in general, as distinct from particular, explanations of and guides for human behavior. The scope and power of his theoretical generalizations are among the criteria by which his professional competence is judged.

His interest in social theory contrasts sharply with the instinctive interests of men who are professionally engaged in public affairs. The latter tend to be pragmatic in judgment, incremental in decision-making, and oriented toward specific concrete cases, not general categories of cases. The intellectual's interest in social theory is transmitted to society via the increasing number of college students who are exposed to academic intellectuals. It is even forcefully conveyed by students to their parents.[18]

It would be rash to attempt to characterize the range of social and political theories that now enjoy significant intellectual currency. But they would appear to be closer to Rousseau than to Hobbes, closer to Marx than to Madison. They often disclose a kind of utopian expectation of man's goodness or social perfectability. They convey a certain resistance to the individualism that character-

[18] This growing interest in theory has probably stimulated an increased receptivity among students to leftist or Marxist theory. As Daniel Yankelovich has written, "Generation after generation of college students pick up, almost by osmosis, the compelling but false picture of our society generated by vulgarized Marxism . . . [because] our leadership groups outside of the academic community have historically shown little interest in theory and have produced no widely accepted explanation of the contemporary American political/economic system" ("The Real Meaning of the Student Revolution," *Public Affairs Conference Board Record,* March 1972, p. 12).

ized the English and early American philosophers. They express a resistance toward market-mechanism economics with its reliance upon individual energies and private incentives. Until recently, mechanisms for collective choice seemed to have been preferred over mechanisms of individual choice.

The intellectual's ideas must be new. Only a very limited academic marketplace exists for balanced, sensible, carefully considered restatements of old ideas. In the present American scholarly culture the premium is placed upon the fresh perspective, the new insight, the innovative mind, in contrast to the synthesizing mind. This means that academic fashions, likue college course offerings and scholarly books, change regularly and often. This may help to account for the fickle way in which the intellectual treats policy ideas.

The intellectual is critical. This is probably a requirement of his career. His very product is often criticism. Those intellectuals who deal with the human condition and human behavior are often especially critical of the social status quo, whatever it may be.

The intellectual is particularly critical of organizational authority, and he resists it. This may partly reflect his recognition of the basic requirements for the free exercise of his own craft. Organizations do not happily tolerate the intellectual's product when it is directed against them. In his own work, he seeks to be free of organizational constraints. He is conspicuously an individualist in his career even when he is a collectivist in social theory or politics. As an individualist, he is philosophically tolerant of individual differences that other people do not so easily accept.

In respect to public policy for complex social situations, the intellectual often seeks to maximize a single desirable value or goal instead of seeking a "practical" balance among several important but competing values. The intellectual's focus upon a single value may result partly from career specialization in his academic field (academic reputations are made in particular, specialized fields, not "in general"), partly from necessary simplification for teaching purposes, partly from an overconcern for logical argumentation, and partly from his realization that it is very difficult to achieve any social change without concentrating upon a single goal. The intellectual may not always see the consequences for an interdependent social system of excessive attention to a single goal. The intellectual's intensity about single goals may help to explain his impatience with compromise and with centrist politics.

A review of these traits makes the intellectual's attitudes toward certain policies more understandable than they might otherwise be. Consider, for example, what some advocate as the desirable way for governments to make decisions. Some intellectuals urge decision-making procedures that maximize the number who participate in the decision. (The single value to be maximized is the proportion of the relevant total population that participates.) This is the logic of one model of democratic political theory driven to a plebiscitory extreme. It displays a curious preoccupation with procedures at the cost of substance. It ignores values that other people might wish to consider, including (1) the desire to reach decisions that are substantively just or wise, (2) the desire to reach decisions consistent with a preexisting body of law or tradition, (3) the desire to reduce the influence upon governmental decisions of sudden extremes of public passion, (4) the desire to assure that voters treat only those issues of which they have some knowledge or in which they have an interest, and so forth. Indeed, maximizing participation in governmental decision-making can produce substantive decisions that are diametrically opposed to the beliefs of the very intellectuals who advocate the procedure. But that, they may say, is another problem. The urge toward logical and theoretical consistency among intellectuals has been known to overwhelm common sense.

In regard to race relations, the single prominent value of recent years has been equality. The intellectual's struggle to help blacks achieve equality has tended to overlook other possibly conflicting values, such as community stability and tranquillity, economic progress for blacks, the reduction of black-white tensions, and so on. (The problem of determining what was meant by equality and determining the possible costs of achieving it also received inadequate attention for a time.)

Perhaps partly because of this attention to a single goal, crime, which has been terribly damaging to good black-white relations, has been either ignored or treated in a theoretical rather than a practical manner. The intellectual has sought to find and treat the "underlying causes" of crime instead of supporting effective, direct actions to stop it.

In respect to the economy, it is not easy to identify the single value that the contemporary intellectual seeks to achieve. Economics is a sophisticated discipline that takes formal, theoretical account of many variables. Thus it is more difficult for the intellectual who has had economic training to seize upon only a single value.

Yet even here one may detect the swing from fashion to successive fashion as the perceptions of the intellectual change and as new ideas gain currency. At one time the major goal was the achievement of maximum production; later, economic stabilization and full employment; then more equal distribution of goods and services. Most recently it has perhaps become the reduction of certain social costs accompanying economic activity.

Regarding the intellectual's attitude toward foreign affairs, the single value to be maximized has come to be the absence of international violence. The attainment of this goal seems to supersede a variety of other goals, such as present and future international stability, the credibility of American diplomatic and military commitments, American material interests, American interests in the morality and justice of certain foreign regimes, and many others. Whatever else is involved, the intellectual's present utopian view is strongly opposed to the direct exercise of force and perhaps of any kind of power.

Perhaps this desire to avoid violence explains the curious fact that the intellectual has opposed the exercise of force by America more vigorously than he has opposed the use of force by our opponents. Especially in the last ten years, he has reserved his full wrath for American force wielded in the international arena. Given his goal, this is perfectly logical. For no matter what actions an adversary may undertake, *no international violence* can occur unless the United States resists or reacts with force. It takes two nations to produce international violence.

A careful survey of both scholarly and popular intellectual writings of the last decade might show that they have largely overlooked the long and continuing history of Marxist-Leninist violence. Yet they have not ignored violent history in general. Some writings have kept alive painful memories of violent rightist history—for example, the Spanish Civil War, the Japanese militarists, and especially Nazi German atrocities.

IV

The media elite—the *New York Times,* the *Washington Post,* CBS and NBC Television News, *Newsweek,* and *Time*—have often distorted the liberal intellectual's complex and sometimes subtle policy views. They have conveyed to the public an oversimplified version of his policy preferences without transmitting his framework of theory, his factual assumptions, his professional standards of evidence, or his criteria of judgment. If anything, this kind of journalism has increased the popular appeal of his policy preferences. It has conveyed his idealistic intentions to a portion of the public that has been very receptive to them, but abandoned the complicated burden of scholarly considerations which are the basis of the intellectual's conclusions but which, of course, could impede popular acceptance of them.

1. The intellectual's interest in words, ideas, and theory has sometimes been journalistically conveyed to the public in the form of crude slogans and oversimplified remedies for complex social situations. For example, the word "establishment" (which implies a simple kind of political theory pitting "the people's legitimate aspirations against the resistant, self-serving establishment") has been pejoratively applied to a range of individuals, organizations, practices, and understandings shared by civilized people which simply cannot be subsumed under the same label. The word certainly serves no useful purpose in explaining them. The phrase "military-industrial complex" has been distorted to convey the misleading impression that the main motive for the maintenance of an American military capability is the self-interest of those who build and operate it. The phrase "white racism" has been journalistically applied to a multitude of difficult human situations that defy analysis—and hence defy solution—in such simplistic terms. The journalistic use of such abstractions has blurred useful distinctions and introduced categories that are analytically obscure.

2. The intellectual's resistance to authority has been so altered that certain media at times appear to advocate anarchy. In the civil

rights context, great exposure was given to the most radical of the agitators. The media justified this exposure by reference to the current "newsworthiness" of the radicals. But the effect was to give an appearance of legitimacy to demands for the destruction of the civil order.

3. The intellectual's tolerance of human differences has sometimes been so journalistically altered as to appear to oppose discipline and to advocate radical permissiveness. News coverage of the student violence that began in 1964, and of the developing student "counterculture," conveyed this impression. When acts of violence were reported without any tone of moral disapproval, large numbers of people interpreted the reporting as expressing approval of violence.

4. The intellectual's professional disposition to criticize was sometimes changed into a process whereby the media elite seemed to seek systematically to discredit men and policies with which it disagreed. This is most evident in respect to American overseas military and diplomatic problems.

5. The intellectual's tendency to maximize a single value has sometimes been changed into the relentless journalistic support of a single public policy goal, heedless of its broader costs or side effects. At a time when Defense Secretary Robert McNamara was popular with journalists, "cost-effective" methods of military weapons procurement was one such goal. Later, "getting out of Vietnam" was another. At the time of this writing, school busing to achieve "equal educational opportunity" is another case of the focus upon a single desired goal.

Even the intellectual's search for new ideas appears in distorted but recognizable form in the restless shifts of certain news organizations from one topical attitude to another. Newsmen obviously have an endless need for new material. This accounts for much of their activity.

But it does not account for outright reversals of position. For example, consider the basic shift of some news organizations during the 1960s from support of the doctrine of American counterinsurgency efforts to total rejection of any part of it, or from support of racial integration to what looked like support for some black separatists, or from a cold war doctrine to a trace of acceptance of the revisionist argument that Americans produced Russian-

American tensions after 1945. Even when successive oversimplifications presented a caricature, the general moral tone of the media elite has been more like that of the more fashionable intellectuals than of any other single social group.

Many monographs of content analysis would be required to demonstrate this statement conclusively. But it is possible to mention here a few bits of evidence. The media elite has had evident favorites in domestic politics. It is not difficult to identify those public figures who have been most and least favored by the media elite writings and television coverage during the last fifteen years.

The favorites have been consistent with intellectual predispositions. The favorites have been highly verbal men, theoretical as distinguished from practical men, men who were sharply critical of some aspect of the status quo, men outspokenly opposed to violence, and men who did not exercise much, if any, governmental authority at the time they were most favored. Among the more obvious favorites have been Adlai Stevenson, John Lindsay, Eugene McCarthy, William Fulbright, John Kennedy, Robert Kennedy, and George McGovern. They enjoyed much more favorable media elite treatment than certain others with whom they might reasonably be compared: Dwight Eisenhower, Richard Daley, Henry Jackson, Dean Rusk, Richard Nixon, Lyndon Johnson, Hubert Humphrey. There is not a clear preference here by political party, but there is by type of man.[19]

Media elite coverage of major events and political issues has

[19] Television man John Chancellor has written a passage that may reveal more than he intended. "Critics of journalism never take into account the fact that journalists are moved by ordinary emotions. The American people respected Eisenhower; so did the press. The American people loved John F. Kennedy; so did the press. The American people were suspicious of Lyndon Johnson; so was the press. About half the American people don't seem to like Richard Nixon, and that's probably the breakdown in the press" (*Playboy*, January 1972, p. 216). One may believe that journalists are moved by ordinary emotions. One might ask if Chancellor has cause and effect sorted out quite right. Did "the American people love" Kennedy *before* he received very favorable media treatment? Were "the American people suspicious of" Lyndon Johnson—the President elected by the largest majority in our history—*before* the media began rather systematically to challenge him? Indeed, a good microfilm library, or a good memory, calls into question the "press respect" for Eisenhower.

been even more consistent with the predispositions of intellectuals. Recall, for example, the height of the civil rights movement of 1961–1964. The media elite focused very largely upon a single value: the black struggle for equality. The media elite interpreted most of the events of this difficult period as they related to this single dimension. The story emphasis was placed upon white resistance to black aspirations, upon black leaders' efforts to overcome continuing obstacles in the path to equality, and upon white violence perpetrated against blacks.

Now the struggle for equality was certainly the major element in the continuing story. But it was not the only element. Generally given much less attention by the media elite because of their focus upon a single theme were other important themes: the effects of the movement upon the attitudes of moderate and liberal Southern whites, who at some risk to themselves had aided blacks in the past; the effects of the Southern example upon the ambitions and tactics of Northern black leaders; the effects of the movement upon the attitudes of Northern whites; the growing white political movement, which, while not simply antiblack, was openly skeptical of the consequences of a very rapid rate of social change; the effects that highly visible and socially approved lawbreaking in the South might have upon respect for other laws in other places; and others.

Obviously, no one of these should have been the sole theme of the media elite during the period, and the country was ill prepared for what was to come later, because these themes were not given careful, continuing attention by the media elite.

When rioting broke out in Northern and Western cities during the mid-1960s, the media elite tended to make the same interpretation. The riots were to be taken as an expression of the desire for equality. This certainly was one motive among several. But to close observers on the scene other motives and expectations were also evident.

Urban riots, high urban crime rates, prison riots, and similar violent phenomena tended to be interpreted in terms of unproven (sometimes untested) social theory. The media elite were more likely to interview a professor of sociology than a police lieutenant. This is not to imply that there is any reason to assume that the policeman's interpretations would have been more correct than the sociologist's. It is to suggest that the media elite implicitly assumed the opposite, and that they may have been wrong.

The impact of the intellectual's propensity to criticize is evident in the media elite critique of business during the decade. The mid-1960s interest in auto safety could not have grown into the national phenomenon of consumerism without substantial critical aid from national media. Story after story alleging defective, unsafe, improperly priced, or unfairly advertised products was given great prominence. One may suspect that neither the business facts nor the consumers had changed much since the previous decade. The media elite had changed.

The sudden popularity of the ecology movement is a model of the penetration of intellectual viewpoints into the journalistic treatment of an extremely complex matter. The protection of aspects of the physical environment had been a matter of serious and gradually growing concern to conservationists for many decades. But the objective seriousness of the problem did not increase in magnitude suddenly and radically during the late 1960s. The intellectual interest, and hence the journalistic interest, did. The topic had suddenly become fashionable in fashionable circles.

The approach to ecology has been highly theoretical (the very idea derives from one academic conception of the proper relationship among physical elements); the ecology movement has been intensely critical of any and all violators of ecological balance and purity (but especially critical of commercial violators); the movement has also turned its critique upon state and municipal governments that have failed to exercise their authority with due diligence; and finally, the whole movement focused upon the single policy goal of purifying and balancing the physical environment. This goal disregards the competing values that are implicated in the context of the physical environment, values such as the direct costs of improvements; the goods, services, and economic developments that must be forgone through focusing upon environmental consequences; the changes that must be made in governmental structures and powers; and, finally, the possibility that many people might just be more interested in other things.

The moral tone of the media elite has been the most consistently obvious in respect to American foreign affairs. One cannot quarrel with the desire to avoid international violence. One can question journalism that has interpreted complex and dangerous events very largely from the perspective of this single goal.

Media elite coverage has steadily criticized or opposed some of the American military weapons, military tactics, and overseas activities that were, or could have been, highly effective in terms of American policy objectives at the time. All American covert activities, and the agencies that conducted them, have been subject to intense criticism. At the same time, the covert activities of the Soviet Union and their effects have been rather casually ignored. (Serious journalistic discussion of the possible uses of nuclear weapons, of course, has long been out of the question.) Great journalistic credence was given to the supposedly scientific evidence against the American ABM. (That evidence has subsequently been subject to very substantial question.)[20]

A review of foreign affairs during the last twelve years reveals a continuing record of media elite opposition to and criticism of the premises of the earlier American foreign policy. The first major instance was Cuba. Castro's 1959 revolution was welcomed in some of the news organizations discussed here; the propriety (not the failure) of the 1961 Bay of Pigs effort was challenged; the 1962 Cuban missile crisis settlement was hailed as a victory, without careful consideration of what brought the crisis about or what its long-term consequences were. Another case was Southeast Asia in 1962 and Russian "proxy war" activity. The media elite opposed American involvement in Laos, supported the 1962 "settlement," but seldom criticized Communist activity.

It is safe to predict unequivocally that when the candid American diplomatic history of the 1960s is written, it will record case after case in which three successive presidents resorted to ineffective military half measures, or fell into inaction, because of the leftward pull upon American opinion of some of the most influential media (coupled, of course, with their allies in the Senate and on the campus).

One of the most historically crucial and journalistically revealing

[20] See especially *Operations Research,* 19 (September 1971):5.

instances was the media elite campaign against the late President Diem of Vietnam during 1962 and 1963. Thoughtful analysts of all persuasions now generally agree that the coup and the assassination of Diem radically altered the character of the Vietnamese war. Yet it is seldom mentioned that some young American journalists contributed mightily to reducing American support for him and to setting the stage for the coup. As one newsman who was on the scene recalls:

> For if anybody had a stake in the overthrow of the Diem regime it was three bright, enterprising young reporters: David Halberstam of *The New York Times;* Malcolm W. Browne of the AP; Neil Sheehan of the UPI.
>
> It was this trio which set the tone of American reporting (and hence of American public opinion) about the Diem regime, and that tone was fundamentally negative. I do not say that any of the three reported anything which he knew to be totally untrue. I do say that none of the three could see anything good in the Diem regime and that each willingly acted as a conduit for forces determined to achieve the overthrow of that regime.
>
> Did the activities of this trio materially affect the success or failure of the Diem regime? President Kennedy obviously thought so, since he unsuccessfully brought pressure to bear on the *Times* to recall Halberstam from Vietnam.[21]

The media elite came to oppose the Vietnam war before most other media or other Americans. But long before they changed their stated editorial opinions, the media elite provided written and newsfilm accounts of the negative aspects of that war which reasonable people could conclude exceeded the requirements of balanced news

[21] Smith Hempstone, *Detroit News,* July 4, 1971, p. 2E. In a book containing many thoughtful observations on press-government relations in foreign affairs, Pierre Salinger comments on these men. "Whether they intended it or not, their articles reflected the bitter hatred they had for the Diem government and their avowed purpose (stated to a number of reporters in Saigon) to bring down the Diem government. It is a deep question of reportorial ethics whether the destruction of a government is within the legitimate framework of journalistic enterprise" (Salinger, *With Kennedy* [New York: Avon, 1966], p. 400).

judgment.[22] The prominence given to antiwar arguments, antiwar protestors, doubts about successive South Vietnamese governments, problems arising in the conduct of the war itself (especially interpretations of the 1968 *Tet* offensive and the My Lai massacre) has been evident.[23] News coverage has been episodic, often focused upon individual tragedies and difficult small unit actions. In surprising contrast to the usual intellectual interest in general considerations, the media elite and especially network television news seldom reviewed what the war was about in general. But the moral tone of that coverage was increasingly and overwhelmingly critical. It criticized not so much the effectiveness (or lack of it) of the American military effort, but by implication its intent.

The greatest emotional force against the war was television news film coverage. As we cannot forget, television showed endless film clips of American troops being killed and injured. As one writer sardonically commented, "Tune in at eleven and see Johnny die."

The best demonstration of the direction taken by the media elite during the Vietnam war is simply to compare it with the newspaper, radio, and newsreel coverage of World War II. The contrasts in the treatment of American defeats and alleged defeats (Bataan, Kasserine Pass, the Bulge, compared with *Tet*) or of atrocities (which went essentially unreported in World War II) should stimulate thoughtful people to ask searching questions.

The media elite was also consistent in what it omitted. One could not fail to note many journalistic criticisms of American intelligence-gathering bureaucracies but few of American welfare bureaucracies. One could find discussions of the purported power

[22] See, for example, Marguerite Higgins, *Our Vietnam Nightmare* (New York: Harper & Row, 1965). See also former ambassador to South Vietnam Frederick E. Nolting, "The Origin and Development of United States Commitment in Vietnam" (unpublished manuscript, 1968), especially pp. 20–21.

[23] Wilbur Elston, "The Other Side: Viet Cong Atrocities Documented," *Detroit News*, December 30, 1971, p. 13A; Don Oberdorfer, *Tet: The Story of a Battle and Its Historic Aftermath* (New York: Doubleday, 1971); Colonel Chandler Goodnow, Colonel Edward A. Partai, Colonel Louis G. Michael, and Colonel Sidney R. Steel, *News Coverage of the Tet Offensive* (unpublished research paper, U.S. Army War College, Carlisle Barracks, Pennsylvania, 1969).

over opinion exercised by communications media owners, but few analyses of the power over opinion exercised by intellectuals.

To document the general trend of media elite journalism it is not necessary to rely exclusively upon the writings of such very different critics as Daniel Patrick Moynihan and Edith Efron.[24] In a good-natured analysis of his own newspaper, *Washington Post* man Richard L. Harwood has written:

> I said . . . that we suffered at times from intellectual arrogance. Our newsroom was full of a lot of highly educated people who sometimes looked down their noses at people who didn't dress the way they did, or didn't talk the way they did, who didn't think the way they did. I said that we got very emotional about the things we were covering. So emotional that we often seemed to be taking sides. And I said in this document that we very often seemed to lack any sense of perspective about our country, about the problems we face here, about the kinds of people who live here and about the diversity that makes this country what it is.[25]

Howard K. Smith on network television:

> Networks, says Mr. Smith, are almost exclusively staffed by liberals. "It evolved from the time when liberalism was a good thing, and most intellectuals became highly liberal. Most reporters are in an intellectual occupation." Secondly, he declares that liberals, virtually by definition, have a "strong leftward bias": "Our tradition, since FDR, has been leftward. . . . The networks have never given a complete picture of the [Vietnam] war."[26]

[24] Daniel P. Moynihan, "The Presidency and the Press," *Commentary,* March 1971; Edith Efron, *The News Twisters* (Los Angeles: Nash Publishers, 1971). One of the best recent analyses is made by respected columnist Robert P. Novak, "The New Journalism," in this volume. The problem is not a partisan matter. "One veteran Washington correspondent, speaking privately, is convinced that what he calls the 'liberal press'—in concert with the Democratic 'doves' in the U.S. Senate, and the insurgent Kennedy and McCarthy factions of the Democratic Party—made it impossible for Lyndon Johnson to function as President" ("Will the Press be Out to 'Get' Nixon?," *U.S. News & World Report,* December 2, 1968, p. 39).

[25] Richard L. Harwood, "Press Criticism: Who Needs It?", *Bulletin of the American Society of Newspaper Editors,* February 1972, p. 10.

[26] Efron, "There *Is* a Network News Bias," *TV Guide,* February 28, 1970, p. 8. On television network news, see Edward Jay Epstein, "News

No less an authority than Richard W. Jencks, former president of CBS/Broadcast Group, has indicated that:

> "History will assign television a major role in the Black Revolution, and in the Anti-Vietnam War Revolution. It is hard to say how any of these changes would have come about without the most energetic, and often empathetic coverage of television." He mentioned specifically the coverage of the violence-marked march by civil rights groups from Selma, Alabama, to Mongomery in March 1965—coverage which was a factor in the subsequent enactment of the 1965 voting-rights bill.[27]

The media elite advocacy of certain viewpoints and policies has produced an additional new problem. Having diagnosed complex public problems, and having taken unequivocal public positions on them, they apparently wish to demonstrate that they were right. They have a substantial journalistic and moral stake in proving their own rightness. This stake helps to account for the negative and self-fulfilling prophecy character of much journalistic comment of the 1960s and 1970s ("People are losing confidence in the [Johnson, Nixon] administration," "The war is unwinnable," "We cannot police the world," and so on) and for the unrelenting attacks and implied attacks upon two successive national administrations (of both parties) and especially of their conduct of foreign policy.

American opinion about public policies has changed substantially in the last decade, and, in vital cases, changed in the directions advocated by intellectuals. The attitudes that changed the most were those regarding the Vietnam war, appropriate levels of military expenditure and foreign aid, American foreign policy in general, national attitudes toward race relations in the South, the status of minority groups in general, the challenges to business (consumerism), and the ecology movement.

Opinion changed the least, or changed contrary to the intellectuals, in cases in which the public did not have to rely for in-

---

from Nowhere: The Selection of Reality on Television" (unpublished Ph.D. dissertation, Harvard University, 1972).

[27] *Broadcasting,* March 16, 1970, p. 36. See also George F. Will, ed., *Press, Politics, and Popular Government* (American Enterprise Institute, 1972).

formation upon the media. That is, people did not accept the media elite policy views when they could *see for themselves* what was happening. This is true of crime, school busing for racial integration, and other aspects of race relations outside of the South. It also defines those matters on which the public seems to feel the greatest skepticism about the mass media.

It is interesting to review the general time sequences of many of these changes. Policy changes were often first advocated by intellectuals who did not work in the mass media. The changes were then generally accepted by some or all of the media elite. Later, many other print media organizations slowly adopted the recommendations for changed policies. Eventually, upper-middle-class and middle-class segments of the population came to accept them. Finally, the working classes and other groups slowly began to accept them.[28]

The diffusion of rough approximations of intellectual attitudes (from universities or other centers to esoteric journals, to elite newspapers, to television network personnel, to local hinterland news-

[28] A large literature documents the opinion changes that have taken place over the decade. A convenient brief summary of some changes is provided by the Roper reports, March 1972. Opinion changes suggesting covariance of certain forms of political liberalism with the college experience are discussed in Yankelovich, *The Changing Values on Campus* (New York: Washington Square Press, 1972).

Similar covariance with increased incomes is suggested in many sources. See, for example, Louis Harris, "Affluent Families Increase," *Chicago Tribune,* January 28, 1971, p. 1A; "Americans Shifting Away from Political Center," *Washington Post,* January 11, 1971, p. A2. Opinion changes regarding the Vietnam War have been carefully analyzed. See, for example, Sidney Verba et al., "Public Opinion and the War in Vietnam," *American Political Science Review,* June 1967; Phillip Converse and Howard Schuman, "Silent Majorities and the Vietnam War," *Scientific American,* June 1970; John E. Mueller, "Trends in Popular Support for the Wars in Korea and Vietnam," *American Political Science Review,* June 1971; Charles Kadushin, "How the American Intellectual Elite Decided to Oppose the War in Vietnam" (unpublished manuscript, 1971); James D. Wright, "Life, Time, and the Fortunes of War," *Trans-action,* January 1972.

Some literature from experimental psychology suggests that "the mere repeated exposure of a stimulus is a sufficient condition for the enhancement of the S's attitude toward it" (Robert A. Zajonc and D. W. Rajecki, "Exposure and Affect: A Field Experiment," *Psychonomic Science,* 17, no. 4 [1969]:216; Robert Zajonc, "Brainwash: Familiarity Breeds Comfort," *Psychology Today,* February 1970, p. 33).

papers, to various publics) may take months, often years. One may even find cases in which local newspapers editorially criticized the editorial positions of, say, the *New York Times* in 1960 but employed junior staff members who implied the same positions in the news columns they wrote in 1970. Those who have followed academic sociology, the intellectual reviews, and popular journalism will recall that sweeping criticisms of American society which are widely discussed today were confined to graduate schools ten years ago, and that they bear a striking resemblance to the writings of, for example, the late C. Wright Mills in the 1950s.

Obviously, many other currents of influence run in the complex channels of American public opinion. Obviously, instances exist in which influences ran in different ways than those suggested here. For example, at certain times during the 1960s, mass media reports deeply influenced the intellectual community rather than vice versa.

But the fact that the flow of influence suggested here does not exist in every case does not negate the general thrust of the argument. Although one may find instances in which intellectuals were not the sources of media elite attitudes, much more media elite policy derived from intellectuals than from any other source.

Some people assert that advertisers exercise some degree of restraining influence over media. But whatever the merits of this proposition—and I find it highly questionable—advertisers are in no sense the *sources* of the moral tone of the media elite. One need only reflect upon the substance of the more striking media elite policies to reject the notion that businessmen are in any way their source or even connected with them. Any lingering doubts on this score will be quickly disabused by frank conversations with the puzzled businessmen (and troubled advertisers) themselves. Neither is government, the military, the law-enforcement system, organized labor, the farm lobby, or any other of the classical interest groups the source of the policies.

Consider a random selection of some of the names initially associated with the moral tone that was conveyed to the country during the last decade: C. Wright Mills, J. Kenneth Galbraith, Theodore Sorenson, McGeorge Bundy, Rachel Carson, Barry Commoner, Ralph Nader, Hans Morgenthau, David Halberstam, Noam Chomsky, Hannah Arendt, Jerome Wiesner, Theodore Draper, and so on. These are not the names of leaders of the classical interest groups. The basic source of the influences that have changed American public opinion is the intellectual community.

If public opinion had changed only in respect to the Vietnam war, one could believe that the altered national mood was solely a rational response to objective reports of a painful situation. But opinions changed about a great range of policy issues. More significantly, public confidence has notably declined, not just in respect to foreign affairs and military leadership, but in respect to other major institutions. Public confidence in government officials, in business, in higher education, and in the news media has eroded.[29]

The intellectual's moral tone has been powerfully transmitted to many Americans. They have witnessed continuing fault-finding, searching criticisms, and allegations of deep national guilt conveyed in ways not always respectful of the criticized men, policies, and institutions.

V

What difference does it make? If one shares the attitudes successfully advocated by the media elite, one might believe the trends explored here simply represent "progress." It is difficult to find fault with the processes of opinion formation when one is on the winning side. But what if, another time, the opinion machine were working against what one believed in?

[29] For data on the apparent decline of general public confidence, see, for example, Louis Harris, "The Emerging Public Responsibilities of the Newspaper Business," address before the American Newspaper Publishers Association, New York, April 25, 1972. One may accept Mr. Harris's survey data without accepting his policy conclusions.

If one wishes seriously to consider the possible future relationships between the mass media and American government, it does not help much to say that the Vietnam war was the "cause" of the opinion changes, or that, if the Vietnam war had not occurred, opinions might not have changed so rapidly. The war did occur. The question is: What can be learned about the behavior and influence of the media under conditions of great strain and division of opinion? Similarly, it does not suffice to conclude that the lesson to be learned from Vietnam is simply that there "must be no more Vietnams." Reasonable men can agree that at some time, in some way, America is likely again to face some tormenting test involving overseas activity in the face of divided domestic opinion. We would do well to reflect upon the question: How will the country arrange better to cope with such a situation?

The processes described in this essay have two kinds of consequences: those affecting choices among alternative public policies and those affecting our very system for making public choices, that is, consequences for the stability, viability, and justice of the governmental regime or constitutional order.

In respect to choices among public policies, it might be argued that the disproportionate influence of certain media is bad for at least three reasons: (1) It is bad because it is monolithic in its moral expression (albeit that expression is a bland liberalism). It represents a new orthodoxy imposed by an elite elected by no one. (2) The influence is bad because it may simply be wrong in substance and may prevent wise or just governmental decision-making. (3) The influence is especially bad in respect to foreign affairs because it may weaken us or kill us by diplomatic accident. The continuing erosion of American confidence and military capability could lead to destruction by causing Americans or our opponents to believe that America would not fight to defend some vital interest.

The domestic policy effects *might* be no worse than those of a fundamental change in American life brought about by a small handful of people and accepted unknowingly by a passive population. After all, how many people have died as a result of fashionable and well-intentioned domestic reforms?

The impact of the media elite upon domestic policies may produce no more than another quiet chapter in the history of American politics. It is conceivable that the major political parties and major candidates will demonstrate the same adaptability that has characterized most of American political history (except that preceding the Civil War). Each candidate may adopt the intellectual's values as his own, modify them to his needs, and develop from them policies that would differ only in nuance from those of the other party or candidates. The genius of American politics has been peaceful accommodation to major changes in facts or beliefs.

The potential effects upon foreign affairs, however, are of a totally different kind. Judgments about foreign affairs do not just distribute goods and statuses among Americans. A domestic decision subsequently viewed as mistaken can always be changed. The effect of a mistake in foreign policy or national security is sometimes irreversible.

Thus, in respect to foreign affairs, the influence of certain mass media (and of the higher education system) is more than an important political fact. It is a possible challenge to survival. The American revisionist left has argued that post–World War II American foreign policy ran dangerous risks of war by adopting an excessively adamant posture and backing it with force. But the contrary case could easily be made about the foreign policies now proposed by the left. By conveying the impression to vigorous foreign powers (we need not even assume here that they are hostile powers) that we lack the will or ability to defend certain territories, we run a great risk of tempting them to test our will and ability. Or we risk unilateral abandonment of commitments painstakingly made and gains painfully won during twenty-five years. We risk all the consequences of attempting to return to 1940.

During the last decade the media elite has acted, at worst, as if it were waging a studied propaganda campaign against the United States in foreign affairs. At times it has acted as if it viewed itself as a neutral agent between the United States and its enemies. The media elite has largely pretended to ignore television's greatly increased power over opinion. It has largely ignored specific foreign tactics, rather apparently designed to use our own news media against us.

During the Vietnam war, Presidents Johnson and Nixon obviously sought to accommodate the media elite (and others) by stopping bombing campaigns, by reduction of troops, and by withdrawals. Our enemies exploited each such move to their own military and diplomatic advantage. It is evident that both administrations required and sought some media elite approval. It is evident that in respect to foreign affairs approval was granted most often when unilateral American gestures toward "peace" were made. Thus presidents may have been constrained by domestic political realities to take actions that violated international political realities. The choices forced by the media elite, in other words, could have been electoral victory at the price of foreign policy weakness or overseas strength at the price of electoral defeat.

In one of the more thoughtful essays on television's broader influence, Robin Day wrote, "One of television's *inherent* limitations is that its coverage contains a built-in bias against free and open societies. Television is far more able to give a critical and unflattering picture of a free society than of any totalitarian one."[30]

Americans seem unable to see the importance in international affairs of the intangible morale factors, such as will, patience, determination, and national unity. More than weapons or grand diplomatic strategies, these factors sometimes define the strengths or weaknesses of nations in the ideologically competitive world. The American public has only a very limited idea of our opponents' tenacity or of the range of political and propaganda techniques they employ. It is just here, in respect to the morale factors, that the media elite has done the greatest disservice.

Our decline in national confidence, our protracted and unjustified public discussions of national guilt, our tendency to withdraw from risk and from the world have resulted not just from events, but from *reports of events* informed by the uniquely debilitating philosophy sketched in this essay.

It may be that American foreign policy could benefit from more of the intellectual's qualities of imagination and ingenuity. But the administration of a successful foreign policy cannot be built upon theory founded more in hope than in fact, upon criticism, the challenge to authority, or single-goal policies. It requires, instead, precisely that quality which the American intellectual community as a group has not recently displayed: calm tough-mindedness.[31]

If the media elite continues to propagate the values and policy preferences of intellectuals, what could be the general consequences? The consequences evidently depend upon how rapidly and how widely the new viewpoint succeeds in gaining public acceptance; they depend upon how much opposition to it persists.

In the past, when only a few Americans shared the intellectual's predispositions, those predispositions were not more than another

[30] Robin Day, "Troubled Reflections of a TV Journalist," *Encounter,* 24, no. 5 (May 1970).

[31] There are some noteworthy exceptions. See Richard Pipes, "International Negotiation: Some Operational Principles of Soviet Foreign Policy," Subcommittee on National Security and International Operations, U.S. Senate, January 10, 1972.

shade of opinion in a genuinely pluralistic society. The media reported them as such—they did not *advocate* an intellectual moral tone.

But today, while the intellectual tone is not dominant in most local media, it is predominant in the major national media. While not everyone uses the same vocabulary about it, the intellectual moral tone is quite apparent to very large parts of the population. The public controversy about it is unclear but loud. Although sometimes portrayed simply as "the truth," the intellectual viewpoint has itself become a subject of political debate.

The obvious controversy has several effects. Passions are raised. Those in favor of the intellectual viewpoint and those against it are more aware of basic differences than they were in the past. The media readers and viewers on either side of the matter suspect and criticize the partisans and media on the other side. The cumulative effects have been a slow decline in public confidence.

If the matter were confined merely to disputes about policies and candidates, challenges to media credibility, or even arguments about differences in moral tone, the situation could be regarded as serious but not grave. But the intensity with which policies have been criticized, and the critics' tendency to increase the stridency and generality of their criticism each time they fail to get everything they ask for, has led to widespread challenges to something much more basic than policies or candidates.

A nation's government involves more than the personalities who happen to occupy public office, the statutes they write and enforce, the court rulings they draft, and the bureaucratic apparatus that is supposed to carry out their intentions. These men and institutions may pursue one policy in contrast to another, and their particular policy judgments sometimes are, as I have indicated, of crucial importance.

But behind the set of men and policies that comprises any particular administration or government, and at a much higher level of significance, lies the constitutional order or regime. This is the accumulated body of widely shared goals, constitutional documents, procedures, unwritten practices, civilities, and understandings by which the nation organizes itself to choose among alternative candidates and policies. The regime is the system by which governments are created and by which they decide how to decide. The regime is a rough reflection of the broader balance of interests, attitudes, and forces that comprise the civil society at any given time. If it is to survive, the regime must be widely regarded as good, trustworthy, and more valuable than any alternative. In a word, people must feel the regime is legitimate.

It is the sense of legitimacy of the American civil order that has been touched and marred by the continuing stridency of a decade of oversimplified and amplified intellectual criticism.

If the media elite believes the highest good is to risk bringing down the present regime and replacing it with some new and as yet undescribed civil order, then it is pursuing the correct strategy. If, on the other hand, it believes that it shares a substantial stake in the basic justice and promise of the present civil order, in the delicate balance of social groupings that it mirrors, then it might wish to reconsider its course. History teaches that a regime can tolerate only so much doubt about its fundamental premises before it is toppled and replaced. But history cannot tell us at what instant that breaking point might suddenly be reached in our own case.

When all men struggle passionately to advance specific policies, few consider the effects upon the regime. The accidental fact that the same kinds of intellectual demands have been forcefully, but with only partial success, thrust upon presidents of both political parties raises the passion and focuses it more directly upon the regime itself. Similarly, the fact that the media elite has violated traditional values, ignored widespread concerns and fears, and given little expression to the interests and viewpoints of large numbers of ordinary people tends to make those people distrustful of the regime itself (although they may express themselves in quite different words).

Relentless criticism has established unreal expectations and eroded public confidence. The media can lead people to hope and to doubt. But they cannot satisfy the hopes for sudden equality or peace or replace the objects of doubt with trusted objects. No one else yet has. Thus the widespread restlessness and unease. The relentless advocacy of single-goal policies puzzles or infuriates citizens whose common sense tells them other desirable but competing goals exist in the real world.

If it is continued, the propagation of the intellectual moral tone through the media could produce an even stronger public reaction against the regime or against the media elite (or all media). It could also produce a new wave of general anti-intellectualism.

One could even imagine some civil unrest resulting from ever sharper contrasts between what people perceive to be reality, on the one hand, and the heavy doses of liberal philosophy provided by the media elite, on the other. These perceptual differences would exacerbate the cleavages between intellectual and nonintellectual. They might also exacerbate other cleavages that are latent in the society.

Some academic students of the mass media make arguments that superficially resemble those made in this essay. They urge as a basic goal that the mass media convey an even greater diversity of viewpoints. But when we closely examine some of these arguments, we may discover that they really seek a greater expression of radical viewpoints. Among such radical viewpoints are to be found the most fundamental challenges to the regime and to those of its goals that are still widely shared. One may ask: How much more basic divergence of opinion can the regime tolerate? Is our heterogeneous population equipped to cope with even more expressions of basic difference and dissent than it endured during the 1960s? To the extent that one values the preservation of the regime, one may wish carefully to reconsider the advocacy of fundamentally diverse opinions for their own sake.

One could imagine an opposite outcome—a case in which the intellectual media and their allies would eventually succeed in imposing their own values and policy preferences upon a very substantial part of the American people. In such a case, traditional middle-class values and nonintellectual preferences would be reduced to a minority status, ironically comparable to the position occupied by American intellectuals of the 1920s. Those who disagreed with the intellectual position would then be defined as the aberrants. They might fall silent and perhaps ultimately disappear. This result might yield a changed regime.

Neither of these two possible outcomes is pleasant to contemplate. In the first case, continuing perceptual and policy disagreements are forecast, leading perhaps to civil unrest. In the second case, the *appearance* of a civil consensus might rise again. But substantial questions about how it was formed and about its substance would also arise. Should the country be guided by the values of any single group that may happen to capture the imagination of a key segment of the mass media industry? Are intellectuals more deserving of guiding American life than any other single group? Could intellectual values properly inform and effectively guide government? Could they assure continuing national security? Could they maintain civil order with justice? (How would intellectuals in power cope, for example, with violent dissenters of the right?)

Consideration of problems of the regime leads us to consider the general processes by which American public policy goals are advocated and adopted. This essay's argument reduces, in its simplest form, to the question: Should the intellectual's goals be imposed upon the country, or should policy goals continue to be the product (admittedly the sometimes tortured product) of the traditional political processes? The virtues and defects of those processes are the same. The virtues include a centrist tendency, a compromising character, and the ability generally to ameliorate most major grievances, given sufficient time. The American constitutional order is so designed that the workings of the processes themselves often provide the necessary time. The defects are that the processes never satisfy everyone, they seldom satisfy extreme advocates of any single viewpoint, they sometimes discard major elements essential to the achievement of the policy goals themselves, they try the patience of the ardent and may spur the zealous into frustrated action. On balance, the traditional political processes have worked to maintain the regime and the substantial opportunity ultimately to achieve justice which it offers.

In the American mythology, if not in fact, the intellectual was regarded as an adviser to government, not as a goal-setter. He was to provide specialized advice about alternative means to achieve widely shared goals. The goals themselves were not created by him, but were to be the outcome of the political processes.

I have argued that the intellectual's influence has become increasingly disruptive as he has increasingly become a goal-setter himself. His recent exceptional access to some mass media and his control of the educational system have permitted him partly to bypass the traditional political processes. As they have been bypassed, he has generated significant support for his policies. But very substantial opposition also remains. The fact is that when the political processes are bypassed, no other method exists—short of resort to violence—to assure that an effort will be made to hear, bargain with, satisfy, or justly treat those who intensely oppose some policy. Government action that disregards sustained opposition can severely damage any regime. Action that disregards reasoned and principled opposition can define injustice.

One may conclude that we should not permit the educative and consensus-building effects of the traditional political processes to be bypassed by direct mass media influence over opinion (or by the influence of intellectuals, institutions of formal education, or any other single source of opinion). Whatever the moral quality of the intentions behind such single influences, the technique would constitute government by propaganda.

The intellectual's special abilities and perceptions contribute to American life in irreplaceable ways. His individual contributions should be praised, not denigrated, and that is certainly the intention of this essay. The intellectual's intelligence, originality, curiosity, detachment, and critical powers fulfill vital moral and social functions.

I argue only that, through accidents of circumstance and force of numbers, a monolithic intellectual viewpoint has to a great extent demoralized and overwhelmed the pragmatic funtionaries of American political life and government in recent years. Intellectual attitudes have—temporarily, I hope—overcome men whose goals and methods were rooted in practical experience, common sense, and traditional values. I submit that this has been unfortunate for the nation.

There exists at least one outcome alternative to the somewhat somber possibilities sketched above. This is that, instead of staying with their present course and either stimulating continuing unrest or imposing monolithic attitudes upon everyone, the most influential media might return to the professional posture and philosophical positions that they occupied during the 1950s and before. They might cease to advocate the intellectual viewpoint but again merely report it, as one among many diverse American perceptions.

Several possible corrective measures follow from the analysis of this essay. They would reduce the influence of a few over all, and they would properly diversify again the content of intellectual opinion.

The public should be better informed about the values and policy preferences of the media. This would permit the public better to evaluate them and to discount them if they wished to. For the same reason, the public should be better informed about the general character traits of the intellectual. Thoughtful but critical essays about intellectuals are long overdue. As a social group they were more protected than most during the 1960s. The practical problem is: Who will bear the message about the messenger?

Efforts could be made to dissolve the consensus among many newsmen. This would require, at least, more careful attention to recruiting and training by news media managements. It might require editors to take a step they have been most reluctant to take: to examine the policy preferences of their news staffs. This would be done not to influence or restrain them, but to assure that highly controverted matters are reported from several balanced and thoughtful philosophical and moral vantage points.

The chain of influence from campus to reporter might be reexamined. Media employment criteria could place greater emphasis upon practical experience and exposure to human diversity and less upon formal academic training.

The link between the young newsman and specific intellectual sources might also be reviewed. Conscious, countervailing efforts might be made to seek out, understand, and sympathetically interview those potential sources of news and opinion who are essentially inarticulate or whose viewpoints are not understood by, or not congenial to, the young reporter. The experienced should be called upon to counterbalance the merely articulate.

The general problem may be of such magnitude as to induce college and university trustees and administrators to rethink the practices that led to near-monolithic campus moods on fundamental policy issues during the 1960s. Faculty recruiting patterns might be subject to closer public scrutiny. Taxpayers and contributors to higher education are not entirely aware of the values that form the current campus fashions. The articulate public still tends to equate universities with intelligence and intelligence with wise and proper policy advice. The public has only begun to perceive the connection between universities and a single set of policy preferences. An intense struggle may be waged to determine whether those preferences will be seen as unequivocally good or as properly subject to question.

Newspapers might try harder to insulate themselves from the influence of network television and of the most influential printed media. This should be done at least in the local newspapers' own self-interests. For competitive reasons, if for no other, local papers must provide materials (including opinions) which are recognizably different from those of the national media. Greater encouragement might be given to those few national news organizations which reflectively convey viewpoints different from the present orthodox liberalism.

If the domestic policy consequences of the processes traced here are no more serious than suggested, no governmental corrective action is required. The domestic implications can be treated by self-corrections undertaken by the news industry itself, encouraged perhaps by a concerned public. If, however, the foreign affairs implications are as grave as suggested, then in time of crisis the government might be justified in taking measures regarding the media as vigorous as any measures national security may require.

If the consequences for the regime are real, responsible people of goodwill should seriously reflect upon the matter.

Paul H. Weaver

•

THE POLITICS OF A NEWS STORY

Few questions arouse more interest these days than that of the influence of the mass media on American politics. Yet despite our obsessive attention to this subject, the fact is that we know very little about it. To be sure, we are fairly certain that there is a media influence, and we have learned something about its origins, its channels, the conditions under which it becomes greater or smaller, and other such matters. What we do not know, however, is the most important thing of all: what difference this influence makes in the way we live, think, and govern ourselves. For we have not yet managed to identify, in any really satisfactory way, the political ends in behalf of which the media speak and the political directions in which their influence pushes us. In short, although we know that a media influence exists, we do not know what, politically, this influence is.

In this particular case, our ignorance does not reflect any want of inquiry or effort. On the contrary: there has been, over the past decade, an endless stream of statements on "the politics of news," and nearly every one of these has been valid enough in its own terms as a statement about the political tendencies of a given sample of media content evaluated from a given point of view. But as theories of the political principles that are inherent in all news, all of these statements are inadequate and may easily be refuted.

For example, critics on the left have argued for years that the media propagate a politics of the status quo, one that is pro-capitalist,

 This paper is a modified version of a chapter of a book scheduled to be published in 1973 by Basic Books, Inc., tentatively titled *The Bias of News: The Form, Governance, and Political Consequences of Daily Journalism in America*.

pro-elitist, pro-imperialist, pro-racist, and pro-sexist; and in behalf of this contention they have adduced instances of news coverage and noncoverage which do indeed illustrate their point. On the other hand, one does not have to look very far to find examples of media content which favor left or liberal causes—two instances that come immediately to mind are the press treatment of the early civil rights movement and the late antiwar movement. So the "news is against leftward political change" theory will not do. But is the argument advanced by Vice-President Agnew and other observers on the right any better? Their theory is that the news media systematically promote liberal or leftist views, and as evidence of this they have pointed to network television hostility to Nixon during the 1968 campaign, to the intensive and generally favorable coverage of the Black Panthers in 1969–1970, to the slanderous treatment of George Wallace since 1964, and so on. Most of these examples are authentic enough, and yet for each such example one can readily turn up another story or episode in modern journalism with a distinctly right-wing slant, the most notable modern instance being the intensive and quite uncritical coverage of Senator Joseph McCarthy in the early 1950s. Thus the theory that the news is a pro-left and anti-right is also inadequate.

Along a slightly different dimension, there are the centrist interpretations of the politics of the news media. The eminent Daniel P. Moynihan, for example, has asserted that the media have adopted an adversary stance vis-à-vis our political institutions and that their "anti-institutionalism" may be seen, for example, in their intense preoccupation with events indicating a lack of "credibility" on the part of recent presidents. Moynihan has offered some striking examples of such coverage—and yet, for all their pertinence, it is an easy matter to discover news stories that anyone would unhesitatingly count as pro-institutional and, even in the Nixon era, pro-presidential. A dramatic and not so very unusual case in point is the intensive and overwhelmingly favorable press and television coverage of President Nixon's trip to China.

The apparent inadequacy of these left-center-right interpretations of the politics of news is often cited by newsmen as evidence for their own view on this subject, which is that the news media adhere to and propagate no particular line or view and thus are politically neutral. The idea that there is no such thing as "the politics of news" is a central tenet of the traditional ideology of American journalism, which has made a sharp distinction between "news" and "editorial" for more than a century. According to this ideology, "editorial" is the journalistic vehicle for political opinion. "News," by contrast, contains no statements of opinion; it is a purely factual mirror of events, and it reflects only what happened, not what the reporter felt or believed about it. In this view, there can be no politics in news except on those occasions, hopefully rare, when an individual reporter's professionalism and self-discipline falter and he injects bias into the news. Inevitably, however, the politics that enter news in this way are occasional and idiosyncratic rather than inherent and systematic, which is why, according to the newsman's view, the popular theories of the politics of news are so easily refuted by counterexamples.

But this newsman's theory will not stand scrutiny either. For although it is true that a proper news story does not contain explicit statements of opinion, opinion is nevertheless pervasively, even massively present in every news story. When an author composes a text, he is making decisions—choosing a subject, selecting information, finding the right words, formulating sentences, putting sentences in a sequence, and so on. The author may be conscious or unconscious of such decisions; he may make them deliberately or intuitively; but whatever his state of mind, decisions are made, alternatives are rejected, and preferences are asserted. In this sense writing is never neutral, and in this sense too every text embodies—and therefore propagates—opinion. Such opinion need not be explicitly political in the sense of taking sides on a current issue; in the case of news writing, explicitly political opinion plays a relatively small role in the construction of stories. Neither does this opinion have to be personal or idiosyncratic: it can be, and in the case of news writing it typically is, institutionalized opinion, embodied in rules defining a form (e.g., the sonnet, the news story) which is maintained by a profession, craft, or tradition. But however that may be, every piece of writing is based on some kind of nonneutrality, and no kind of nonneutrality can ever be totally devoid of implications for political thought, choice, or action. The newsman's theory is therefore incorrect: there is—indeed, there must be—a politics of news, albeit that these politics are not explicit, need not necessarily be describable as left, center, or right, and are as consistent only as news stories are similar to one another. There is a politics of news because a citizen's perception, thought, and action concerning public matters are inevitably altered as a result of learning about them through news rather than through conversation or direct observation or some other means. And the fact that news is not fully neutral makes it less useful for certain ways of perceiving, thinking, and acting, and more useful for other ways. In this manner news channels a citizen's understanding, choice, and political behavior.

We have now arrived at the quandary in which students of the news media find themselves mired: Clearly, the media do exercise a political influence, and yet just as clearly this influence is not to be discovered in the explicit content of news, nor, apparently, can it be described by the conventional left-center-right nomenclature. Under these circumstances, how is one to identify this influence? Obviously, a casual inspection of the media as a whole for overt signs of sympathy with current bodies of opinion is not going to produce an acceptable answer, if only because one cannot be sure what to look for.

I

I therefore propose an experiment. Instead of exploring the news media as a whole—an unmanageable enterprise, really—let us concentrate on a single news story. This narrow focus should help us to see more clearly what news is and what poitical influences it might exert. Of course, this experiment has some shortcomings as a way of identifying the political consequences of our mass media industry. The conclusions we draw about our single story will be no more applicable to all news than the story is typical of all stories. Moreover, analyzing the story without reference to its context (in an issue of a newspaper, in time, in a reader's experience) may lead to certain distortions. But any approach has disadvantages, and it is hard to see that the disadvantages of this strategy are greater than those of the other approaches one can imagine. So, with these caveats, let us proceed.

The story I have chosen for our experiment is in all important respects a typical news story. It scrupulously observes all the conventional rules of news writing; its subject is a sudden and discrete event; and it was written, as are most news stories, under the pressure of a deadline. It is unusual in only in two respects. For one thing, this is an exceptionally good news story—invariably clear, interesting, easy to read, strictly neutral and nonpartisan, full of information, and extremely accurate. The fact that this is a genuinely excellent story means that it approximates the ideal type of the news story as a form, and this enhances the value of our experiment as a means of learning about news as a whole. The excellence of the story increases the likelihood that whatever political implications it contains derive from the form of the news story itself, rather than from any merely personal deficiencies, quirks, or idiosyncratic lapses on the part of its author. In the second place, the story is unusual because it describes an event of great interest and historical importance: the arrest of 800-odd demonstrators on the campus of the University of California at Berkeley, which inaugurated a new era in American higher education and politics. The story itself was written by a veteran newspaperman and published on the front page of the *New York Times* on December 4, 1964.

796 Students Arrested as Police Break Up
Sit-In at U. of California

BERKELEY, Calif., Dec. 3—The police arrested 796 University of California students in 12 hours today, dragging many on their backs down flights of stairs to end a sit-in demonstration.

The mass arrests were made in removing demonstrators who took possession of the administration building on the campus last night.

The Free Speech Movement, the protesting student group, retaliated by calling a student strike. Faculty members, at a special meeting, gave evidence of some support for the students. The dispute over students' political and protest activities has shaken the university for almost three months.

The strike was called after Gov. Edmund G. Brown ordered early this morning that sit-in demonstrators be removed by force from the corridors of Sproul Hall, the administration building. Mr. Brown said that the students' action constituted "anarchy."

Charges of police brutality were made as a result of the removals and arrests today.

In this 27,500-student university, the effectiveness of the strike was difficult to measure. In the morning pickets wheeled in front of the doors of all the classroom buildings and, although students continued to pass through the lines, there were reports that many classrooms were empty.

Clark Kerr, president of the university, issued a statement tonight declaring that the Free Speech Movement represented an "understandable concern" last September but that it "has now become an instrument of anarchy and of personal aggrandizement."

Representatives of about 75 of the 82 academic departments at the university, in a meeting this afternoon, found that about 20 departments were functioning normally in the face of the strike. Prof. Charles Hulten, chairman of the Journalism Department, said that individual faculty members would decide tomorrow whether to hold classes.

A meeting of 500 of the 1,200 members of the faculty voted a resolution this afternoon stating that the university faced a "desperate situation."

The faculty members favor new and liberalized campus rules for political activity and setting up a committee to which students could appeal administration decisions on penalties for violating university rules on political action.

Plan Telegram to Brown

The resolution also asked "that all pending campus action against students for acts occurring before the present date be dropped."

At the meeting, faculty members drafted a telegram to be sent to Governor Brown. It condemned the use of the California Highway Patrol on the campus and the exclusion of faculty members from Sproul Hall.

Last night about 1,000 sit-in demonstrators filled the corridors of Sproul Hall before the doors were locked at 7:00 P.M. They sat there, sleeping, singing, studying and talking until about 3:10 A.M., when Edward W. Strong, the chancellor for this campus of the multi-campus university, went to Sproul Hall.

Mr. Strong read a statement asking the students to leave. A few did, but most stayed. They had put up barricades at the stairways and were concentrated on the second, third, and fourth floors.

The police took an elevator to the fourth floor and began removing students there.

Capt. Larry Waldt of the Alameda County sheriff's office made the estimate of the number of students arrested.

By midday, the routine was standard, as illustrated by the arrest of Jean Golson.

When she found herself at the head of the line of demonstrators, Sgt. Don Smithson of the Berkeley police force told her, "You are under arrest for tresspass and unlawful assembly."

Another Berkeley policeman held a microphone to record her answers and the sergeant's statements. A third made notes on a booking form.

"If you walk out, you will not be charged with resisting arrest, but if we are forced to carry you out, you will be charged with resisting arrest," the sergeant said.

"Female on the Way"

Miss Golson said she would not walk out. A number was held to her chest and her photograph was taken. The Berkeley police pulled her by the arms for a few feet and then turned her over to two sheriff's deputies from Alameda County. They dragged her quickly down the corridor on her back, shouting, "Female on the way."

At a booking desk, she was pulled erect and was fingerprinted. Then she was pulled into an office for searching by two matrons from the sheriff's office.

Then she was dragged back into the elevator, where other girls were being held. When the elevator was full, the girls were taken to the basement and were loaded into a van for transportation to the county jail.

The bail schedule was $75 each on the trespass and unlawful assembly charges and $100 for resisting arrest.

Total Bail is $150,000

Booking officers at the Alameda County sheriff's office said that about 25 of the demonstrators posted bail soon after being booked. Meantime, lawyers, parents and others were meeting with a municipal judge attempting to obtain an order freeing the demonstrators on their own recognizance. The total bail involved will be more than $150,000.

For men, the handling was significantly different once they were turned over to the sheriff's deputies after arrest. Those men who would walk were jogged down four flights of steps to the basement. Those who remained limp were dragged by the arms down the steps, departing to the cries of "Good luck" from their friends.

There were about a score of sheriff's deputies whose job was to drag the men down the steps. As the day passed, their humor became more acid. Some bumped the buttocks of their male prisoners as they dragged them down the stairs.

"There'll be some sore rumps in jail tonight," one deputy said.

After the corridors of Sproul Hall were closed, a floor at a time, the litter of the sit-ins remained. There were empty fruit cartons, crushed soft-drink cans, a guitar, stacks of textbooks, sleeping bags and blankets and scores of notebooks with lecture notes in them.

Shouts "This Is Wonderful"

When Mario Savio, a protest leader, was taken away by the police, he shouted, "This is wonderful—wonderful! We'll bring the university to our terms."

Another leader, Arthur Goldberg, said as he was led away, "Good! The kids have learned more about democracy here than they could in 40 years of classes. This is a perfect example of how the State of California plays the game."

Mr. Savio is a New Yorker who is the president of the Berkeley chapter of Friends of S.N.C.C., the Student Nonviolent Coordinating Committee. He was involved last spring in the recruiting of demonstrators who slept in at the Sheraton Palace Hotel. He was arrested on a charge of disturbing the peace. He also worked in the S.N.C.C. program in Mississippi last summer.

Another leader of the Free Speech Movement is Bettina Aptheker. She is a member of the W. E. B. DuBois Club, which has been described by Department of Justice sources as a front among college students for the Communist party.

The dispute that led to the arrests began last September when the university administration announced that it would no longer permit the use of a strip of campus property for soliciting political funds and recruiting protest demonstrators.

The students objected, and a series of demonstrations resulted. Eight students were suspended and the demonstrations were stepped up.

Last month, the university regents ordered that the students be permitted to recruit demonstrators and collect political contributions on campus. But the regents said the students must be held accountable for off-campus violations of the law in projects begun on campus.

They also said that discipline must be tightened.

Earlier this week, four students received letters from the administration indicating that they were to be disciplined, and perhaps expelled. Yesterday the newest demonstration began in protest.

Conservatives Quit Group

The Free Speech Movement was organized with an executive committee of about 69 members, each representing some campus organization. Initially, conservative groups belonged, including the Young Republicans, but these recently disassociated themselves.

The leadership is concentrated in an 11 member steering committee that appears to be dominated by representatives of campus chapters of the Congress of Racial Equality, the Young Socialist League, the Young Socialist Alliance, Slate (a student political organization) and the W. E. B. DuBois Club.

At a noon rally of about 5,000 students, Steve Weisman, a leader of the Free Speech Movement, called for an investigation of what he termed police brutality. He also demanded the removal of the police "from this campus now and forever" and the removal of Mr. Kerr as president of the university.

In his statement tonight, Mr. Kerr denied that freedom of speech had ever been an issue and said, "The protest has been over organizing political action on campus."

Mr. Kerr accused the Free Speech Movement of violating the law, of intolerance, distortion of the truth, irrationality, indecency, and ill will.

In Sacramento, Governor Brown said, "We're not going to have anarchy in the state of California while I'm Governor, and that's anarchy. I did plan to go to Berkeley, but I have other things to do."

Opposition to the Free Speech Movement was in evidence here today. Some students standing at the noon rally held signs reading, "Throw The Bums Out" and "Law Not Anarchy—The Majority of Students Do Not Support This Demonstration."

What are the politics of this story? How does it channel a reader's political attention and thought about the events it describes? The answer is to be discovered in the cognitive uses of the story—in the kinds of questions it invites a reader to pursue and enables him to answer—and in its cognitive nonuses, or in the kinds of questions it discourages and does not equip a reader to answer or think about. So let us now turn to the issue of what this story is and is not useful for thinking about, and how these uses might affect a reader's notion of what happened at Berkeley.

II

The first and most obvious use of this story, one that it serves consistently and superbly, is that of identifying unambiguously true facts about events that occurred in Berkeley on December 3, 1964. Anyone who read the story for that purpose, and that purpose alone, would have had his curiosity entirely satisfied: his purpose in reading the story would have been identical with one of the author's effective purposes in writing it. I say "effective purposes" here because, from the text itself, there is no way of knowing what the author actually had in mind as he wrote; but whether he intended it or not, almost every feature of this story—the nature of its subject matter, its vocabulary, its structure and narrative voice—is ideally suited for the function of identifying unambiguously true facts about events.

The clearest indication that the story serves this use is to be found in the fact that literally every statement the reporter makes in the story is a statement of fact. That is, every sentence describes some feature or features of a person, thing, or action that the reporter (or someone) actually witnessed with his own eyes or ears. Moreover, the statements in this story are not about just any kind of fact; with only a few exceptions, they are statements of directly and unambiguously observable fact, as is indicated by two further features of the text. First, the subject of these statements of fact is almost invariably a single person, a single thing, or a single action; only a very few statements of fact are made about aggregate phenomena, such as distributions of opinion or collective behavior. And second, the reporter couches his descriptions in a broad, categoric vocabulary that neither requires nor permits fine distinctions. For example, people in this story generally "say" things when the reporter wants to describe them in the act of verbal expression; they rarely "mumble," "shout," "sigh," or "insist" what they have to say. Similarly, students are always referred to as "students," and never as "undergraduates," "chemistry students," "seniors," "honors students," and so on. The result of the reporter's focus on single rather than plural subjects and his reliance on broad, relatively uninflected descriptive categories is that the facts in the story are of a sort that is especially hard to be mistaken about, and therefore especially easy to believe. Of course, this focus on unambiguously true facts imposes certain limitations on the story, as we shall see later: it excludes any very precise description, and it makes it impossible for the reporter to offer his own deductions, inferences, interpretations, opinions, or feelings directly, for what they are. But it does guarantee that this story is thoroughly and genuinely useful for learning unambiguously true facts.

I emphasize this use because the story itself emphasizes it, through two expository devices that call a reader's attention to the individual facts as such rather than as a means of understanding the thing the facts describe and which reinforces his belief in the authenticity of the facts. One of these devices is the story's strictly impersonal narrative style. The author never speaks in the first person and never reveals anything in particular about his point of view or purpose; he merely records, impersonally, the facts he observed. In this way the story suggests to the reader that the author's only concern was to find and record facts and keeps to an absolute minimum what a reader can infer about the observational and empirical context of the facts. In the second place, the story as a whole is organized according to an arbitrary journalistic principle (the so-called inverted pyramid), as a result of which facts are not presented in, for example, the chronological order in which they occurred or were observed. These two features of the story, in sum, help ensure that the various facts are presented in as much isolation from one another, and with as little evocation of their real-world context, as is possible without degenerating into total randomness and unintelligibility.

But granting the centrality of unambiguous facts to this story, there still remains the further question of what these facts are about.

Obviously the story presents only a tiny, highly selective sample of all the facts that were observable in Berkeley on December 3. In order to form a complete picture of the content and uses of this story, we need to know the basis on which the reporter selected facts for the story.

The first thing to be noted here is that these are invariably facts concerning events or the constituent elements of events, such as actors, settings, antecedents, rhetoric, and the like. This focus on events is clearly visible both in the headline, which describes an action (the arrests), and in the lead paragraphs, which present the most "newsworthy" or central facts in the story, which, in this case, also describe the event of the arrests. A similar preoccupation with events can be seen throughout the story, which describes people, conditions, inert objects, and the like only insofar as they contributed to, or were connected with, events. When not connected with events, stable things and conditions—that which merely exists, as opposed to that which happens—are not described in our story.

The particular events described by the facts in this story are obvious enough and require no discussion here. What does require discussion, and is crucial in our attempt to identify the uses of the story, is *how* the reporter defined or understood those events, since this understanding determined which facts about them he selected and emphasized. To begin with, it is clear that our reporter defined them as events of conflict: Hardly a paragraph does not in some way refer, directly or indirectly, to conflict. But what kind of conflict does the reporter appear to have had in mind? Conflict over what and between whom? Here the story is ultimately ambiguous, and there seems to be no truly intelligible organizing principle at work behind the reporter's choice and presentation of facts. To be sure, the story does present these events as conflict between various sides or parties; but although the sides are described with sketchy and shifting reference to their political, institutional, verbal, behavioral, and legal characteristics, they are described primarily in terms of their mutual hostility and their mutual acts of conflict. Thus, in the initial paragraphs, the police are described not as an organization that duly enforced the law against breakers of the law, but rather as enemies of the sit-in demonstrators whose principal action was not the enforcement of law but the ending of the sit-in.

("The police arrested 796 University of California students . . . *to end a sit-in demonstration*"; "The mass arrests were made *in removing demonstrators. . . .*") Similarly, the FSM demonstrators are described not as a political group organized around certain ideas of justice and acting in behalf of certain grievances, not as a group that in this instance was in violation of law, but rather as a group defined by its enmity toward the university administration (". . . demonstrators who took possession of the administration building . . ."; "The Free Speech Movement . . . retaliated by calling a student strike").

The ambiguity here lies not only in the vagueness with which the various sides are identified—were there two sides? three? five? —but, also, and more importantly, in the circularity of the principles of selection at work in the story. Facts were selected for their capacity to illustrate events of conflict between certain parties. But whereas the parties appear to have been defined in terms of their participation in conflict, the conflict appears to have been defined primarily in terms of the parties that joined it. Ultimately, therefore, there is in this story a certain confusion as to its real subject, and as we shall see, this confusion profoundly affects its uses and political implications. But at this point, it means only that, at the margin, there is a degree of indeterminacy that creeps into our picture of the way the facts were selected and what precisely the story is useful for in its own terms.

As a whole and on its own terms, then, this story clearly is useful for identifying unambiguously true facts about events of conflict between certain vaguely specified parties. Both the formal characteristics of the story and its particular contents as we have surveyed them guarantee that anyone who read the story in order to find out about such facts on such subjects would have been entirely satisfied. It goes without saying that the story serves the entire range of lesser included uses; thus, any reader whose purpose in reading was to learn a fact or two about Mario Savio, the governor of California, the faculty's reaction, or the litter in Sproul Hall would also have found the story perfectly satisfactory. By the time he reached the end of the story he would have become aware of the desired information. One may doubt that anyone in his right mind ever reads anything for precisely this fact-collecting purpose—it is the height of gradgrindism—but it is nevertheless the principal purpose the story is designed to serve.

Is the story also capable of enabling a reader to achieve some kind of actual political understanding of the subject, as opposed to a mere awareness of some facts about the subject? The answer, as we shall now see, is yes; the story does seem to have a further use, this one explicitly political in nature. But this use, and the understanding it permits, is of an extremely low order.

III

Now that we have described the contents of this story, we are in a position to think about its political consequences. We shall approach this problem by looking for the political uses of the story, its uses to an individual reader not in his role as a gatherer of current facts or as an observer of Mario Savio, but rather in his role as a citizen, as a participant in sovereignty. His concern in this role is with the just allocation of values in society and with the regulation of public policy and public officials in behalf of such a just allocation, and in this role he reads a news story in order to identify matters that bear on this concern, understand the nature of that bearing, and then come to some decision about what, if anything, ought to be done about these matters. Of course, the *particular* nature of a citizen's concern depends on his distinctive views; presumably there are as many sorts of concerns as there are citizens. But the *general* nature of this concern is always and in every case the same: it is a concern with the relationship between general notions of justice and specific conditions and events.

To a reader in his role as citizen, then, the Berkeley events called for this sort of political analysis, and he would therefore read our story with a view toward evaluating the various actions and statements by his own standards of justice. At a minimum he would want to form some judgment about the conduct of the various public officials and institutions, since as a voter he participates in their election and control. In light of the fact that the University of California is a public university, he might want to come to some conclusion about its rules, organization, funding, and the like. Probably also he would want to evaluate the justice of the conduct of the FSM, of the faculty, of the police and sheriff's deputies, of the university administration. In fact, there is no necessary limit to the kinds of questions a citizen might want to ask and the kinds of judgments he might want to form in this matter. But whatever their range and number, a citizen-reader of this story would necessarily ask questions concerning the justice of what happened at Berkeley.

Is this story of any use in pursuing such questions? The answer to this question depends critically upon our citizen-reader's sympathies and standards, which determine both the kinds of issues he will raise and the kinds of information necessary to their resolution. It is possible, for example, that a citizen will adopt what I shall call a partisan mode of thought and judgment, one in which questions of right and wrong, praise and blame, are decided on the basis of who is involved rather than what was done. Thus it is possible that a citizen identified himself so strongly with Governor Brown, or with the police, or with university administrators, or with young people, or with the FSM, or with any person or organization connected somehow to the civil rights movement that, for him, it was enough to know that these persons or groups were involved in these events to decide where justice in this case lay. Conversely, it is possible that a citizen had such animus *against* the governor or the FSM that the mere fact of the governor's involvement was sufficient evidence for deciding that the FSM was in the right and its actions praiseworthy. For such a partisan citizen, all questions of justice are resolved into questions of who benefits and who is harmed: what benefits his side or party is good, what harms it bad; whoever supports his party is in the right, whoever opposes it is in the wrong; whatever his party does is just, whatever its opponents do is unjust.

This story enables a citizen-reader to form a broad range of partisan judgments concerning the justice of what happened in Berkeley; anyone who identified as a partisan or enemy of any side in this dispute is given more than enough information to make up his mind, in a partisan manner, about who was and was not in the right. Thus we have discovered a second clear use of the story. Its focus on events of conflict makes it a veritable catalog of symbols identifying the various sides in terms of name, rhetoric, behavior, organizational associations, age, institutional status, and so forth. A quick inspection of the text reveals the following symbols for the various parties: "police," "students," "sit-in demonstration," "mass arrests," "Free Speech Movement," "University of California," "student strike," "dispute over students' political and protest activities," "Governor Edmund G. Brown," "anarchy," "police brutality," "Clark Kerr, president of the university," "instrument of . . . personal aggrandizement," "trespass and unlawful assembly," "Mario Savio," "Arthur Goldberg," "the Berkeley Chapter of Friends of S.N.C.C.," "Bettina Aptheker," "W. E. B. DuBois Club," "Department of Justice," "front among college students for the Communist party," "university administration," "Young Socialist League," "Young Republicans," "Young Socialist Alliance," "intolerance, distortion of the truth, irrationality, indecency, and ill will"—and this is only a partial listing.

To be sure, there presumably are people with clear partisan sympathies and a habit of making partisan decisions who, on the basis of this story, would be unable to form a partisan judgment of the justice of these events, either because they were truly indifferent to the parties to the Berkeley dispute, or else because the story fails to provide enough symbols for identifying the parties. On the other hand, it seems unlikely that very many Americans would find nothing in the story to excite their approval or animosity. Moreover, the story's massive preoccupation with the actions and words of conflict at Berkeley positively encourages a reader to define and think through the issues raised by the events in the participants' own terms, which in turn invites a partisan judgment. There can be little doubt, then, that the story both permits and encourages a partisan judgment of what happened at Berkeley.

IV

For rendering an independent and nonpreconceived judgment, however, this story is as close to useless as makes no difference. Anyone for whom the justice of what happened was initially an open question, one to be resolved honestly and independently by evaluating actions in accordance with general principles of justice, by assessing the participants' claims in light both of the evidence and of standards of truth and justice, and by resisting any temptation to draw hasty or uncritical or preconceived conclusions—any such person would find in this story none of the information required by such an enterprise. For purposes of such a nonpreconceived evaluation, that is to say, this story is not of use. This holds true in the case of an effort to assess the claims and charges made by the actual participants in the Berkeley events, and it also holds true *a fortiori* in the case of an effort to pursue questions or issues other than those raised by the participants. As we shall see, it is not by accident that the story is of such little help to this kind of evaluation. On the contrary: the same features of the story that enable it to serve the two uses that it clearly does serve are directly responsible for its inability to assist this third sort of inquiry.

To test these assertions, let us see to what extent the information presented in the story enables a reader to think independently about two basic questions of justice raised by the Berkeley events, one of them an issue raised by the FSM, the other a question that it might occur to a reader to pose on his own. The first question is: Was there police brutality? And the second: Was it prudent or wise of the governor to order the arrests when he did?

Was there police brutality? Since the question of police brutality was raised initially by spokesmen for the FSM, our open-minded reader might want to begin his inquiry into this issue by inspecting the texts of their charges in order to see what evidence and implied standard of brutality they had in mind and what specific police behaviors they were referring to. With this information, our reader would know the specific problems his inquiry should focus on. But when he scans the story for the FSM statement, he discovers in the third paragraph (and again in the fortieth) only the paraphrase "Charges of police brutality were made as a result of the removals and arrests today." This extremely truncated and uninformative account of the charges prevents our reader from beginning at the beginning, by identifying the precise referent of the charge and by criticizing the charge on internal grounds.

In the absence of this information, our reader must fall back on his own common-sense understanding of what the charge might refer to and what kind of evidence would validate or falsify the claim. This is not too serious a difficulty in this case, since the concept of police brutality is simple enough and its manifestation physical and easily identified. So, to begin with, our reader searches the story for evidence about the behavior of the policemen. The first evidence is provided by the passage describing the arrest of Jean Golson, but it clearly has no bearing on the question of brutality: a single arrest does not necessarily indicate any aggregate pattern of police behavior, which is what the charge of police brutality seems to refer to; the behavior of the police in this case is depicted as a model of procedural rectitude; and in any case the story sharply differentiates Miss Golson's experience from that of the male demonstrators—and it was, one infers, in connection with these latter that the charge of brutality was raised.

Our reader then scrutinizes the remainder of the story for further evidence about police behavior or its effects on the demonstrators. He finds:

1. The fact that sheriff's deputies dragged male prisoners who resisted arrest down four flights of stairs and that some deputies "bumped the buttocks" of their prisoners as they dragged them down these stairs.

2. The fact that the deputies' humor became "more acid" as the day passed.

3. The fact that one deputy remarked, "There'll be some sore rumps in jail tonight."

The bearing of these bits of information on the question of police brutality is resolutely ambiguous. The fact that deputies were in an "acid humor," presumably illustrated by the "sore rumps" remark, says nothing about their physical behavior and reveals nothing relevant about their intent, since an "acid humor" is as compatible with the intention of being nonbrutal as it is with the intention of being brutal. As for the dragging and buttock-bumping, here too the story's information is ultimately insufficient for deciding the question of brutality one way or the other. To take the buttock-bumping first, it was inevitable that dragging prisoners down stairs was going to cause *something* to bump, and that it was the prisoners' buttocks rather than, say, their heads or ankles that bumped on the stairs would suggest, if anything, the absence of brutal intentions. So the question of police brutality comes down to the question of how, why, and with what effects the deputies dragged their male prisoners down the stairs, and why they did not carry them down or take them down in elevators, as they did the women.

The story is determinedly silent on each of these critical points.

The dragging might have been slow, gentle, painless, uninjurious, and done in a neutral or even solicitous spirit, or it might have been rapid, rough, painful, injurious, and done in a spirit of malice and brutality. The story reports only the fact of dragging, not its method, consequences, or spirit, and the result is that our reader cannot even begin to make the distinctions that must be made before an intellectually honest conclusion about brutality can be drawn. Similarly, it makes a difference if the deputies decided to drag the male prisoners reluctantly and dispassionately, as the least objectionable method of removing them under the circumstances, rather than gleefully and in the expectation or hope that the men would be hurt. On this point the story says absolutely nothing at all; again, our reader is deprived of the all-important contextual information that is necessary to his effort to interpret the fact of dragging. In consequence, our open-minded reader is simply unable to decide whether there was or was not police brutality in Sproul Hall; indeed, he is even unable to begin ruling out extreme possibilities. The story simply does not provide the information necessary for this order of judgment. To decide the issue of brutality, our reader needs information about the intentions of the deputies, whereas the story provides information only about that which is unambiguously observable; our reader needs information about aggregates, whereas the story describes only single things; our reader needs the contextual information that is inherent in facts when they are organized chronologically in an eyewitness narrative account, whereas the story presents facts in descending order of newsworthiness; and our reader needs information gathered by an author who takes the question of brutality as one part of his subject, whereas the subject of this story is simply the existence and nature of conflict. In all these ways, then, and for all these reasons, the story is useless to an open-minded reader who attempts to form a nonpreconceived judgment about the question of police brutality.

Suppose, then, that our reader turns to the second question: *Was it prudent of the governor to order the arrests?* The governor in this case was faced with two broad practical questions: first, what are the practical advantages and disadvantages, costs and benefits, of (*a*) arresting the demonstrators, and (*b*) not arresting them; and second, if it is decided to arrest them, what are the advantages and disadvantages of each of the various ways in which these arrests might be carried out? In order to assess the governor's resolution of these issues, of course, our open-minded reader must answer the same questions himself. In this he has the seeming advantage of hindsight, since the actual consequences of the governor's analysis and decision are there for our reader to observe.

He might well begin his inquiry, therefore, by scrutinizing the story for information about what happened after the arrests. He discovers at least the following:

1. The removal of all demonstrators from Sproul Hall.
2. The dragging of male demonstrators downstairs.
3. The FSM's call for a student strike in retaliation.
4. The alienation of a substantial segment of the faculty, who have given "evidence of some support" for the FSM, resolved that the university faces a "desperate situation," and requested amnesty for the demonstrators.
5. The reduction or termination of "anarchy" on campus, according to Governor Brown.
6. Public statements charging police with brutality.
7. The alienation of a substantial part of the student body and their mobilization in support of the FSM strike.
8. "Bumping" and possibly hurting or injuring demonstrators who were dragged downstairs.
9. Mario Savio's statement that the arrests would assist the FSM in achieving its goals.
10. Arthur Goldberg's statement that the arrests discredited the government of the state of California.
11. Public statements demanding the resignation of Clark Kerr as president of the university.
12. Student demonstrations against the FSM and its strike.

All these things are identified by the story as having taken place or existed during or after the arrests in Sproul Hall.

Our reader now begins to analyze these data for their bearing on the prudential wisdom of ordering the arrests. Immediately he discovers his effort blocked by a series of seemingly insurmountable difficulties. To begin with, there is the question of whether this is an exhaustive list of consequences or sequels of the arrests; only if it is exhaustive does it constitute an adequate evidentiary basis for a cost-benefit analysis of the decision to order the arrests. Clearly, however, the story does not provide an exhaustive inventory of such information. For one thing, it was written during and immediately after the arrests, as a result of which it is capable of describing only those consequences that were immediately apparent; consequences that took more than a few hours to become manifest are not described by the story, even though the long-term consequences of an event are of more lasting importance than short-term consequences. In the second place, the story describes the effect of the arrests on only the principal self-identified "parties to the dispute"; how the arrests affected individuals, groups, or institutions that did not identify themselves by statement and action as "participants" in the dispute—and how the arrests affected interests and values without any organized or self-conscious representation—are subjects on which the story is silent. As a result, if our citizen, in making his analysis of the governor's decision, wanted to take account of the way the arrests would affect the future of the University of California football team, or the way they bore on the state of social science research at the university, or what they boded for the future of the university's capacity to govern itself effectively, or how they would affect some other group or value that did not have spokesmen taking a position on the conflict, he would find in this story none of the desired information. Clearly, then, this is a hopelessly inadequate data base upon which to build a serious analysis of the consequences of the actual arrests; for such a purpose, this story is simply useless. Indeed, the sample of information in this story is so arbitrary and limited that any analysis one might attempt with it would be almost certain to be worse than no analysis at all.

But even if this story did offer a reasonably comprehensive survey of the consequences of the arrests, our reader would still be unable to pursue his concern over the wisdom of the governor's decision. Three additional difficulties would render his inquiry impossible. To begin with, there is the problem of causality. It is impossible to weigh the advantageous and disadvantageous consequences of an action without first knowing what was a consequence of the action and what merely a sequel that would have occurred whether or not the action had taken place. The story does indeed describe many things that happened after the arrests, but it gives our reader no information with which even to begin to differentiate the consequences from the mere sequels. Of course, even in the best of circumstances such judgments are always difficult and uncertain, resting as they do on inferences based on a sense of context, pattern, and nuance. As we have seen, this story's structure suppresses to a very low level what it suggests about the context of the facts and events it describes. The virtue of this is that a reader can rely on the story to tell him only what is certainly true, but it also reduces almost to zero our reader's ability to make the probabilistic and inferential judgments that must be made if consequences of the arrests are to be identified as such.

A second barrier in our reader's path arises from the fact that he is judging the prudential wisdom of the governor's decision retrospectively, whereas the governor was making decisions about the prospective prudence of various courses of action. Such prospective decisions are always based on probabilistic predictions. This fact is important because it determines the terms in which one may fairly judge the governor's decision. Probabilistic predictions are never invalidated by an occurrence other than the one predicted. If, for instance, I state that there is a 10 percent chance of rain within twenty-four hours, and it then proceeds to rain during that period, the statement that there was a 10 percent chance of rain is not thereby refuted. Similarly, one cannot properly judge the governor's decision solely, or even primarily, on the basis of what actually resulted from it; the question for our open-minded citizen is rather whether the governor's assessment of the future probabilities associated with the course of action he chose was correct—not whether it encountered bad luck. In a story that limits the governor's own statements to fewer than thirty words and which radically restricts indications of context, very little information about the governor's prospective judgments of probability can be gleaned. Strictly speaking, then, this makes it quite impossible for our reader to form a judgment of the governor's decision.

The final barrier to our citizen's inquiry arises out of the fact that practical action is never ideal or unmixedly desirable, and that any practical decision represents an attempt to select the least of evils or the greatest of benefits. The fact that the adopted course of action turns out to have negative consequences, or was initially thought to have a high probability of such consequences, is meaningless in evaluating a decision until one has compared those probable or actual negative consequences with the negative consequences of the alternative courses of action. In order to come to some reasoned conclusion about the wisdom of what the governor did, therefore, our reader must compare the costs and benefits of what the governor did do with the costs and benefits of the alternatives he rejected, and then decide which alternative, on balance, was preferable. But this story contains not a single shred of evidence on these critical matters, with the result that in this respect as well as in all the other respects this story prevents our open-minded citizen from answering, or even beginning to think about, the question of the prudential wisdom of the governor in ordering the arrests.

Our reader could turn to other questions of this general sort, and in each case the result would be the same. Whether it was the elementary matter of the legal justification for the arrests in the first place, or the complex issue of the higher morality of the demonstrators' and authorities' actions, or the classificatory and interpretive question of the uniqueness and potential replicability of what happened at Berkeley, our reader would find in this story none of the requisite information, and his inquiry would immediately come up against a blank and impenetrable wall. In all these matters our citizen needs information about the intentions and goals of the various actors, whereas the story focuses on conflict alone; he needs information about aggregate and intangible phenomena, whereas the story presents statements only about unambiguously observable physical particulars; he needs facts and events that are securely located in their natural context, whereas the story presents them in an arbitrary and ambiguous journalistic context; and finally he needs information about things that might have happened but didn't, whereas the story concentrates single-mindedly on what did happen. For these reasons, then, the story is inevitably useless for pursuing the questions that are always asked by a citizen—the questions about justice.

I had better add quickly that the point of all this is not to decide whether the reporter did a good job or a bad job on this story, or whether he deserves our praise or blame, or whether his brief account provides enough information to permit one to answer definitively every conceivable question that one might manage to dream up. What is at issue here is not whether he did a good job but rather what job it was that he did, and what kind of question this job enables a reader to pursue. To put it another way, we have merely been attempting to identify what is in this story. After scrutinizing and testing it in a variety of ways, we have established that what is in this story is—and what the reporter was doing was gathering—information relevant to questions of fact about events of conflict and information useful for rendering partisan decisions about the justice of what happened. What is not in this story, and what the reporter was not gathering, was information useful for rendering independent and nonpreconceived decisions about the justice of what happened. In short, we have established what this story is and is not good for and good at; to borrow a phrase from Philip Selznick, we have identified, in cognitive terms, the "distinctive competence" of the story, and along the way we have also managed to learn something about its distinctive incompetence as well.

V

Now that we know something of the content and uses of this story, we are in a position to think about its political consequences. This is best done by assuming that a citizen's knowledge of what happened in Berkeley on December 3 derives exclusively from this one story. Of course, nobody in the real world is ever entirely dependent on news stories, though in many areas of our knowledge we come uncomfortably close to this condition. I make the assumption merely because it enables us to think about the direction or character of the influence of this story upon a citizen's political thought and action, and because it forces us to ignore the very different and almost unrelated questions of degree of influence and of contrary influence from other sources. So, assuming a citizen totally dependent on this one story, let us now ask what its impact would be on his notion of what happened at Berkeley, his evaluation of who was right and wrong and in what degree, and his conclusions about what, if anything, should be done, and by whom, about the people, organizations, and problems involved in these events.

The mental picture our citizen would form from this story would be one of intense conflict at Berkeley, manifested in dramatic, large-scale events like mass occupation of buildings, mass arrests, and a university-wide strike preceded by some vague dispute over university rules and discipline. His principal impression of this conflict, aside from its bitterness and physical manifestations, would be that it is joined by two principal sides—one the party of established authority, including the governor, the university president and administration, and the police and courts; the other the party of student dissent and activism. These parties he would define and identify in accordance with their members' institutional roles (e.g., student, policeman), certain bits of political symbolism (such as the sit-in demonstration itself, rhetoric, organizational affiliations), and their mutual hostility. He would have the impression, moreover, that the events in Berkeley defined not merely a problem, but an authentic crisis—mass conflict, a great university paralyzed, major questions hanging in the balance; in all, a situation of importance, requiring serious attention, discussion, and at least the possibility of action by outside forces. His picture of what was happening in Berkeley, then, would be one of a problem of mass conflict between an establishment and an anti-establishment party requiring intense public attention and decision.

By defining the Berkeley events in this way, the story invites a citizen to formulate his opinion on the basis either of the parties to the conflict or of the problem of conflict between parties. Thus this story prompts four primary reactions and reinforces four types or bodies of opinion: (1) for party A and against party B, a *partisan reaction*; (2) for party B and against party A, also a partisan reaction; (3) concern for the problem of conflict in itself, implying a desire to resolve it by splitting the difference, the *liberal reaction*; and (4) unconcern for the problem of conflict and unconcern for its resolution, the *indifferentist reaction*. Obviously various combinations and permutations are possible among these four positions, but they need not concern us here. The point here is that this story presents the Berkeley events in a way that encourages the mobilization of partisans and liberals and the withdrawal of the indifferent, with the result that public discussion and action are dominated by the partisans and liberals, who act out their roles before the cynical indifferentists.

We have already observed the utility of this story for a committed partisan, and we may dispose of this aspect of the political influence of the story simply by noting that it reinforces partisan identifications, if any, in its readers, and that it encourages the partisanization of those who are not already committed. As for the liberal and indifferentist reactions it facilitates, what is interesting is their cognitive similarity to the partisan reactions. For they are no less automatic and unthinking, in their way, than those of the simple partisans of the FSM or the police. The liberal reaction, for example, is based on the notion that conflict as such is undesirable and a problem that needs to be solved, and that the appropriate response is not to consider the issues in dispute on their substantive merits, but rather to search out some middle ground on which a compromise may be arranged and the conflict brought to an end regardless of the way the outcome may affect values and interests other than those of conflict resolution alone. Similarly, the indifferentist reaction is based on the premise that all partisan bickering and conflict are beneath notice, and that the minute one becomes aware of such a dispute one should resolutely ignore it, again regardless of the issues at stake. Thus both reactions proceed in as much indifference to the full range of political issues involved, and in as much ignorance of the true relationship between general ends and particular actions and conditions, as do the more obviously partisan reactions. The difference lies not in the quality of the opinion, but only in the symbols to which it is responsive. The partisan responds to everything in accordance with his party's position, the liberal in accordance with his commitment to the symbol of conflict resolution through compromise, and the indifferentist in accordance with his sincere disdain of conflict.

And this brings us to the final and most important political tendency in our story: its encouragement of the partisan mode of discussion and judgment and action, and its correlative systematic discouragement of a more thoughtful and less simplistic and preconceived sort of politics. As a result of its underlying conceptualization of what happened in Berkeley, the story ends up as both a conveyor belt for the symbolic propaganda of the two parties and a case study ideally suited to the symbolic propaganda of liberals and indifferentists. As among these four bodies of opinion, it does not have favorites. And it clearly does not favor—indeed, it systematically thwarts—another type of opinion or cast of mind: that which attempts to understand the world of events from a comprehensive rather than partial viewpoint, which is committed to intellectual honesty rather than to simplistic preconception, and which treats all practical questions of policy and administration for what they undeniably are—practical problems of finding means that efficaciously bring about desired ends in a world where policy must serve many ends, all of them conflicting. In the nation as a whole, then, this story encouraged needless conflict (among the various parties) and mindless consensus (among the groups of partisans), and to this extent it was an instrument of political drift rather than of public mastery of events.

Walter Berns

THE CONSTITUTION AND A RESPONSIBLE PRESS

The Constitution, especially in the First and Fourteenth Amendments, sets out to protect the freedom of the press and the freedom of newsmen and others to speak, but it does not, in any of its parts, set out to protect the public from an irresponsible press, or from the mendacious, unfair, or indecent speech of newsmen and others. It does not, for example, make any provision for the education of citizens, including newsmen, by which I mean, of course, their moral education; and if it should happen that newsmen are restrained by a sense of shame from telling lies or from being unfair and indecent in what they write, and perhaps most of them have been, that is the happy result of chance. Indeed, the First Amendment, in another of its parts, has been interpreted to forbid any official concern with moral education, on the part of the states as well as on the part of the national government, even though Washington, in his Farewell Address, said the moral education of citizens was an "object of primary importance." In this omission, as well as in what is explicitly set down, the Constitution reveals the extent to which it is anchored in the principles of modern political philosophy.

Critics and especially victims of the press used to be able to mount a more formidable array of weapons in their battle with irresponsible newsmen. Editors could be formally "called out" to satisfy the honor of their victims and to defend themselves, which they did not always do successfully: the *Vicksburg Sentinel*, for example, lost four of its editors in duels during the period 1833–1860. And they could always be assaulted—"horsewhipped" would be the term expressing the moral outrage involved—in the streets, usually, apparently, with impunity. But dueling, in addition to being illegal, passes naturally into desuetude in democratic times, and common assaults have been made more difficult either by a more efficient police force or by the greater anonymity of editors.[1]

It was understood by the Founders that the problem could be kept within manageable limits by appropriate recourse to the laws, if not the laws of the national government—and of course there was considerable disagreement as to whether the national government had been given authority to adopt such laws—then at least of the states, and there was no disagreement as to this. He who enforces the state laws "against false and defamatory publications," Jefferson said in his Second Inaugural Address, "renders a service to public morals and public tranquillity." The problem threatens to become unmanageable today because the Supreme Court has, speaking generally here, declared even such state laws to be forbidden by the Constitution. America, the Court said a few years ago, is a society that places a primary value on freedom of expression,[2] and this, as we shall see, leaves almost no room for laws designed to promote a responsible press. Thus a free press is a command of the Constitution, whereas a responsible press has become merely an unendowed wish or prayer.

Until this change wrought by the modern Supreme Court, the states and to a lesser extent the national government were permitted to enforce laws that must have constituted some restraint on the press. There were laws respecting what could be said by way of political comment, or disclosed to satisfy a vulgar curiosity on the part of the public, or printed or distributed or exhibited under the label of literature and the arts; and these laws had the effect of reminding editors and other newsmen that there were limits they were bound by the law to respect, whether or not they were independently inclined to do so. There were libel laws, laws protecting privacy, and censorship laws, and laws protecting the judicial process by punishing, in the words of the federal statute, "attempts to in-

[1] Anonymity obviously does not protect television newsmen, and one can only suppose that Sandor Vanocur, for example, and George Herman owe their good health to the efficiency of the police or to some other factor, perhaps bodyguards. Surely horsewhips are still available?

[2] *Time, Inc.* v. *Hill,* 385 U.S. 374, 388 (1967).

fluence the action or decision of any grand or petit juror . . . upon any issue or matter pending before such juror . . . by writing or sending to him any written communication, in relation to such issue or matter. . . ."[3] These laws were, generally speaking, official attempts to promote responsibility on the part of the press, but of course they have been challenged—and in our time with increasing success—in the name of freedom of the press.

I

Consider first the fate of laws designed to protect the judicial process from out-of-court contempts. So venerable a Supreme Court justice as Oliver Wendell Holmes, Jr., was the author of the federal rule of law on the subject; he wrote the opinion of the Court rejecting an appeal on the part of a publisher who had been held in contempt for printing articles and cartoons reflecting upon the motives and conduct of a Colorado court in a case pending before it. "The theory of our system," he wrote, "is that the conclusions to be reached in a case will be induced only by evidence and argument in open court, and not by any outside influence, whether of private talk or public print."[4] Press comment is an attempt to bring other influence to bear; in punishing it, the Court held, the Colorado judge was not violating the constitutional principle of freedom of the press.

That was in 1907, a long time ago in constitutional affairs, and especially in affairs involving the First Amendment, and a more contemporaneous generation of judges has tended to read the Constitution differently. In 1941 the Court, by the narrowest of margins, reversed contempt citations brought against Harry Bridges, the labor leader, and the *Los Angeles Times,* at that time, at least, an anti-labor newspaper, for their separate comments on a case still pending before a California judge. The Supreme Court held that to justify the contempt citations it would have to be shown that the comments constituted a clear and present danger of actually obstructing justice.[5] The Court continued to apply this rule, with the same result, in subsequent cases, leading Justices Jackson and

[3] 18 U.S.C.A. 1504.
[4] *Patterson* v. *Colorado,* 205 U.S. 454, 462 (1907).
[5] *Bridges* v. *California,* 314 U.S. 252 (1941).

Frankfurter to say a decade later that the Court had "gone a long way to disable a trial judge from dealing with press interference with the trial process."[6] But of course the Warren Court carried this still further by applying the rule to attempts to influence a grand jury of laymen, rather than, as had been the situation in the previous cases, the judges. This difference was thought to be important, because the judges, assumed to be "men of fortitude, able to thrive in a hardy climate," are also to be presumed better able to withstand the kind of pressure the press can generate under some conditions.[7]

It cannot be said that the Supreme Court is, or was, unaware of this power of the press. One year before the Wood case it had reversed an Indiana murder conviction on the ground that the jury had not been impartial, and it had not been impartial because the press had succeeded in destroying the conditions of impartiality, or of a fair trial generally. Justice Frankfurter, who had dissented in the Bridges case, pointed to the consequences of the inability of a trial judge to restrain the press:

> How can fallible men and women reach a disinterested verdict based exclusively on what they heard in the court when, before they entered the jury box, their minds were saturated by press and radio for months preceding by matter designed to establish the guilt of the accused? A conviction so secured obviously constitutes a denial of due process of law in its most rudimentary conception.[8]

And, of course, the Court was familiar with the problem of "trial by newspaper," and especially trial by southern newspaper. In 1949 a seventeen-year-old white girl reported that she had been raped, at pistol point, by Samuel Shepherd and three other Negroes, and the local Florida press had, among other things, incited mobs to burn the homes of the parents of the accused Negroes, and with cartoons of electric chairs and accompanying comment called for their conviction and electrocution. They succeeded in getting the conviction, but the Supreme Court of the United States reversed,

[6] *Shepherd* v. *Florida,* 341 U.S. 50, 52 (1951). Concurring opinion.
[7] *Wood* v. *Georgia,* 370 U.S. 375 (1962).
[8] *Irvin* v. *Dowd,* 366 U.S. 717, 729–30 (1961).

thereby preventing the electrocution, on the ground that the jury had been selected in a manner discriminating against Negroes.[9] Thus an obvious and horrible injustice was prevented, but the injustice in this case was not wrought in the selection of the jury, but rather by the "prejudicial influences outside the courtroom," as Jackson and Frankfurter put it in their concurring opinion, influences that were brought to bear on the jury "with such force that the conclusion is inescapable that these defendants were prejudged as guilty and the trial was but a legal gesture to register a verdict already dictated by the press and the public opinion . . . generated."[10]

An irresponsible press does not confine its abuse to the poor and the weak; it abuses the rich and the seemingly strong as well—so long as they are in no position to retaliate. Consider the case of still another Sam Sheppard, this one the Cleveland physician convicted of murdering his wife. Here was a case featuring swarms of press men at the city hall when Sheppard was brought there under arrest; and live broadcasting of a coroner's inquest; and a courtroom given over to the press during the trial, with a press table erected inside the bar of the court and extending the entire width of the room, within three feet of the jury box and so close to the counsel table that the defendant and his counsel could not consult without being overheard by reporters; a radio station allowed to broadcast from a room next to the jury room; television interviews with the judge; a viewing of the murder scene by the jury in the company of hundreds of reporters and others; constant publicity concerning the jurors, and constant pressure from the headlines and editorial comment, pressure to get on with the indictment, the trial, and the conviction of Sam Sheppard. "Why No Inquest? Do It Now, Dr. Gerber." "Why Don't Police Quiz Top Suspect?" "Why Isn't Sam Sheppard in Jail?" "Now proved under oath to be a liar. . . ." And from Walter Winchell in New York the report that a woman under arrest in New York for robbery had stated that "as Sheppard's mistress, she had borne him a child." "Blood Is Found in Garage." "Sheppard 'Gay Set' Is Revealed by Houk." And when, in an effort to show the necessity for a change of venue

[9] *Shepherd* v. *Florida,* 341 U.S. 50 (1951).
[10] 341 U.S. at p. 51.

as the result of this publicity, defense counsel conducted a random survey of public opinion, the press said the "survey 'smacks of mass jury tampering.'" And so on. This is what a "crusading," "public-serving," "fearless," "staunch," "robust," "vigorous" press can descend to when it is set free from any restraint, which of necessity means restraint by the law. There appears to have been no disposition on the part of the trial judge here to impose any restraints on the Cleveland press, perhaps because he was up for reelection (which, of course, is also a comment on another aspect of the press's power), but it is not clear what powers were left him. In the event, however, the Supreme Court, faced with the lurid details of Sheppard's trial and pretrial treatment, had the temerity (and good sense) to order a new trial on the ground that the trial judge had improperly allowed the news media to inflame and prejudice the public.[11] This probably surprised trial court judges around the country, who must have thought they had been deprived of any authority to control the press by the Supreme Court's effort to ensure the absolute freedom of the press.

It was this behavior of the Cleveland press in the Sheppard case and of the Dallas press (and police) after the assassination of President Kennedy that gave rise to two quasi-official studies and reports dealing with this problem, the first by a committee of the American Bar Association and the second by a committee of the Bar of the City of New York. The first, although acknowledging the constitutional obstacles, nevertheless proposed a renewed use of the power to punish out-of-court contempts; the second took the position that, in the light of these obstacles, the courts were, on the whole, powerless to control the media, and suggested that the problem might be alleviated through the adoption of voluntary codes of behavior by the police (respecting the dissemination to the public of information concerning crimes and arrests and suspects) and by the press in their reporting of these matters. Inevitably, of course, this was greeted by a cry of censorship from the American Newspaper Publishers Association, thereby reminding us of what William Allen White, the famous editor of the Emporia, Kansas, *Gazette,* once said on this subject:

[11] *Sheppard* v. *Maxwell,* 384 U.S. 333 (1966).

> The most serious danger that menaces the freedom of the American press is the obvious anxiety of rich publishers about the freedom of the press. They make so much noise about the threat to the freedom of the press that they have persuaded many people, particularly unthinking people, that the freedom of the press is merely a private snap for editors who wish to exploit the public by selling poisoned news. It is not a universal rule, but the rule is fairly workable that a newspaper which is eternally agonizing about the freedom of the press is a newspaper which is endangering the freedom of the press by abusing that freedom.[12]

II

It used to be that the press was also restrained by the libel laws, being permitted to make defamatory statements about public persons (to say nothing of private persons) only if it could be shown that these statements were based on facts; but the Supreme Court began its reconstruction of this body of law in its 1964 decision in *New York Times* v. *Sullivan,*[13] so that today the most outrageous comments pass as "fair comment," and nothing in the law restrains men like Jack Anderson from rushing into print with malicious statements for which there exists no better authority than the unsupported whispers of a former political opponent of the victim. In the more remote past, and even in the United States, as I pointed out earlier, Senator Eagleton could have sent his seconds to Anderson, or "called him out," but the libel laws were designed, in part, to put an end to dueling and this private method of settling disputes. Having now put an effective end to public libels, the Supreme Court ought, in justice, to overturn the antidueling statutes, thus permitting a measure of justice to be meted out to the likes of Jack Anderson.

The new law of libel was originally confined to cases involving public officials, but it has since been extended to libels of candidates

[12] As reprinted in *Freedom of the Press from Hamilton to the Warren Court,* ed. Harold L. Nelson (Indianapolis, 1967), p. 363.

[13] 376 U.S. 254 (1964). The new rule requires the victim of the libel to prove actual malice, which is defined as the making of statements known to be false or made with "reckless disregard" of whether they are false. Not surprisingly, this is proving to be a difficult thing to prove, although Senator Goldwater succeeded in doing so in his case against *Fact* magazine (*Ginzburg* v. *Goldwater,* 396 U.S. 1049 [1970]).

for public office[14] and even to libels of persons who are not even remotely public officials but who happen to be connected in one way or another to a matter of public or general concern.[15] Justice Douglas, employing his customary tactic of solving a problem by denying its existence, insists that the First Amendment forbids all libel laws, both civil and criminal,[16] because to him, ever ready to look on the sunny sides of things, even an irresponsible free press performs a public service—in fact, under some conditions, even lies are good. "Extravagant, reckless statements and even claims which may not be true seem to me an inevitable and perhaps *essential* part of the process by which the voting public informs itself of the qualities of a man who would be President."[17] Thus Jack Anderson performs a public service when he falsely accuses Senator Eagleton of having been many times arrested for drunken driving.

Douglas is alone on this frontier now, but his colleagues are not too far behind him. Collectively they have held the First Amendment to place severe limits on the authority of the states to provide remedies for the injuries caused by speech and press, either because, after consideration, they regard these injuries as a necessary price to be paid for freedom of the press, or because they deny that words, in themselves, can cause an injury. This accounts for what has happened to the right to privacy. It used to be understood that speech could invade privacy, but while there is a good deal of talk today about the invasion of the right to privacy, and quite properly so, what is usually meant by this is the sort of invasion, or intrusion, committed by agents of government when they engage in electronic surveillance, or establish data banks, or engage in administrative searches as part of the effort to enforce various health and regulatory measures, or in the words of Justice Douglas's hyperbole, "search the sacred precincts of marital bedrooms for telltale signs of the use of contraceptives."[18] But, except for Jacqueline Kennedy Onassis's quarrel with that cameraman, there is almost no concern

[14] *Monitor Patriot Co.* v. *Roy,* 401 U.S. 265 (1971).

[15] *Rosenbloom* v. *Metromedia, Inc.,* 403 U.S. 29 (1971).

[16] *Dun and Bradstreet, Inc.* v. *C. R. Grove,* 92 S.Ct. 204 (1971). Dissenting opinion.

[17] *Ginzburg* v. *Goldwater,* 396 U.S. 1049, 1051–52 (1970). Dissenting opinion. Italics supplied.

[18] *Griswold* v. *Connecticut,* 381 U.S. 479, 485 (1965).

with the invasions of privacy committed not by government but by the press. We seem not to be offended by them, or worse, incapable of finding them offensive; yet, in the day of *Candid Camera* and candid cameramen and the almost ubiquitous reporter with the microphone, there would appear to be a good deal more to be offended with now than there was in 1890, the year of Warren and Brandeis's famous *Harvard Law Review* article, "The Right to Privacy." It was here that they uttered their famous complaint against the press, being concerned not with its falsehoods or libels, but with, and only with, public disclosure by the press of true details of what they insisted were essentially private affairs: "The press is overstepping in every direction the obvious bounds of propriety and of decency. Gossip is no longer the resource of the idle and of the vicious, but has become a trade, which is pursued with industry as well as effrontery." Such conduct not only is offensive to the persons whose privacy is involved, but it corrupts the public taste and even works to undermine one of the conditions of democracy: an intelligent concern with public affairs.

> When personal gossip attains the dignity of print, and crowds the space available for matters of real interest to the community, what wonder that the ignorant and thoughtless mistake its relative importance. Easy of comprehension, appealing to that weak side of human nature which is never wholly cast down by the misfortunes and frailties of our neighbors, no one can be surprised that it usurps the place of interest in brains capable of other things. Triviality destroys at once robustness of thought and delicacy of feeling. No enthusiasm can flourish, no generous impulse can survive under its blighting influence.[19]

It may be difficult today to imagine anyone being made indignant by publicity, and in particular being outraged by press coverage of his wedding to the daughter of a United States Senator and of their entertaining of friends in their newly established Back Bay town house. Yet this is what is said to have led Warren to propose to Brandeis, his friend and former law partner, that they write the article that was so influential in the establishment of a

[19] *Harvard Law Review,* 4:196.

legal right to privacy.[20] Warren's counterparts today are more likely to employ public relations men to ensure such coverage and to complain only when they do not get it. The desire for publicity is a characteristic of modern life. The producers of the television show *Candid Camera*, for example, apparently encountered no difficulty whatever in obtaining permission to use the surreptitiously made films, no matter how foolish the subjects were made to appear in them and no matter how ashamed they ought to have been to have themselves displayed to the world in this fashion. On the contrary, it seems that the typical person was eager to have his episodes used, and importuned employees of the show to this end. Such a person is incapable of shame, and instead of arguing for a right to privacy, to which he is in fact indifferent, he clamors for what he regards as the privilege of being made an object of public attention, if not of ridicule.

No doubt Warren and Brandeis appear absurdly patrician, or even undemocratic, in this affair, but it is worth remembering that Brandeis, at least, would have to be counted among the greatest of American democrats. Nevertheless, while neither he nor Warren saw any incompatibility between democracy and the development of their legal remedy for invasions of privacy, the fate of that legal right suggests that a right of privacy exists only uneasily with democracy, and particularly with a First Amendment interpreted in a contemporary democratic fashion. (This is so even though in some contexts the First Amendment is cited as the constitutional basis of privacy. For example, the First Amendment is one of the amendments with "emanations" that cast "penumbras" within which the connubial bed can be hidden from the inquisitive eyes of Mr. Douglas's imaginary police.[21]

Surely the right has not had an illustrious history. It was given a statutory basis in a number of states, beginning, apparently, in New York in 1903, but in the process pretty much confined to the unauthorized use of a person's name, portrait, or picture for commercial purposes; and its career probably came to an end in a 1967 case (argued and lost by Richard M. Nixon) involving that statute.

[20] Alpheus Thomas Mason, *Brandeis: A Free Man's Life* (New York, 1946), p. 70.

[21] *Griswold* v. *Connecticut* p. 484.

Time magazine ran a story linking a play made from a novel with an actual episode in the life of a family named Hill, printing some inaccuracies along the way. The New York court had awarded $30,000 in compensatory damages in an action brought by Hill under the privacy statute, and the New York Court of Appeals affirmed. After the case had been argued before the Supreme Court of the United States, the New York Court of Appeals handed down a decision in the case of Warren Spahn, the great baseball pitcher, who had sought and won an injunction to prevent the publication of an unauthorized and fictionalized biography of himself. In its opinion the New York court had said that the rule of *New York Times* v. *Sullivan* did not apply because Spahn was not a public official and because no public interested "is served by protecting the dissemination" of this fictionalized biography. To which Mr. Justice Brennan, in his opinion for the Court in the Hill case, responded as follows:

> If this is meant to imply that proof of knowing or reckless falsity is not essential to a constitutional application of the statute in these cases, we disagree with the Court of Appeals. We hold that the constitutional protections for speech and press preclude the application of the New York statute to redress false reports of matters of public interest in the absence of proof that the defendant published the report with knowledge of its falsity or in reckless disregard of the truth.[22]

Thus the new law of libel and slander, which effectively removes any restraint on the press in that area, is now applied to the right of privacy, where it will have the same effect. It is so applied not because the right is being claimed by a public official, but because the person claiming it is, or has become, willingly or unwillingly, an object of news. And since the press is much better qualified than the Supreme Court to determine this—Professor Kalven says newsworthiness will come to be defined as whatever is published in the press[23]—Warren and Brandeis's right of privacy is reduced to this: those affairs or details of a life in which the public has no interest,

[22] *Time, Inc.* v. *Hill,* 385 U.S. 374, 387–88 (1967).

[23] Harry Kalven, Jr., "The Reasonable Man and the First Amendment: Hill, Butts, and Walker," in *The Supreme Court Review,* ed. Philip B. Kurland (Chicago, 1967), p. 284.

or is thought by the press to have no interest. Beyond that, a person's remedy against an irresponsible press will depend on his ability to prove actual malice, defined according to the rule of *New York Times* v. *Sullivan*, and the typical newsman is much too clever to allow this to be proved against him. So it is that privacy gives way to the freedom of the press, buried by the Supreme Court in *Time* v. *Hill*, and without the obsequies that usually attend such events. Instead Justice Brennan said this for the Court:

> The guarantees for speech and press are not the preserve of political expression or comment upon public affairs, essential as those are to healthy government. One need only pick up any newspaper or magazine to comprehend the vast range of published matter which exposes persons to public view, both private citizens and public officials. Exposure of the self to others in varying degrees is a concomitant of life in a civilized community. The risk of this exposure is an essential incident of life in a society which places a *primary* value on freedom of speech and of press.[24]

Warren and Brandeis lived in a world that still held it possible to combine democracy and privacy, and beyond that, democracy and delicacy of feeling, and cultivation of the mind and of the public taste, and, most relevantly in this context, democracy, meaning especially the principle of equality, with the principle of merit. The truly qualified to rule would be freely chosen to rule. Perhaps it was a delusion, and surely the mass press has done its best to make it so, but they were not unique at that time in thinking it possible to educate liberally the great body of citizens in the American democracy. This would allow public men, although dependent on the suffrage of the people, to be disdainful of vulgar opinion and of appeals to it during elections, which, it was hoped, would serve an educative function. Living at a time when democracy had not yet become altogether the rule of public opinion, or had not yet worked itself out in the direction Tocqueville had feared for it, Warren and Brandeis were of the opinion that what mattered was the opinion of their peers (including newsmen such as Walter Lippmann) and not of an uninformed public or of an ignorant press; and they there-

[24] *Time, Inc.* v. *Hill*, at p. 388. Italics supplied.

fore did not cultivate the press or attempt to ingratiate themselves with it. Their character was such that they could retain their dignity in the presence of newsmen—even television newsmen, had there been any—in marked contrast to the behavior of the typical public man or politician today. The situation today can be characterized this way: What the layman is to *Candid Camera,* the politician is to *Face the Nation* or *Meet the Press,* a man lacking in dignity and inclined to be slavish in his manner. George Herman matters more to him than his own opinion of himself or than the dignity that ought to be attached to his office, because George Herman, by inviting him to appear on *Face the Nation,* can give him unparalleled access to the nation; and if George Herman wants to crack a figurative egg over his head, he will oblige with the appropriate barnyard cackle. "Senator, this is a television program, and everybody watching you can see that you're perspiring considerably and that your hands have a slight shake to them."

Brandeis would not have permitted that attitude of utter contempt to be struck with him; he would have forgone public office rather than become contemptible, especially in the eyes of ignorant people. His friend and political associate Woodrow Wilson would never have submitted to the impertinence to which contemporary politicians, at whatever level, are regularly subjected by Vanocur and Brinkley, or to being ordered about by Rather, Wallace, and McGee[25] ("Step aside, Governor, you're in the way of the camera"). He would have refused to talk with Jack Anderson, the newsman who first broke into the news himself when discovered on his hands and knees bugging a hotel room. Thanks largely to television, that has now become a posture that politicians are finding more and more comfortable. Woodrow Wilson was incapable of acting in a slavish manner, and when one realizes that this can also be said of his

[25] In 1914 Wilson told a news conference that he deeply resented the "treatment" the ladies of his family were receiving in the press. "Take the case of my oldest daughter. It is a violation of my own impulses even to speak of these things, but my oldest daughter is constantly represented as being engaged to this, that, or the other man in different parts of the country, in some instances to men she has never even met in her life. It is a constant and intolerable annoyance..." (cited in Arthur S. Link, "Portrait of the President," in *The Philosophy and Policies of Woodrow Wilson,* ed. Earl Latham (Chicago, 1958), p. 24.

three Republican presidential opponents, William Howard Taft, Theodore Roosevelt, and Charles Evans Hughes, it becomes apparent that something has happened to American politics and American politicians.[26]

III

In a society that places a primary value on freedom of the press, not only does the press have the right to determine what and who is news, but it has the right to decide what news is fit to print, and what is fit to print even if it is not news. This is most clearly demonstrated in the case of the pornography that is now published without apology even by the erstwhile respectable press. It would seem to follow, then, that the government is not entitled to prevent the publication of anything, including, and especially, government documents such as the Pentagon Papers, even if they are stolen documents. Indeed, it is not necessary to adopt the extreme position of granting freedom of the press the primary place to conclude that the government has no such right, for to allow the government to prevent publication would be to establish the legality of prior restraint, or prior censorship, at least under some conditions, and even Blackstone's understanding of freedom of the press allowed no room for prior restraint.[27] In its brief in the Pentagon Papers case, petitioner *New York Times* put it this way: What the government seeks to do is "to impose on a newspaper the kind of prior restraint which holds an especially disfavored position under the First Amendment."[28] In short, whereas there might still be argument concerning the farther reaches of the First Amendment, there would seem to be no argument that it extends at least so far as to protect the press

[26] There are of course, exceptions. Mayor Daley of Chicago is one. He does not need the press, which is one reason the press hates him. But how many American politicians are similar to Canadian Prime Minister Pierre Elliott Trudeau, who is disliked by the press because, among other reasons, he is so obviously more intelligent, more knowledgeable, and more eloquent than the members of the press who come into contact with him, and because he frequently makes no effort to conceal his contempt for them?

[27] Blackstone's *Commentaries on the Laws of England,* bk. 4, chap. 11, sec. 13.

[28] *New York Times Co.* v. *United States,* 403 U.S. 713 (1971). Brief for Petitioner, p. 24.

from being prevented in advance from publishing news of public affairs.

The *New York Times* did not, however, press this argument on the Court, and the Court, or at least a majority of the justices on the Court, did not adopt it in its decision. The *Times* said that it "need not be contended, and we do not contend, that the First Amendment always carries all before it, regardless of countervailing considerations."[29] In principle, it conceded the right of the government to obtain a court order restraining publication, but the government would have to convince the court that publication would lead directly and almost unavoidably to a disastrous event. "The probabilities must be very high, near to certainty, and the chain of causation between the publication and the feared event must be direct. Anything less will risk having the exception swallow the rule."[30] In its *per curiam* opinion the Court agrees that the government, by its failure to show the probability of such consequences, had not successfully rebutted the presumption against prior restraint.[31]

Of course, there are those justices and members of the press who are not satisfied to assert so relatively modest a claim on behalf of freedom of the press. On the Court, Black and Douglas held to their familiar view that any restraint of news "would make a shambles of the First Amendment,"[32] and *New York Times* associate editor Tom Wicker thinks that the mere attempt to get an injunction had the effect of "scaring ideas out of the market."[33] He and many other journalists argue that they have the right to publish anything they can get their hands on, including, in the case of Jack Anderson, transcripts or accounts of secret, high-level discussions of national security affairs. They acknowledge that it is probably within the legitimate powers of government to punish (under a

[29] Ibid., pp. 24–25.

[30] Ibid., p. 51.

[31] 403 U.S. 713, 714 (1971).

[32] Ibid., p. 715.

[33] *New York Times,* July 18, 1972. Apparently ideas were also scared out of the market by the Vice-President's attacks on the press. This suggests that journalists are not the most intrepid of men, and that therefore the First Amendment, in order to guarantee the right of newsmen to say whatever they choose about politicians, is going to have to be interpreted as preventing the politicians from saying anything by way of criticism of the press.

properly drawn criminal statute) anyone who divulges official secrets directly to an enemy or indirectly to an enemy through the press; but they nevertheless continue to insist that the government may not prevent them from publishing what they obtain as the result of an illegal act on the part of someone else. The stealing of a document may be made a felony, as may the willful communication of certain information, but the use of that document or that information is a constitutional right. So they contend.

Furthermore, when asked whether the government, in the effort to enforce a law against the stealing of documents or the communicating of certain information, has the right to ask newsmen to testify as to the sources of the stories they print—that is, to disclose to a grand jury, for example, the names of the persons who give them the documents or the information—they reply that such information, although no federal statute has made it so, is privileged as a matter of constitutional right. To hold otherwise, they contend, would have a deterring effect on "First Amendment activity," by which they mean that when a newsman and his news source cannot maintain a confidential relationship there will be an "impairment of the flow of news." Jack Anderson depends absolutely on informers, and to be required to disclose their names would put an end to their usefulness and to his column. Walter Cronkite, Eric Sevareid, Mike Wallace, Dan Rather, Wallace Turner, John Kifner, Frank Morgan, Marvin Kalb, and a variety of other journalists all testified in the Caldwell case in support of the proposition that the flow of news would be impaired if news sources could not be held in confidence;[34] and it follows for those who have an exalted notion of the importance of the press that an impairment of the flow of news is too heavy a price to pay for anything so ephemeral or evanescent as the public interest. It may be an old maxim, honored in theory as well as in the practice of all other English-speaking countries, that "the public has a right to every man's evidence,"[35] but, according to the newsmen, there is no right to a newsman's evidence—not, at least, in America. There is no right to the testimony of a newsman even when he has knowledge that a crime has been committed, and even though

[34] *Branzburg* v. *Hayes; In re Paul Pappas; United States* v. *Caldwell,* 91 S.Ct. 2646, 2677, n. 20 (1972).

[35] John H. Wigmore, *Treatise on Evidence,* sec. 2285 (Boston, 1940).

there is a federal crime of misprision.[36] What applies to other citizens does not, he insists, apply to him. He is a journalist. He is a journalist in a country that places a primary value on freedom of the press.

By the narrowest of margins, and with considerable apologies, the Supreme Court denied this claim to extraordinary status, at least in the circumstances of the three cases before it.[37] Justice White said for the Court that there was no "basis for holding that the public interest in law enforcement and in ensuring effective grand jury proceedings is insufficient to override the consequential but uncertain burden on news-gathering which is said to result from insisting that reporters, like other citizens, respond to relevant questions put to them in the course of a valid grand jury investigation or criminal trial."[38] Whether the Court would be able to muster a majority in favor of the proposition that a newsman must disclose to a grand jury or in a criminal trial the name of the thief who passes a government document to him, or of the person who willfully communicates certain information, may be another question. Yet without such power it would seem almost impossible to enforce this sort of statute, but that is of no concern to the press as press. Its "constitutional mission," according to Justice Stewart in his dissenting opinion in *Branzburg* v. *Hayes*,[39] is to gather as well as to publish the news, and news-gathering requires a constitutional right to a confidential relation with news sources.

The typical newsman will insist there is no danger in allowing the press an absolute freedom to publish what it chooses or in granting to newsmen an absolute privilege respecting their professional

[36] "Whoever, having knowledge of the actual commission of a felony cognizable by a court of the United States, conceals and does not as soon as possible make known the same to some judge or other person in civil or military authority under the United States, shall be [guilty of misprision]" (18 U.S.C. 4). This has been construed to require, in addition to knowledge of the crime, some affirmative act of concealment. See *Branzburg* v. *Hayes,* at p. 2664, n. 36, and cases cited.

[37] Paul Branzburg, a reporter for the Louisville, Kentucky, *Courier-Journal;* Paul Pappas, a television newsman-photographer for a New Bedford, Massachusetts, station; and Earl Caldwell, a reporter for the *New York Times,* all refused to answer questions put to them by grand juries that were conducting criminal investigations.

[38] *Branzburg* v. *Hayes,* at p. 2661.

[39] Ibid., p. 2671.

relations with their news sources. Their reason is not that these privileges cannot be abused—on the contrary, there seems to be some recognition among newsmen today that there are times when the public interest requires information to be withheld[40]—but rather that the press can be trusted not to abuse them. The public has "a right to know," but the public interest would not be served by allowing the public to know the sailing dates and destinations of troop transports, and fortunately the press can be trusted not to divulge this information if it should reach its hands. This is to say, the press will decide, and can be trusted to decide, when the public good will be served by publication, and this is the same thing as saying that the press, in those matters coming within the ambit of the First Amendment, is entrusted by the Constitution with the duty of defining the public interest.

But who elected Jack Anderson, Tom Wicker, and the editors of *Ramparts* and thereby entrusted them with this awesome authority? And when do they come up for reelection so we can throw them out? If there is at least an element of truth in the maxim that when annual elections cease tyranny begins, what can be said of a system that puts the definition of the public good in the hands of journalists subject to no man's suffrage? And not merely in the hands of our favorite journalists, but—since we are discussing a rule of constitutional law that is to apply generally and without exception—in the hands of all journalists operating under all conditions.[41]

[40] Writing on the op. ed. page of the *New York Times* (July 12, 1972), CBS producer Norman Morris said this: "The right to know and the right to publish what is known are held to be inalienable in a democracy. Most of us who deal intimately with the flow of events arch our backs at the suggestion that there may be times when circumstances warrant silence to be the better part of journalistic valor. Yet a case can be made for those extraordinary instances in which factual information should be withheld." He gives skyjacking as his particular example.

[41] "News today has become another commercial product to sell, and competition between news gathering organizations is sufficiently keen to take precedent [*sic*] over judgment and reservation. The problem for journalists is exacerbated by a number of factors: what is assumed to be the public's unquenchable thirst for information; growing awareness of credibility gaps between the source and the report; and steadily increasing attacks on the news media on the grounds of unfair presentation.

"By its very nature the newsroom atmosphere serves to unhinge judg-

Of course there are grave objections to allowing the executive branch of the federal government to classify documents and to decide what may be published. Are there not, however, graver objections to giving these powers to the editors, publishers, and network presidents? And of course elections do not constitute a wholly adequate check on executive officeholders. But a vote against an incumbent public official is surely superior in this respect to a canceled subscription or a letter to the editor, to say nothing of a switching of television channels.

As it turned out, of course, the final authority to decide what shall not be published was given not to the executive branch and not to the press, but, by a narrow Supreme Court majority, to the courts. This is the effect of the decision in the Pentagon Papers case. The government bears the heavy burden of convincing the courts that the public good will be dangerously jeopardized by the publication of an item before the courts will enjoin its publication by the press. As for communications between a newsman and his news sources or informants or informers, in the absence of a statutory privilege (and there is no federal statute granting the privilege)[42] such communications are not privileged, and the newsman, like his fellow citizens and his fellow journalists in the rest of the English-speaking world, has a duty to testify when properly asked. These decisions recognize that what is good for the press, as was true also in the case of General Motors, is not necessarily good for the United States. The typical journalist finds it difficult to accept this, and has been encouraged in this attitude by all those judges who, with familiar insouciance, assert that freedom of the press is a primary value in the United States. It is not. It is subordinate to the public good, to which, we all hope, it will contribute, but which, we all should know, it has the capacity to harm.

---

ment. Decisions, in large measure, are formulated by Pavlovian response to wire service bulletin bells and buzzers, consequential human clustering about the news machines and a piqued sense of competitive urgency" (ibid.).

[42] On August 17, 1972, Senators Sam Ervin and James Pearson introduced a bill designed to protect newsmen from compulsory disclosure of information in federal criminal proceedings "when such disclosure is not necessary for the proper functioning of the criminal justice system."

IV

When a society places primary value on freedom of speech and press, the various laws designed to promote a responsible press are given a secondary or subordinate place, and we have seen what happens to them there. What Professor Kurland has said about truth and the law of libel after *New York Times* v. *Sullivan* can be said of the other qualities and laws as well: "...assuring the freedom of the press is the Court's business, but assuring the responsibility of the press to the truth will have to come from elsewhere."[43] And elsewhere may prove to be nowhere. But even that is not the whole of our problem. There is also the likelihood that the kind of emphasis we have put on freedom of expression will lead us to forget the purpose of expression and the reason it is protected in the Constitution.

A First Amendment interpreted to protect the arts from censorship, for example, is intelligible: the arts, properly understood, are something deserving of protection and something requiring protection. A First Amendment interpreted to protect every crude, vulgar, and ugly form of expression is not intelligible. It does not make sense. It does not make sense because, as is now readily apparent to anyone with a modicum of taste, the effect of a policy of permitting all expression (or placing a "primary value" on freedom of expression) is the loss of any sense of what is beautiful expression. A Matisse painting, in the eyes of the New York Civil Liberties Union, deserves no more from the law than a crude tattoo on a sailor's biceps,[44] which reduces the one to the other. This, it

[43] Philip B. Kurland, "1970 Term: Notes on the Emergence of the Burger Court," in *The Supreme Court Review, 1971,* ed. Kurland (Chicago, 1971), p. 290.

[44] "Just because a design is tatooed on a man's arm or chest instead of painted on canvas, it doesn't make it any less of an art form.

"That is the contention of the New York Civil Liberties Union, which announced last night that it would file a brief tomorrow in the state Court of Appeals challenging a New York City ordinance forbidding tatooing.

"The A.C.L.U. argues that tatooing is a 'recognized art form introduced to Europe and America by returning sailors from the South Seas,' and contends 'no art form may be absolutely prohibited even though it may lend itself to instances of crudity and debasement.'

"Noting that the city adopted the ordinance for health purposes, the A.C.L.U. argued that the law should instead provide rules specifically designed to provide safe tatooing, including sterilized equipment" (*New York Times* [Paris ed.], March 21, 1966).

can be said with some confidence, is not what the authors of the First Amendment had in mind when they set out to protect freedom of expression. Nor did they have in mind topless go-go dancing, regardless of the decision to the contrary handed down by Superior Court Judge Robert W. Winsor in Seattle, Washington. The judge, and apparently the *New York Times* editor who thought it cute or amusing to make a feature, complete with cartoon, of the judge's opinion, think that all dancing is alike and must by the law be treated alike, that there can be no distinction in the manner in which the law treats Dame Margot Fonteyn and Miss Ruby Code of the Lucky Lady Tavern, because the only esthetic distinction between them is in the eye of the beholder.[45]

It is usually said that a censorship law depreciates the arts. No doubt such a law gives rise to difficult problems and lends itself to familiar abuses; but a censorship law that distinguishes between art and trash, the beautiful and the ugly, is a law that serves to remind us why the arts are protected and thereby, perhaps, of the nature of the arts. In theory, even if not in practice, it appreciates or exalts the arts; whereas the equation of Matisse and a bicipital tattoo, and of Margot Fonteyn and Ruby Code, is an insult and a denigration of the arts and of artists truly understood.[46] This, thanks to the Supreme Court, is where our law now stands.

According to the orthodox view today, freedom of expression, being primary, serves no purpose beyond itself. All expression is equal, not only in the arts, or so-called arts, as we must now say, but in the area of political speech as well. There can be no distinction in the manner in which the law treats good speech and bad speech, the speech we like and the speech we hate. The venerable Holmes said it first:

[45] *New York Times,* July 27, 1972. This is an excellent example of the natural tendency of the press in America—even the best of the daily press—to contribute to the vulgarization of American life. Vulgarity has always existed, of course, but it used to be looked upon with disgust and as an unfortunate concomitant of the lack of education. The particular kind of vulgarity involved here was understood to be illegitimate, and existed only on the fringes of society. What Judge Winsor has done is to make it legitimate in the law, and the *Times,* by the manner of its treatment of the judge and his decision, has done its part to make it legitimate generally.

[46] I have argued this at greater length in "Beyond the (Garbage) Pale, or Democracy, Censorship, and the Arts," in *Censorship and Freedom of Expression,* ed. Harry M. Clor (Chicago, 1971), pp. 49–72.

"... if there is any principle of the Constitution that more imperatively calls for attachment than any other it is the principle of free thought—not free thought for those who agree with us but freedom for the thought that we hate."[47] Unless limited to freedom of thought, and not to freedom of thought that is communicated, this is nonsense, and cannot be in accord with the intentions of the authors of the amendment. They obviously were of the opinion that freedom of expression is good, which means good for something, and because it is good it must be protected. But if the privilege is extended to the speech we hate, why is freedom of speech good? Because when "truth grapples with falsehood" truth will prevail? But Holmes and the modern civil libertarians do not make this contention. Because monarchists (fascists, communists) can thereby advance the cause of monarchy (fascism, communism)? If we accept this answer, and it is today the accepted answer,[48] we commit ourselves to being indifferent to the outcome of the debate among the advocates of these opposing doctrines, which means—and there should be no concealing of this fact—we do not prefer free government to the alternatives, monarchy then or either of the varieties of slavery now. However well established is this view today, it was demonstrably not the view of the men who wrote the Constitution and the First Amendment.[49] They had a purpose in protecting freedom of expression; they sought to foster free government, and while in practice they might have tolerated the advocacy of monarchy (fascism, communism), they would not have done so as a matter of constitutional right. Whatever is said in libertarian circles today, this is not proof of their illiberalism. On the contrary, a law of political expression that distinguishes between advocacy of free government as

[47] *United States* v. *Schwimmer,* 279 U.S. 644, 654–55 (1929). Dissenting opinion.

[48] Holmes, again, stated it first in his dissenting opinion in *Gitlow* v. *New York:* "If in the long run the beliefs expressed in proletarian dictatorship are destined to be accepted by the dominant forces of the community, the only meaning of free speech is that they should be given their chance and have their way" (268 U.S. 652, 673 [1925]). Dissenting opinion.

[49] Leonard W. Levy, *Legacy of Suppression: Freedom of Speech and Press in Early American History* (Cambridge, Mass., 1960); Walter Berns, "Freedom of the Press and the Alien and Sedition Laws: A Reappraisal," in *The Supreme Court Review, 1970,* ed. Philip B. Kurland (Chicago, 1970), pp. 109–59.

opposed to advocacy of the others, rather than to depreciate freedom of expression, serves, once again, to remind us of its purpose and thereby to appreciate it.

Whatever the tension that exists between them, a responsible press need not be the opposite of a free press; and a government that, through its law, acts to promote a responsible press is not by that fact the opposite of a free government. Not only are such laws not incompatible with free government, they may be a necessary condition of it. That is why the Constitution, until recently, was understood not to forbid such laws.

A. Stephen Boyan, Jr.

●

THE ABILITY TO COMMUNICATE: A FIRST AMENDMENT RIGHT

A new type of First Amendment issue is coming to the attention of the courts. The issue is: who has access to the media? Stated differently, does the First Amendment in any circumstance require the owner or licensee of a communications facility to open up his facility to ideas (or persons with ideas) different from his own? The problem stems from a First Amendment concern for "uninhibited, robust and wide-open"[1] discussion of all issues of significance to the public. It arises now because centralization and monopolization increasingly characterize ownership in the media of communications.[2] The First Amendment does not supply any obvious answers in this area. Those who wrote it had different concerns. They thought primarily in terms of preventing government interferences with press freedom. Whether by prohibiting prior restraints or seditious libel prosecutions, or both, the theory of the First Amendment was that if the government kept hands off, a multitude of voices expressing competing ideas about public matters would be heard. The framers were justified in that supposition. In their day, almost anybody who wanted to print a newspaper could do so without much difficulty. Existing newspapers were printed sheets from small printing shops; presses were inexpensive. What was published potentially could get into the hands of the minority of the population who had the suffrage.

Likewise, each reader could choose a paper that reinforced his own prejudices. Much choice, much variety existed. The newspaper was a "cue-giver," as V. O. Key put it—like an actor, with beliefs,

[1] *New York Times* v. *Sullivan,* 376 U.S. 254, 270 (1964).
[2] V. O. Key, Jr., *Public Opinion and American Democracy* (New York: Alfred A. Knopf, 1963), pp. 371–72.

likes, and hates.[3] Through it a reader could make sense of the world. Then the various opinions would confront each other as people talked face to face, in group meetings, in town meetings, and the like. It was in this sense that the framers saw that if the government would stay its hand, truth could emerge from the competition of ideas.

Today it costs $50 million to start a general circulation newspaper.[4] Not everybody can afford it. At the same time the electorate now to be served by newspapers is huge: Polsby and Wildavsky estimate that 74.5 percent of the population is registered to vote.[5] Thus there is a marked reduction in the number of units of the press relative to the reading electorates. Moreover, the mere absence of government interference does not guarantee that a man who has something to say has a chance to say it to the public. On the contrary, in many communities across the United States there is one newspaper (or two, with common ownership). It determines what facts, what interpretation of the facts, and what ideas are told to the public, and by whom. Partly because the government has not interfered, moreover, these communities may have but one television station—owned by the same newspaper. All this is happening at a time when alternative forms of communication are somewhat in eclipse—when people spend "more and more of their time in their air-conditioned homes watching television, and less and less time listening to speakers in the public parks, attending town meetings and reading handbills on the streets."[6]

Even when there is more than one newspaper in a community, and/or more than one television station, diversity in points of view presented is virtually nonexistent. The press used to be an appendage of political parties; today it is an appendage of business interests. All of the media—newspapers as well as TV—are heavily dependent on

[3] Ibid., p. 396.

[4] U.S. Senate, Subcommittee on Constitutional Rights of the Committee on the Judiciary, *Hearings, Freedom of the Press,* 92nd Cong., 1st sess., October 12, 1971 (unpublished). Hereafter cited as Senate Hearings.

[5] Nelson W. Polsby and Aaron B. Wildavsky, *Presidential Elections,* 3rd ed. (New York: Scribner, 1971), p. 255.

[6] Nicholas Johnson and Tracy A. Western, "A Twentieth-Century Soapbox: The Right to Purchase Radio and Television Time," *Virginia Law Review,* 57 (1971):574.

commercial advertising. Newspapers in particular have been beset with economic problems; many have folded. This does not mean that "big business" exercises a measurable control over the content of the media, although in some cases it tries.[7] In the first place, it doesn't have to. The media themselves are "big business." The producers of soap opera know just as well as the manufacturers of soap products that it is better business to "reinforce the values of the system and to maintain an indifference to questions that might touch on controversial matters."[8] People don't watch shows that upset them as much as shows that entertain them. This does not mean that all controversy is absent from the media. Newspapers and television do present to their audiences the various sides of well-recognized or respectable points of view. It is the unrecognized, "touchy" subject in which some people wish to interest the public that the mass media as a whole don't cover or else merely caricaturize.[9] To do more hurts business.

Second, the ethic of the media is different today than in the past. Newspapers formerly were expected to be biased. Today, to hurl such a charge against the media brings forth wringing of hands and assertions of pained innocence—however true the charge may be.[10] Representatives of the media assert that they report the facts—and then the public can decide what the facts mean. Several things may be said about this. First, some facts are presented and others are not. David Brinkley has said that there is no "intentional" bias on television. "We are criticized by both the far right and far left—we must be doing something right."[11] Perhaps. Equally possible,

[7] For example, on March 7, 1972, the *New York Times* reported that Bumble Bee Seafoods had withdrawn all advertising from the Columbia Broadcasting System. Bumble Bee objected to network news coverage of Senator Phillip Hart's investigation of fishing industry practices. In withdrawing their ads, Bumble Bee declared that CBS was not a "hospitable vehicle" for their advertisements.

[8] Key, *Public Opinion and American Democracy,* p. 396.

[9] Dan Lacy, *Freedom and Communications,* 2nd ed. (Urbana: University of Illinois Press, 1969), p. 69.

[10] Key, *Public Opinion and American Democracy,* p. 392. See also the CBS documents "CBS Comments on *The News Twisters,*" October 1, 1971, and "CBS News Releases First Independent Study on Bias Charge," October 13, 1971, submitted for the record of the Senate Hearings, February 2, 1972.

[11] Senate Hearings, October 19, 1971.

however, is that television does not fairly cover the far right or far left.[12] Second, what does it mean, in any event, to say that the press is without bias? It means that it doesn't openly, at least, question the veracity, the underhandedness, or the contradictions of what a political actor is doing. The press becomes a "common carrier of neutral, and often meaningless, political intelligence."[13] It makes no sense of politics. It permits easy manipulation. He who can make the most startling charges (such as a Joe McCarthy) or engage in the most dramatic behavior (such as a George Wallace) can fill the front pages or be seen on television day after day. The media themselves are either entertainers or spectators, inducing a spectator or audience attitude toward political things. As purveyors of entertainment the media do not explain the significance of events, or who is really doing what to whom—or, as Key put it, the "identity, motives, and objectives of political antagonists."[14] Furthermore, the "unbiased" media—if there are such things—are media of bland centrism. "Objectivity" tends to mean, in practice, reducing dissonance about a matter—giving a "reasonable" interpretation of what is going on. What often is "reasonable" then turns out to be something between two opposing points of view. That is centrism, and that is bias.

Whatever the problems of the media as a whole may be, they apply with special force to television. Television broadcasters, those "lineal descendants of operators of music halls and peep shows,"[15] cannot even pretend that they are anything more than headline services, when they cover public events at all. At least newspapers can cover news in some depth. News interests some of their readers. Sports interest others. Comics are great for still others. The women's pages are of special interest to the fair sex, especially the unliberated ones, and everybody likes the TV program listings. The point is that newspapers can print lots of different things—even news—and each of these different things, within limits, adds to readership. More

[12] Edith Efron, summarizing the findings in her book *The News Twisters* (Los Angeles: Nash, 1971), said, for example, that network news during the latter part of 1968 had a pro-Humphrey and antiwar bias. She concluded that views on the right and on the extreme left of the political spectrum did not receive fair treatment (Senate Hearings, February 2, 1972).

[13] Key, *Public Opinion and American Democracy,* p. 392.

[14] Ibid., p. 393.

[15] Ibid., p. 389.

readers mean more advertising—or more highly priced advertising. In short, they mean more profits. Television, on the other hand, to the extent that it covers news, is not "doing" entertainment. News doesn't get the audience of good entertainment. This means lower advertising revenues. News, moreover, is expensive to produce. It's an all-around bad business proposition.

Moreover, television, even more than newspapers, is easily manipulated. The thoughtful politician is not nearly as good copy as the gregarious or charismatic one. An idea can only be read by a commentator—and it takes time. An event can be filmed and seen. If it is a little novel, or if it has some "action"—i.e., violence—it is more newsworthy than just some politician's speech. Besides, compared to a speech, after a short film clip the TV broadcaster can more quickly get back to the commercials with which the news competes for time.

Moreover, TV advertisers are more closely associated with the programs they sponsor than newspaper advertisers are to any particular section or item in the paper. So the advertiser on television in particular does not need or want controversy, which may upset people. He may fear that some people may be upset with *him* as one of the sponsors of the program. Today it is often forgotten that radio entertainment was usually produced by the sponsor himself. Until recently, the same was true of television. Even assuming, then, that a provocative program wouldn't make people angry at a television network itself, why should a network air a program that attracts no sponsor? Television, unlike newspapers, doesn't even have a history of opinionated political muckraking, a noble tradition to which a TV broadcaster can point to justify his controversial or heretical broadcasts.

All this casts some doubt on whether the media today are serving First Amendment values. Freedom of speech and freedom of the press are essential to a functioning democracy. A democratic regime assumes that the government may err. It assumes that no person or institution possesses a monopoly of political truth. The truth emerges out of the *competition* of ideas. Liberty in a democratic regime, therefore, is not merely the right of the citizen. The regime has the duty to protect liberty in order to retain its essential character as a democracy.

Furthermore, since the truth is not known but rather emerges out of the competition of ideas, the regime fosters the pursuit of truth by protecting free expression. The regime must protect the expression of ideas or opinions even when they seem untrue, irrelevant, or unpopular. As John Stuart Mill concluded a century ago, if an opinion is bad, the community gains by being reassured of the grounds of its own correct opinion. On the other hand, if an opinion is not entirely base, the community gains by taking from it that which is not entirely bad or which may even be good.

Beyond being an instrument for discovering truth, free expression is also the necessary condition for adequate public discussion of public matters. The value of public discussion is that it promotes a level of public education or public spiritedness in the community. It helps to translate grievances into demands on the regime. It alleviates a sense of "alienation" which many people feel about public matters. It thus also generates support for the regime—the consent of the governed. Consent without free expression, without communication of information, without competition of ideas, is consent obtained in a nondemocratic way.

If the government keeps its hands off the press, these purposes will be achieved, according to the traditional understanding of the First Amendment. But will they? It is true that the government must keep its hands off the press in a certain way. It cannot tell the press to publish or not to publish the *substance* of something, or punish it for doing otherwise. But if the government does keep its hands off, and there is no debate, and only limited communication of information, is the purpose of the First Amendment served?

A reasonable argument can be made, especially in the case of television, for a negative answer. Indeed, in the case of the broadcast media, I believe the government must intervene "to open up the channels of communication." Speech that "invites dispute, induces a condition of unrest, creates dissatisfaction with conditions as they are, or even stirs people to anger"[16] has as much right to be broadcast under the First Amendment as any "centrist" commentary by an Eric Sevareid. The argument that the First Amendment requires the government to keep its hands off, which *might* have

[16] *Terminiello* v. *Chicago,* 337 U.S. 1, 4 (1949).

relevance for newspapers, doesn't even apply in the case of the broadcast media. The government has already intervened. It has not kept its hands off. It has enacted the Communications Act of 1934.

The purpose of that statute is

> to maintain the control of the United States over all channels of interstate and foreign radio transmission; and to provide for the use of such channels, but not the ownership thereof, by persons for limited periods of time, under licenses granted by Federal authority, and no such license shall be construed to create any right, beyond the terms, conditions, and period of the license.[17]

The government licenses the use of the airwaves, in short, to some persons. It necessarily denies licenses to use the limited radio spectrum to other persons. As Fred Friendly has put it, the government has said that a few citizens can operate "a super public address system that can, in effect, drown out that [historically expected] multitude of diverse and robust voices."[18] The government in effect says who shall print and who shall publish, not on the printing presses, as three hundred years ago, but on the airwaves. Government intervention constitutes a form of prior censorship.

Thus when we describe the television broadcasting industry as one that gives little attention to public affairs, and bland, biased attention at that, we in fact describe a government-created and government-sanctioned system of broadcasting. The government could have created and sanctioned an entirely different broadcasting system. It could have allocated channels to itself, as in Great Britain. "[T]he government could surely have decreed that each frequency should be shared among all or some of those who wish to use it, each being assigned a portion of the broadcast day or the broadcast week."[19] It could have simply refused to renew licenses beyond the initial three-year period for which they are granted, if any other qualified applicant appeared. Less drastically, it could have re-

[17] *U.S. Code,* vol. 47, sec. 301 (1964).

[18] Senate Hearings, October 12, 1971.

[19] *Red Lion Broadcasting Co.* v. *Federal Communications Commission,* 395 U.S. 367, 390–91 (1969).

stricted or prohibited network programming. The government instead established what has been called a "permit to print money" for a privileged few. It has then said that these licensed few can broadcast almost anything they want over the airwaves.

The few limits the government has imposed on its licensees are mostly technical in nature. They have to do with the power of the signal, the equipment, the hours of broadcasting, and so forth. None have to do with permitting those who were denied licenses the use of the airwaves. Some have to do with fairness. If a licensee discusses a controversial issue, he is required by the Federal Communications Commission to deal with that issue fairly. This means, generally, that he must present the various points of view concerning that controversy in a balanced manner. If he openly takes a position on a controversial issue, he must offer reasonable opportunity for a spokesman on the other side of that issue to reply. If he personally attacks a particular person or group, he must inform the person or group of the attack and offer a reasonable opportunity to respond. If he offers his facilities to one candidate for a political office, he must offer equal time to all other candidates running for that political office. It should be noted that none of these rules requires any licensee to offer any time to anybody for any office, or to editorialize on any issue, or to deal with any controversy. No one may use a licensee's facilities to reply to silence.

But television network spokesmen vigorously object to even this much FCC regulation. CBS president Frank Stanton complains that FCC rules actually inhibit both the amount and the quality of public affairs broadcasting. His argument seems to be that network journalists have enough to do to handle complaints by their station affiliates when they do present controversial programs. If, in addition, they have to worry about government evaluation of the fairness of what they've done, then why go to the trouble of doing the show at all?[20] Moreover, if this evaluation, as NBC president Julian Goodman interprets it, involves such matters as FCC officials' deciding what was the issue, what represents a position on the issue, who is to present other positions on the issue and how, the counting of minutes devoted to each position, and so on, the whole business becomes ridicu-

[20] Senate Hearings, September 29, 1971.

lous.[21] Network spokesmen claim that fairness is a quality that cannot be regulated.[22] They claim it means that government bureaucrats decide what issues a journalist must cover; that is, they, and not journalists, decide what meets journalistic standards of relevance and urgency.[23]

Dr. Frank Stanton cites Jefferson as his authority to warn against government interference, whatever the problems of television. Jefferson saw worse problems with the press of his day, and yet he opposed interference:

> Indeed the abuses of the freedom of the press here have been carried to a length never before known or borne by any civilized nation. . . . But it is so difficult to draw a clear line of separation between the abuse and the wholesome use of the press, that as yet have found it better to trust the public judgment, rather than the magistrate, with the discrimination between truth and falsehood. And hitherto the public judgment has performed that office with wonderful correctness.[24]

It is not difficult, moreover, to cite recent cases of government intervention against the broadcast media which had an impact having nothing to do with achieving fairness, access, the competition of ideas, robust debate, or any other value arguably protected by the First Amendment.

The Nixon administration, for example, which was unhappy with the news reporting of CBS reporter Daniel Schorr, ordered the FBI to investigate him.[25] The administration said it wanted the investigation in connection with a federal job possibility of which Schorr knew nothing. The investigation involved interviews by the FBI of CBS officials, Schorr's neighbors, and fellow reporters. CBS officials wondered whether Schorr was about to leave his job for another one. Others wondered if he was "in trouble" with the FBI, if his "FBI tail" was with him, or whether it was "safe" to talk

[21] Ibid., October 12, 1971.
[22] Ibid.
[23] Ibid., September 29, 1971.
[24] Ibid.
[25] Ibid., February 1, 1972.

on the phone.[26] All of this made Schorr's work as a reporter very difficult. Schorr said it also tended to push him into an antagonist role, which the administration then could cite as confirmation of its allegation that Schorr was biased against it.[27]

But the seriousness of this rather clumsy effort becomes clear only after some understanding of other incidents that preceded it. Nicholas Johnson has described in some detail administration pressure on the media in 1969 and 1970 to stifle debate on the Vietnam war.[28] It started with President Nixon's speech of November 3, 1969. Among other things, Mr. Nixon condemned a planned "Mobilization Against the War." According to Johnson, Herbert Klein, White House "Director of Communications," and other White House officials made at least twenty telephone calls that night to television stations asking them if they planned to make any comment on the speech. The next day Dean Burch, chairman of the FCC, called the presidents of all three television networks demanding transcripts of the commentaries—even though the White House already had the tapes. Ten days later Vice-President Agnew made a speech attacking television news coverage and commentaries, and reminded the networks that the government had licensing powers over them. The television networks responded not by broadening the variety of perspectives they broadcast on the war, but by blocking out almost all coverage of the biggest demonstration ever held in the history of Washington. They also reduced their commentary on subsequent Nixon announcements and speeches. But the administration kept up the pressure. An official of the Subversive Activities Control Board called television stations for logs of their coverage of Vietnam war policy, pro and con. A group of business friends of President Nixon challenged the license renewal of a television station owned by the *Washington Post*—which in its *newspaper* editorials consistently attacked administration war policy. White House officials kept dossiers on Frank Reynolds, anchor man on the ABC Evening News. They let this fact be known. One year later ABC removed Reynolds from his position over his objections. In the fall of 1970,

[26] Ibid.

[27] Ibid.

[28] Nicholas Johnson, "Government by Television," *Earth Magazine*, March 1971.

ABC also refused to telecast the half-time show of the Holy Cross–Buffalo football game; the Buffalo band had a show entitled "America the Beautiful," which contained critical comments about the war and pollution. But several weeks later ABC did not refuse to televise the half-time show of the Army–Navy game. It had a pro-war theme.

The White House encouraged CBS affiliate board members to complain to the network about their network's coverage of the war. Vice-President Agnew proposed that television commentators be publicly examined "by a group of people in government to explore the depths of [their] opinions [and] prejudices."[29] Network news officials argue that all this and more—which the limits of space prevent me from documenting—had a "chilling effect" on their activities. It deters them from doing programs that express controversial viewpoints. Fred Powledge quotes a CBS television newsman who told him of a CBS interview with a United States official in Laos. The official had critical things to say of United States policy there; the interview was not aired: "It becomes a matter of deciding not to do things. The network that owns us is aware of its difficulties with the feds in the past, and they're unwilling to trust their own news judgment to do something which might be controversial.... What happens, says CBS News president Richard Salant, is that there is a 'tendency' to say, 'Oh, well, this isn't the ideal one to fight, so let's let this one go.' "[30]

In light of all this, the soundness of Jefferson's laissez-faire philosophy toward the media seems to be in need of no further demonstration. Government should keep out. When it interferes, it may do so with the most laudable of motives to end the most serious evils. But the *principle* that government has the right to interfere is likely to mean in practice that government will intervene for bad purposes. Most likely, government will not promote the competition of ideas, but try to make the media serve governmental policy preferences. Therefore, there is greater safety in the principle of simply keeping the government out, and letting the public make its own judgment of the press.

[29] Ibid.

[30] Fred Powledge, *The Engineering of Restraint* (Washington: Public Affairs Press, 1971), pp. 33, 36.

But before we rest with this conclusion, let us recall the other side of the question. Most of the defects of the broadcast media which we have already catalogued have nothing to do with government action. Profits, not government, cause television to cover public events so minimally and to cover public discussion of ideas not at all. Timidity, not government, caused CBS to censor such things as 75 percent of the entertainment programs produced by the Smothers Brothers. Arrogance, not government, caused television networks to blackball a Dr. Spock, a Pete Seeger, or a Joan Baez. If any of these individuals wants a permit to use a public park actually to attack government policy, that same government gives the permit. If, on the other hand, a television producer wished to put a Pete Seeger on a show for five minutes to sing a folk song, television corporate executives may veto it, on grounds that Seeger is "controversial." The worst of governmental censorship in recent years pales into insignificance compared to the everyday, arbitrary censorship of what has been presented on the public airwaves by television executives.

Furthermore, some of the governmental attacks on the media have been legitimate. Vice-President Agnew's speeches against the media were surely proper. From his own rightist perspective, he sees the media as "liberal," just as a leftist sees the media as "conservative." He demanded television time—for which reason alone he got it—and criticized the networks, reminding them of their privileged position and their public responsibilities. One may quarrel with the Vice-President's particular perspective. One may not reasonably quarrel with his right to attack the media. The speeches represented no threat, no coercion, no government action—except in a political sense. FCC chairman Dean Burch has stated that Dr. Stanton's "conspiracy" theory—that is, that the FCC would back up Vice-President Agnew's charges with license decisions—"is false and he knows it is false."[31] Burch said he was "disgusted" with these allegations, because there isn't a single fact to back them up. The evidence confirms Burch's statement in this respect.

Nevertheless, there can be no doubt that many of the tactics used by the administration have gone beyond mere criticism of the

[31] Senate Hearings, October 20, 1971.

media or that the FCC on at least one occasion was widely understood to have enforced an administration complaint.[32] FBI and Subversive Activities Control Board inquiries go beyond the rough and tumble of politics. The objective of administration machinations, moreover, was to shift the bias of the media to a more pro-administration point of view and to coerce them simply not to cover, or to give less coverage to, the critics of the administration. The means and the end were to abridge the freedom of the press.

However, does it follow from this that the government must have nothing to do with the media at all? If the government may abuse power, must it therefore be denied all power? When it is stated in this manner, we have before us a question with which political philosophers have wrestled throughout the ages. We shall not solve that problem here. Suffice it to say that the authors of the Bill of Rights answered that question affirmatively in certain ways. One way was to say that, except in the most extreme circumstances, where words have the effect of force, the government may not abridge freedom of speech or press.

Common sense tells us, however, that this injunction is not the same as keeping hands off. As Alexander Meiklejohn has pointed out, government abridges speech procedurally—constitutionally and necessarily:

> In the town meeting the people of a community assemble to discuss and act upon matters of public interest—roads, schools, poorhouses, health, external defense, and the like. Every man is free to come. They meet as political equals. Each has a right and a duty to think his own thoughts, to express them, and to listen to the arguments of others. The basic principle is that the freedom of speech shall be unabridged. And yet the meeting cannot even be opened un-

[32] Powledge, *Engineering of Restraint,* p. 46. The FCC action might have been widely misunderstood. On March 5, 1971, it issued a public notice stating that if broadcast licensees do not make a judgment "whether a particular record . . . promotes illegal drug use . . . it raises serious questions as to whether continued operation of the station is in the public interest." This followed by six months a complaint by Vice-President Agnew about drug lyrics in popular songs. But the FCC notice did not actually threaten license termination on the basis of merely playing drug-oriented popular songs. The standard remained "whether a licensee's programming efforts, on an overall basis, have been in the public interest."

> less, by common consent, speech is abridged. A chairman or moderator is, or has been chosen. He "calls the meeting to order." And the hush which follows that call is a clear indication that restrictions on speech have been set up. The moderator assumes, or arranges, that in the conduct of the business, certain rules of order will be observed.... His business on its negative side is to abridge speech. For example, it is usually agreed that no one shall speak unless "recognized by the chair." Also, debaters must confine their remarks to "the question before the house." If one man "has the floor," no one else may interrupt him except as provided by the rules.... [T]he talking must be regulated and abridged as the doing of the business under actual conditions may require.... If a speaker wanders from the point at issue, if he is abusive or in other ways threatens to defeat the purpose of the meeting, he may be and should be declared "out of order"... [I]f he persists in breaking the rules, he may be "denied the floor" or, in the last resort, "thrown out" of the meeting. The town meeting, as it seeks for freedom of public discussion of public problems, would be wholly ineffectual unless speech were thus abridged.[33]

Jefferson obviously understood this point. If one needs specific evidence, note that this champion of free speech proposed a House manual that contained rules similarly abridging speech. Speech must necessarily be so abridged in order for speech to be heard. The town meeting

> is called to discuss and, on the basis of such discussion, to decide matters of public policy.... The community has agreed that... [matters of public policy] shall be freely discussed and that, when discussion is ended, decision upon them will be made by vote of the citizens. Now, in that method of political self-government, *the point of ultimate interest is not the words of the speakers, but the minds of the hearers*.... What is essential is not that everyone shall speak, but that everything worth saying shall be said. To this end, for example, it may be arranged that each of the known conflicting points of view shall have, and shall be limited to, an assigned share of the time available... [T]he vital point... is that no suggestion of policy shall be denied

[33] Alexander Meiklejohn, *Political Freedom* (New York: Oxford University Press, 1965), pp. 24–25.

> a hearing because it is on one side of an issue than another.[34]

Meiklejohn concluded, on the basis of this understanding, that if it is ever appropriate for someone to take one side of a public question, it is equally appropriate for someone to take the opposite side. "If a public building may be used in which to say, in time of war, that the war is justified, then the same building may be used in which to say that it is not justified."[35] The Supreme Court has also agreed with this understanding in numerous decisions. Speech, of course, cannot be prohibited "merely because public officials disapprove the speaker's views. It must act in patent good faith to maintain the public peace, to assure the availability of the streets for their primary purpose of passenger and vehicular traffic, or for equally indispensible ends of modern community life."[36] More than this, a law that vests in a public official enough discretion so that he might or *could* prohibit speech of which he disapproves is unconstitutional.[37] This is true whether it is a law purporting to regulate, among other things, traffic in the streets,[38] the use of parks,[39] noise,[40] loitering,[41] demonstrations near public buildings,[42] fraud,[43] obstruction of public passages,[44] or solicitation.[45] The Court has further held that some public facilities are forums for the expression of First Amendment rights:

> In considering the right of a municipality to control the use of public streets for the expression of . . . views, we start with the words of Mr. Justice Roberts that "Wherever the

[34] Ibid., pp. 26–27. Emphasis added.

[35] Ibid., p. 27.

[36] *Kunz* v. *New York,* 340 U.S. 290, 282 (1951). Concurring opinion.

[37] *Cantwell* v. *Connecticut,* 310 U.S. 296 (1940); *Cox* v. *Louisiana,* 379 U.S. 536 (1965); *Shuttlesworth* v. *Birmingham,* 394 U.S. 147 (1969).

[38] *Shuttlesworth* v. *Birmingham,* 394 U.S. 147 (1969).

[39] *Niemotko* v. *Maryland,* 340 U.S. 268 (1948).

[40] *Saia* v. *New York,* 334 U.S. 558 (1948).

[41] *Thornhill* v. *Alabama,* 310 U.S. 88 (1940).

[42] *Edwards* v. *California,* 372 U.S. 229 (1963).

[43] *Schneider* v. *Irvington,* 308 U.S. 147 (1939).

[44] *Cox* v. *Louisiana,* 379 U.S. 536 (1965).

[45] *Thomas* v. *Collins,* 323 U.S. 516 (1945); *Staub* v. *Baxley,* 355 U.S. 313 (1958).

title of streets and parks may rest, they have immemorially been held in trust for the use of the public, and time out of mind, have been used for purposes of assembly, communicating thoughts between citizens, and discussing public questions."[46]

The exercise of First Amendment rights cannot be prohibited in such places, even on an impartial basis, without weighty reasons:

> It is clear that if the shopping center premises were not privately owned but instead constituted the business area of a municipality, which they to a large extent resemble, petitioners could not be barred from exercising their First Amendment rights there on the sole ground that title to the property was in the municipality. *Lovell* v. *Griffen; Hague* v. *C.I.O.; Schneider* v. *State of New Jersey*. The essence of those opinions is that streets, sidewalks, parks and other similar public places are so historically associated with the exercise of First Amendment rights that access to them for the purpose of exercising such rights cannot constitutionally be denied broadly and absolutely.[47]

The fact that title to the property may be in private hands is not, in itself, a weighty enough reason to deny access to the property for the exercise of First Amendment rights.[48]

> Ownership does not always mean absolute dominion. The more an owner, for his advantage, opens up his property for use by the public in general, the more do his rights become circumscribed by the statutory and constitutional rights of those who use it.[49]

The Supreme Court has not held to date that the public airwaves are a public forum whose use by the public cannot be totally prohibited. But in *Red Lion Broadcasting Company* v. *FCC*[50] it

[46] *Kunz* v. *New York,* 340 U.S. 290, 293 (1951), citing *Hague* v. *C.I.O.,* 307 U.S. 496, 515 (1939).

[47] *Amalgamated Food Employees Union* v. *Logan Valley Plaza, Inc.,* 391 U.S. 308, 315 (1968).

[48] Ibid., p. 316.

[49] *Marsh* v. *Alabama,* 326 U.S. 501, 506 (1946).

[50] 395 U.S. 367 (1969).

came close to adopting that position.[51] Broadcasters, as lessors of publicly owned property, are subject to the rule that "conduct that is formally 'private' may become so entwined with governmental policies or so impregnated with a governmental character as to be subject to the constitutional limitations placed upon state action."[52]

As Judge (now Chief Justice) Warren Burger has written: "[A] broadcaster seeks and is granted the free and exclusive use of a limited and valuable part of the public domain; when he accepts that franchise it is burdened by enforceable public obligations."[53] A broadcaster has a power—control of a broadcast frequency—which the Federal Communications Act defined as governmental in nature. As such, it can be argued that a broadcaster "become[s an] agenc[y] or instrumentalit[y] of the State and subject to its constitutional limitations."[54]

The Supreme Court unanimously ruled in *Red Lion* that "broadcasting is clearly a medium affected by a First Amendment interest"[55] and declared that a licensee "has no constitutional right to be the one who holds the license or to monopolize a radio frequency to the exclusion of his fellow citizens."[56] The Court declared that so far as the First Amendment is concerned, the government may force a licensee to share his license with others, or to present the views of others in his community:

> It is the right of the viewers and listeners, not the right of the broadcasters, which is paramount.... It is the purpose of the First Amendment to preserve an uninhibited marketplace of ideas in which truth will ultimately prevail, rather than to countenance monopolization of that market, whether it be by the Government itself or a private licensee.... It is the right of the public to receive suitable

[51] "Freedom of the press from governmental interference under the First Amendment does not sanction repression of that freedom by private interests" (ibid., p. 392, quoting *Associated Press* v. *United States,* 326 U.S. 1, 20 [1945]).

[52] *Evans* v. *Newton,* 382 U.S. 296, 299 (1966).

[53] *Office of Communication of the United Church of Christ* v. *FCC,* 359 F. 2d 994, 1003 (1966).

[54] *Evans* v. *Newton.*

[55] *Red Lion Broadcasting Company* v. *FCC,* p. 386.

[56] Ibid., p. 389.

access to social, political, esthetic, moral and other ideas and experiences which is crucial here....[57]

Whatever may be the full implications of this decision, several points are quite clear. First, the Court emphatically rejects the view of network spokesmen that government regulation of what they broadcast necessarily invades their First Amendment rights. The right of the listener to hear a variety of ideas prevails over the broadcaster's right to present his ideas. This does not suggest that if a broadcaster, for example, had broken the Pentagon Papers story instead of the *New York Times,* a court would have viewed the case any differently than in the case of the *Times.*[58] In that situation, the right, if any, of the listener and broadcaster would coincide. Broadcasting the Pentagon Papers would contribute to increased public information about the war. But where the right to receive information conflicts with a broadcaster's unwillingness to present it, then the broadcaster's right must give way.

Second, the *Red Lion* decision sanctions government procedures that will "preserve an uninhibited marketplace of ideas" on the public airwaves. It does not sanction censorship of the substance of any radio communication. Like Meiklejohn's moderator of a town meeting, government may establish procedures ensuring that "everything worth saying shall be said,"[59] including arranging that "each of the known conflicting points of view shall have, and shall be limited to, an assigned share of the time available."[60] The FCC's fairness and personal attack doctrines, which *Red Lion* specifically upheld, do no more than this.

Third, the logic of *Red Lion* suggests that the FCC must do more than it has thus far done to protect the "crucial" public right to receive suitable access to various ideas and experiences. The broad-

[57] Ibid., p. 390.

[58] In *New York Times Company* v. *United States,* 403 U.S. 713 (1971), the Supreme Court said that the government could not enjoin publication of a classified study of the history of the Vietnam war. It held that "any system of prior restraints of expression comes to this Court hearing a heavy presumption against its constitutional validity..." (citation omitted). It held that the government had not met the "heavy burden of showing justification for the enforcement of such a restraint" (citation omitted).

[59] Meiklejohn, *Political Freedom,* pp. 26–27.

[60] Ibid.

caster today stands in the same relation to those who wish to use the public airwaves as police chiefs and custodians do to those wishing to use the public streets and parks. "Broadcast licensees... serve as administrators of a highly valuable communications resource...."[61] If the resource is open to one point of view, FCC regulations require a broadcaster to present the other side of the question. But there is no right on the part of the public to any use of airwaves to discuss any point of view. Furthermore, those who actually *have* the point of view have no right to express it; it is up to the broadcaster to control the way he achieves "fairness." Even a person who wishes to *purchase* time to comment on public issues has no right to do so. FCC rules sustain the right of a broadcaster wholly to deny the use of the radio spectrum to those wishing to make editorial comment. A broadcaster can permit favored interests—in this case, merchants of commercial goods—to use the public airwaves, while denying them to interests out of favor. He is not bound by the rule that once he permits access to public facilities to some speakers or users, he cannot arbitrarily deny access to other speakers or users.[62] Ironically, broadcasters permit commercial advertising while prohibiting editorial comment, while the First Amendment favors the dissemination of political, social, and religious ideas over commercial information.[63]

Taking its cue from *Red Lion,* a court of appeals declared the

[61] *Business Executives' Move for Vietnam Peace* v. *FCC,* 450 F. 2d 642, 654 (1971).

[62] *Cox* v. *Louisiana,* 379 U.S. 536, 557 (1965), and cases cited therein.

[63] *Breard* v. *Alexandria,* 341 U.S. 622 (1951); *Valentine* v. *Christensen,* 316 U.S. 52 (1942). Broadcasters justify their position on grounds that editorial advertising is "controversial." They say they cover such matters in their news programs. But see text references to notes 7, 8, and 9 above. Consider also: "All too often in our society one particular ideology—that of passivity, acceptance of things as they are, and exaltation of commercial values—is simply taken for granted, assumed to be of a nonideology, and allowed to choke out the rest" (*Business Executives' Move for Vietnam Peace* v. *FCC,* p. 661). Thus "a lumber company may advertise its wood products, but a conservation group cannot implore citizens to write the President or Governor about protecting our national resources. An oil refinery may advertise its products, but a citizens' organization cannot demand enforcement of existing air pollution statutes. An insurance company may announce its available policies, but a senior citizens' club cannot plead for legislation to improve our social security program" (ibid., quoting *Wirta* v. *Alameda–Contra Costa Transit District,* 64 Cal. Rpts. 430, 435; 434 P. 2d 982, 987 [1967]).

broadcasters' policy and the FCC ruling that sustained it a violation of the First Amendment.[64] Broadcasters cannot flatly ban editorial advertising. They may limit such advertising, much as a public body may set narrowly drawn regulations for time, place, and manner of using streets and parks. But robust, wholesome debate cannot be achieved merely by "fair" news coverage, pursuant to the FCC's fairness doctrine. Self-expression involves "matters of style and intensity of feeling,"[65] which cannot be achieved in "supervised and ordained discussions."[66] This landmark ruling is now being reviewed by the Supreme Court.[67]

Even if the Supreme Court upholds the Court of Appeals, and a limited right to purchase air time as well as the fairness rule is applied to broadcasters, it is doubtful whether these measures in themselves are sufficient to make the airwaves a forum where public policy questions may be adequately presented—that is, informing the public sufficiently for it to make decisions on them. Recent legal developments are interesting and helpful, but it may be that more drastic changes are required, which would involve legislative action. We start with the premise that the airwaves should be as wide open as possible for the expression of ideas. An idea not presented on television does not compete in the marketplace for acceptance. Just as the shopping mall is replacing the downtown street as the primary marketplace for Americans,[68] the television set is replacing the soapbox orator and the leafleteer as America's primary means of communication.[69] Just as there is a limited right to speak in a shopping center,[70] so there should be a limited right to speak on television.[71] In both cases, that's where the listeners are.

[64] Ibid.

[65] Ibid., p. 657.

[66] Ibid., p. 656, citing *Tinker* v. *Des Moines Independent Community School District,* 393 U.S. 503 (1969).

[67] *New York Times,* February 29, 1972, p. 15.

[68] *Amalgamated Food Employees Union* v. *Logan Valley Plaza, Inc.,* p. 324.

[69] Indeed, during a handbilling or soapbox speechmaking experience, one gets the impression that segments of the public are hostile to these activities as such. The demonstrator is stereotyped as a "kook" before he is heard. Possibly a reason for this is that the public expects to hear "reasonable" matters expressed on television.

[70] *Amalgamated Food Employees Union* v. *Logan Valley Plaza, Inc.*

[71] *Business Executives' Move for Vietnam Peace* v. *FCC,* p. 653.

But commercial television, however many rules and regulations may be imposed upon it, exists to make money. It needs advertising revenues, which are a function of the audience ratings. In short, there is an inevitable tension between government rules requiring public affairs presentations and controversy and the *raison d'être* of a commercial broadcaster. In that kind of situation, a broadcaster tends to do only the minimum necessary to conform technically to the established rules, and government tends to pile on more and more rules to accomplish its objectives. The danger is that a comprehensive scheme of regulation will emerge which not only will have the effect of censoring the substance of speech, but which will at the same time be ineffective. Government can tell television officials to produce public affairs programs, but it can't guarantee that they will be produced with the expense and imagination to be interesting. And if government then tells television broadcasters to produce certain types of shows and formats, it comes close to the kind of censorship forbidden by the First Amendment.

Experience under the fairness doctrine demonstrates the difficulty of government regulation of the broadcast media. The FCC is unwilling to be a moderator of the town airwaves, and wholly allocate television time. Instead, it leaves fairness up to the licensee, subject to its review. That review mires us in a quagmire: what is the issue, what represents a position on the issue, and the extent and manner of presenting other positions. Then, rejecting the implication that it second-guesses the "journalistic judgment" of the broadcaster, the FCC defers to that judgment in almost all cases.[72] Unlike a higher court's deference to the judgment of a lower court, or a lower court's deference to a specialized administrative agency, the FCC defers to a party with an openly vested interest. The difficulty is that if the FCC did the opposite, a licensee would tend to evade the requirement of fairness by doing the weather reports.[73]

Additional approaches should be considered to achieve First Amendment values on the public airwaves. One way might be to use antitrust laws to break up the network dominance over the

[72] Senate Hearings, October 20, 1971, testimony of Dean Burch, chairman, Federal Communications Commission.

[73] Ibid., September 30, 1971, testimony of Walter Cronkite. Cronkite says, moreover, that this is already happening.

airwaves. This seems to be a popular American response to combating supposed evils that result from concentrations of power. But the FCC tried to limit network power in the 1940s and failed. And a case can be made that the networks make possible the telecasting of many useful and entertaining events, like sports events and movies, "free" to the public. Without networks, these either wouldn't be shown or people would have to "pay" for them. Either alternative would be politically unpopular.

Another possibility is to do nothing. Then cable television will develop, providing much more diversity and choice to the listener, and competition on that medium will bring about the democratic objective of robust debate. We cannot discuss here all the implications of the development of cable television. But while cable theoretically holds forth the possibility of broadcasting diversity, that result is unlikely. First, television networks are buying into cable. Second, they oppose its free development. Broadcasters recently worked out a "treaty" at the White House with cable television interests.[74] It limited cable's development in the fifty top television markets.[75] It seems that as broadcasters had enough political muscle to prevent the FCC from breaking them up, they will also have enough political muscle to restrict competition by cable. Nevertheless, over the long run, this solution would still seem to have promise. Cable will develop in rural areas. Its technology may make possible the development of specialized broadcasting, in addition to mass broadcasting. Cable interests will accumulate political power. In the past, laws and agreements have retarded but not stopped technological developments.

Perhaps the most fruitful possibility for opening up the airwaves would be for the United States simply to copy the example of other governments around the world—free and unfree—and to establish a government broadcast service. It is unimportant whether the government operates the service itself or whether it merely provides financial support for an independently run system. The experience of Great Britain shows that a governmentally run system need not be one-sided, a servant of the government. To say that

[74] *New York Times,* November 13, 1971, p. 67.
[75] Ibid.

government operation necessarily has this consequence is simply false. Moreover, in Britain and in Canada, commercial broadcasting successfully competes with the government operation. What *is* important is that the government-supported broadcasting service be financed out of some sort of trust fund—that is, independently of appropriated public funds. In Britain, a household pays the equivalent of $16 annually for a black-and-white television set, $31 for color, and $3.25 for radio only.[76] The BBC got $170 million from these taxes in 1969–1970.[77] By contrast, in the United States, the Corporation for Public Broadcasting depends on annual appropriations from Congress. Its proposed budget for the next fiscal year is a mere $45 million.[78] That budget figure is so mediocre for a country this size that some of public broadcasting's best entertainment programs—*The Forsyte Saga, Masterpiece Theatre*—are not its own productions, but are imported![79] The Corporation for Public Broadcasting may not even get the $45 million. Although it sometimes censors its broadcasts to avoid offending the administration, the White House attacks it for its "controversial" and national programming.[80] Thus, because it has the power of the purse, government now can censor public broadcasting. Independent financing would at least give public broadcasting the power to fight back, while stations would still be subject to FCC licensing requirements for fairness, equal time, and the like.

Alternatively, government could provide for diversity on the public airwaves by issuing a different kind of broadcast license. A license now states the hours and frequency on which a licensee may broadcast; the FCC could provide that during a certain hour each day or a certain number of hours each week, on a rotating basis, the use of that frequency reverts to the government. An independently financed public broadcast service could use those frequencies during those times, and/or could turn it over to citizens'

[76] Senate Hearings, February 17, 1972, testimony of Dean Elie Abel, Columbia Graduate School of Journalism.

[77] Ibid.

[78] Ibid.

[79] Ibid.

[80] Ibid., February 2, 1972, testimony of Clay T. Whitehead, director, Office of Telecommunications Policy. Ironically, these attacks strike at the *raison d'être* of public broadcasting.

groups on a first-come, first-served (or lottery) basis to do what they want with it, including the production of local entertainment. Funds from the independent financing source could be used to compensate the broadcast licensees for the use of their technical broadcasting equipment and studios. The broadcasters could be expected to fight such a proposal, and it might meet the same fate as the antitrust and cable-TV alternatives. But unlike cable or antitrust, to give up an hour a day or three hours a week does not strike at basic network control over broadcasting. The networks would be in the same position as they are today, 90 percent of the time. They might have to charge their sponsors somewhat more during the time at their disposal. But if the principle of government reversion can be established, the main political battle will be over how much time should be given to public broadcasting purposes—a debate that, however resolved, involves no overtones of censorship.

In sum, we have argued that the changes that have taken place in the means of communication in American public life require government action to protect First Amendment values. The character of this governmental action, procedural regulation of speech, was always permitted and sometimes required under the First Amendment. But this aspect of the First Amendment has historically been largely unrecognized because the thrust of its development was directed against *government* interference with the "free competition of ideas." Today, while government must continue not to restrict the expression of ideas, it can enact a variety of procedures to enable those who have something to say to the public to be heard. When governmental action has established patterns of use of a public forum which restricts the free communication of ideas, it *must* enact such procedures. A democratic society can tolerate no less.

George Anastaplo

•

SELF-GOVERNMENT AND THE MASS MEDIA: A PRACTICAL MAN'S GUIDE

Delenda est Carthago.
—Cato the Elder

I

It may be instructive, in considering the significance among us of the mass media, to consider how we deal today with the press and the television industry.

Our ways of handling television and the press remain quite different, both for historical reasons and for reasons bearing on what is distinctive (even natural, one might say) to each. There is considerable effort made by some theorists to have us treat these two means of communication the same way—but to treat them the same way not only would overlook vital differences between them but would also threaten the integrity of our regime even more than it may be threatened already. We must, above all, be practical about these matters.[1]

Thus, we must take care, whatever we may say or do, not to undermine the privileges and hence the usefulness of a press that has traditionally had a vital role to play in our constitutional system,

[1] Consider what leads the unpolitical Socrates, in Plato's *Gorgias,* to declare himself the only statesman in Greece. See Laurence Berns, "Two Old Conservatives Discuss the Anastaplo Case," *Cornell Law Review,* 54 (1969): 920, 924; notes 67, 112, this paper.

Consider also Plato's *Republic,* 540d–41b. See Leo Strauss, *The City and Man* (Chicago: Rand McNally, 1964), pp. 126–27. Cf. note 75, this paper.

a role that is ratified by the First Amendment to the Constitution of the United States. The First Amendment, it may be argued, prohibits Congress, in its lawmaking capacity, from cutting down in any way or for any reason "freedom of speech, or of the press." The extent of this freedom is to be measured not merely by the common law treatises and cases available on December 15, 1791—the date of the ratification of the First Amendment—but also by the general understanding and practice of the people of the United States, who insisted upon, had written for them, and ratified (through their state legislatures) the First Amendment.[2]

Although the prohibition in the First Amendment is absolute—we see here a restraint upon Congress which is unqualified, among other Bill of Rights restraints which *are* qualified—the absolute prohibition does not relate to all forms of expression but only to that which the term "freedom of speech, or of the press" was then taken

[2] An important indication of the extent of this freedom is to be seen in the teachings of the Declaration of Independence and in the events leading up to the American Revolution. See George Anastaplo, book review, *New York University Law Review,* 39 (1964):753; note 57, this paper. For an extended discussion of the First Amendment, see Anastaplo, *The Constitutionalist: Notes on the First Amendment* (Dallas: Southern Methodist University Press, 1971); C. Herman Pritchett, book review, *California Law Review,* 60 (1972):1476. Cf. Willmoore Kendall, *Contra Mundum* (New Rochelle, N.Y.: Arlington House, 1971), e.g., p. 290; *Nation,* September 18, 1972, p. 218.

The bare minimum meaning of liberty of the press, as indicated by common law treatises such as Blackstone, would have been freedom from "previous restraints." See notes 6, 9, this paper.

To the extent that Congress is restricted by a constitutional guarantee, to that extent the executive should usually be restricted as well. See notes 24, 29, this paper. Cf. note 20, this paper. See also Senator Sam J. Ervin, *Congressional Record,* 118 (August 16, 1972):S13613 ("The basis for the exercise of executive privilege is executive fiat"); William W. Crosskey, *Politics and the Constitution in the History of the United States* (Chicago: University of Chicago Press, 1953), e.g., p. v; Malcolm P. Sharp, "Crosskey, Anastaplo and Meiklejohn on the United States Constitution," *University of Chicago Law School Record,* 20 (Spring 1973):3. (All citations in this paper to the *Congressional Record* are to the daily edition, not to the bound edition.)

I have not attempted to incorporate in this paper (which was written in the summer of 1972) the revelations of the "Watergate" investigations. My general impression is that these revelations reinforce much of what is said in this paper. See, e.g., notes 65, 79, and 116, this paper. Cf. note 56, this paper. See also, note 117, this paper.

to encompass: political speech, speech having to do with the duties and concerns of self-governing citizens. Thus, for example, this constitutional provision is not primarily or directly concerned with what we now call artistic expression or with the problem of obscenity. Rather, the First Amendment acknowledges that the sovereign citizen has the right freely to discuss public business, a privilege theretofore claimed only for members of legislative bodies.

II

This can be said to be the "theory" of a constitutional privilege that we all sense to be at the heart of American republicanism. It is a theory that does conform fairly well to current practice in the United States with respect to the press. But how does it bear on regulatory practices with respect to the television industry?

The rules governing the press and television are, at this time, quite different.[3] Thus, for example, the press is barely regulated as such; the television industry as such is quite extensively regulated. I will try to show that there are vital differences in the nature and effects of these two means of communication, differences that are reflected somewhat in current regulatory practices and in immunities from regulation. These differences with respect to regulations may reflect, among other things, some awareness of what each means of communication is likely to do to people.[4]

A discussion of the centuries-old problem of "previous restraints" can provide us, on this occasion, an instructive way of seeing not only what the mass media are like, but also what the char-

[3] See Harry Kalven, Jr., "Broadcasting, Public Policy, and the First Amendment," *Journal of Law and Economics,* 10 (1967): 15. See also note 82, this paper; Jeffry Burnam, "Freedom of Speech and the Public Interest in Broadcasting," University of Chicago Ph.D. dissertation, 1971.

[4] It is my hope that the sometimes presumptuous suggestions I deliberately make for this volume of papers (in the manner of an advocate, at least in the text, less so perhaps in the notes), about the differences between the press and television and about what should follow from these differences, will provoke others (who know both the press and television far better than I) to think seriously about these matters as they supply information and observations to test my diagnoses or to improve my prescriptions. See notes 107, 109, 110, 112, this paper. Cf. notes 67, 78, and 117, this paper.

acter and requirements of our way of life are.[5] The press has long been, among us, virtually free of previous restraints—that is, restraints imposed by the government on a publisher prior to publication (and imposed in the national interest, not as with curbs on public comment upon pending court cases, for the purpose of ensuring justice in a particular trial).[6] The television industry, on the other hand, has always had many previous restraints to contend with (in the broadest sense of the language, "previous restraints," which can extend to the licensing of transmitters, to the determination and supervision of program content, and to the allocation of broadcast power, frequencies, and hours).

I propose to begin to examine what sense there is (with a view to the common good) in the extensive freedom we traditionally accord the press. That is, I propose to examine such things as the risks run and the safeguards provided as well as the advantages offered by our traditional way of regarding what the press may do. I also propose to consider the rationale of the extensive regulation of the television industry to which we are accustomed.[7]

A somewhat detailed discussion of the June 1971 Pentagon Papers litigation should remind us of what the press means to us.[8]

[5] "Mass communication media" is "a concept originating in the English-speaking world" (Consultative Assembly, *Symposium on Human Rights and Mass Communications* [Salzburg: Council of Europe, 1968], p. 13). On "mass media," see Part V, sec. ii, this paper. Perhaps this "concept" reflects the influence of physics in the English-speaking political science tradition. (I am reminded of Thomas Hobbes.) Perhaps, also, this concept has emerged among us as our substitute for the Enlightenment of the Continent. See notes 70, 75, 87, 96, this paper.

[6] "Previous restraints," which are also called "prior restraints" by judges and legal scholars, have been discussed in William Blackstone, *Commentaries on the Laws of England,* 4:151–53. See note 9, this paper. Cf. note 21, this paper.

[7] The need to allocate frequencies has led the government to claim wide-ranging control over broadcasting. Cf. Kalven, "Broadcasting, Public Policy, and the First Amendment," *Journal of Law and Economics,* 10 (1967):13, 30–32; note 111, this paper.

[8] *New York Times* v. *United States,* 328 F.S. 324; 444 F. 2d 544; 403 U.S. 713 (1971); *United States* v. *Washington Post,* 446 F. 2d 1322, 1327; 403 U.S. 713 (1971). (See note 58, this paper.)

The only generally available extensive record of this litigation (because of pressure of time, no printed record was filed in the Supreme Court of the United States) seems to be *The New York Times Company* v. *United States: A Documentary History* (New York: Arno Press, 1971), hereafter cited as

We will consider, first, how we live with an absolute prohibition (in practice) of previous restraints on the press, what that means, and why it should be that way.[9] We will consider thereafter (in Parts V and VI of this paper) what television is like and what should be done about it.[10]

I am prepared to defend the proposition that, for the sake of our way of life, there cannot be (in ordinary constitutional circumstances) *any* previous restraints of the press and that there should be even more previous restraint than we now have of the television industry.[11]

III

i

The publication of excerpts from the Pentagon Papers archives began in the *New York Times* on June 13, 1971, and continued for two

---

Documentary History. Summaries of the briefs of counsel may be found at 29 L. ed. 1104–09 (Supreme Court Reports).

On the Pentagon Papers themselves, as well as on the related litigation, see Anastaplo, "Preliminary Reflections on the Pentagon Papers," *University of Chicago Magazine* (January–February 1972, March–April 1972, reprinted in *Congressional Record,* 118 [July 24, 1972]:S11560); Kalven, "Even When a Nation Is At War—," *Harvard Law Review,* 85 (1971):3; Stanford J. Ungar, *The Papers and the Papers* (New York: Dutton, 1972).

[9] For discussions bearing on the problems raised by the Pentagon Papers, see Anastaplo, *Constitutionalist,* e.g., pp. 41–48, 65–71, 94f, 209–13, 228, 237–39, 294f, 304, 324–30, 454, 469–81, 471, 487, 501f, 512, 515, 518, 520–21, 523, 527, 531, 537, 541, 543, 549, 572, 581, 593, 596, 598, 612–13, 626–27, 652, 659, 680, 703, 711–12, 723, 733, 735, 737, 740f, 760. See also note 21, this paper.

[10] For discussions bearing on the problems raised by television and the mass media, see Anastaplo, *Constitutionalist,* e.g., pp. 122–23, 274, 277–81, 499–500, 544, 549–50, 554–57, 592, 595, 606, 612f, 628, 651, 662–63, 735–36, 756–57, 760, 783, 789–90, 802. See also ibid., p. 277 ("... television is for most peoples, perhaps inevitably, a net loss"). Cf. note 110, this paper.

[11] On other occasions I have considered the limitations of the press. See, e.g., Anastaplo, *Constitutionalist*, p. 544. See also notes 32, 92, 101, this paper. Zechariah Chafee, Jr., has been quoted as writing in 1948, "The press is a sort of wild animal in our midst—restless, gigantic, always seeking new ways to use its strength ... the sovereign press for the most part acknowledges accountability to no one except its owners and publishers" (*Congressional Record,* 118 [June 8, 1972]:S9022). See also Richard M. Weaver, *Ideas Have Consequences* (Chicago: University of Chicago Press, 1948), e.g., pp. 27–28, 51, 87, 92f, 102–03, 123, 167. But, it should be added, the press the Founding Fathers knew was far wilder than ours in certain respects.

more installments before being enjoined in the federal courts until June 30, at which time it resumed again for seven more installments. In the meantime, publication started in the *Washington Post,* the *Boston Globe,* and the *St. Louis Post-Dispatch,* all of which evidently drew extensively on copies of the top-secret archives (of some seven thousand pages) originally made available to the *Times* and all of which were similarly enjoined as they appeared in print with the story.[12] The Supreme Court decision of June 30 permitted newspapers with access to the archives to publish what they chose. These archives, as probably every reader of this paper knows, dealt with the history of American involvement in the Vietnam war.[13]

[12] A *Washington Post* editor said "that a desire to demonstrate to the Justice Department that silencing the [*New York*] *Times* would not kill the story was 'one of the reasons' for publishing the start of the *Post*'s series" (*New York Times,* June 19, 1971, pp. 1, 11). In a televised statement Clark MacGregor, President Nixon's 1972 campaign director, "singled out the *Washington Post,* charging the newspaper [in its articles about alleged Republican surveillance and sabotage of Democratic party activities] with malice, hypocrisy, and a visible double-standard. 'While the *Post* itself openly and actively collaborated in the publication of stolen top secret documents [the Pentagon Papers] of the U.S. Government 16 months ago, today, it is faking shock and outrage at some obvious volunteers who were allegedly spying on Larry O'Brien [then Democratic national chairman],' MacGregor's statement said" (*Chicago Sun-Times,* October 17, 1972, p. 12). See notes 65, 79, and 116, this paper. Cf. note 15, this paper.

Perhaps as many as fourteen journals printed firsthand revelations from the secret documents.

[13] "The story of the Pentagon Papers is a chronicle of suppression of vital decisions to protect the reputations and political hides of men who worked an amazingly successful scheme of deception on the American people. They were successful not because they were astute but because the press had become a frightened, regimented, submissive instrument, fattening on favors from those in power and forgetting the great tradition of reporting..." (Justice Douglas [dissenting], *Gravel* v. *United States,* 92 Sup. Ct. 2614, 2636 [1972]). Cf. John P. Roche, "The Pentagon Papers: A Discussion," *Political Science Quarterly,* June 1972, reprinted in the *Congressional Record,* 118 (August 17, 1972):S13859; note 14, this paper.

It seems that the *New York Times* could use no more than 10 percent of the archives material made available to it. Even so, the Bantam paperback edition of the *Times* articles comes to 677 pages. Editions of the Pentagon Papers have been published as well by the U.S. Government Printing Office and by the Beacon Press. An appraisal of the three editions may be found in *Parade,* November 28, 1971, p. 5. For recommendations of the Beacon Press and G.P.O. editions, see Daniel Ellsberg, *Papers on the War*

ii

Had there been more that was truly new in the Pentagon Papers than there was, the adverse effect of publication upon security might have been more of a problem for the courts than it was. But it would be rash to insist that no possible harm has resulted from the massive publication on that occasion. The *Times* did insist in its editorials that it would not have made its decision to publish "if there had been any reason to believe that publication would have endangered the life of a single American soldier or in any way threatened the security of our country or the peace of the world." I do not believe that this is a prudent test: any course of action (ranging from rigorous censorship to uninhibited publication) runs risks and endangers lives.[14] What must be determined is which course is most likely, in our circumstances, to serve the common good: an episode-by-episode "body count" does not suffice.

It should be noticed that the government was obliged to concede during the Pentagon Papers litigation that it is, strictly speak-

---

(New York: Simon & Schuster, 1972), p. 14, note 3; p. 31, note 22; pp. 34, 44. Cf. ibid., p. 158, note 5.

Much of what appeared in various newspapers can be conveniently gotten by combing the *Congressional Record* for June and July of 1971.

[14] The quotation in the text is from a *New York Times* editorial of June 16, 1971. The most important revelation for some people was that there was not really much that was both new and important to be learned from the Pentagon Papers.

My own opinion has long been that the importance both of secrecy and of government deception has been exaggerated (see my 1966 talk drawn upon in the *Congressional Record,* 118 [July 14, 1972]:S11569). Much more important is the serious inadequacy of moral and political judgment in public servants and hence in the public which is supposed to be informed and instructed by its servants. See notes 33, 41, 69, 104, this paper.

Consider, in this connection, several comments by Senator George McGovern (after becoming the Democratic party candidate for President): "McGovern said he didn't think much of White House briefings on the Viet Nam War. 'I frankly learn more about the realities of Viet Nam from following the dispatches of good newspapermen,' he said . . ." (*Chicago Tribune,* August 16, 1972, sec. 1, p. 6). "I am skeptical that I'll learn anything new" (*Chicago Tribune,* July 24, 1972, sec. 1, p. 7). "But, he said, 'My own assessments of the realities of Vietnam have been much better than the assessments made by those men in the basement over at the White House' " (*Chicago Sun-Times,* July 24, 1972, p. 6). Cf. *Chicago Sun-Times* editorial, August 20, 1972, sec. 2, p. 11.

ing, irrelevant to consider as a cause of harm, and hence as a basis for suppression by injunction, the fact that the documents in question might have been stolen. (Indeed, American newspapers frequently publish, and are even expected to publish, purloined documents.)[15] The government would have been foolish to make much in court of the "theft" of the documents: to have done so would have misled the judges relying on guidance from the attorneys appearing before them.[16] The traditional American opinion about the publication of documents concealed by the government from public view is such that even so "antiliberal" a journal as the *National Review* began its report on the publication of the Pentagon Papers with the concession, "We regretfully conclude we cannot fault the *New York Times*."[17]

It should also be noticed that the government was also obliged to concede during the litigation that the fact that a document has been designated a state secret by an "authorized" official does not

[15] Counsel for the *New York Times* observed, in the New York District Court, June 17, 1971: "... a newspaper has a great many sources of information, a great many documents, a great many employees, a great many secrets, which is the essence in good part, Your Honor, of journalism" (*Documentary History,* p. 275). On the same day and in the same court, the Washington bureau chief for the *Times* filed an affidavit describing journalistic practices which included the observation "But for the vast majority of 'secrets,' there has developed between the Government and the press (and Congress) a rather simple rule of thumb: The Government hides what it can, pleading necessity as long as it can, and the press pries out what it can, pleading a need and a right to know. Each side in this 'game' regularly 'wins' and 'loses' a round or two. Each fights with the weapons at its command. When the Government loses a secret or two, it simply adjusts to a new reality. When the press loses a quest or two, it simply reports (or misreports) as best it can. Or so it has been, until this moment" (ibid., pp. 403–04). See notes 27 and 64, this paper. See also ibid., pp. 965–66 (*London Times* of 1851); Arthur M. Schlesinger, *Prelude to Independence* (New York: Vintage Books, 1965), pp. 150–51 ("The treasure-trove had come from Benjamin Franklin ..."). Cf. notes 12 and 65, this paper.

[16] See, e.g., *Documentary History,* pp. 898–99. See also *New York Times* v. *United States,* 403 U.S., at 732; notes 20, 53, 55, this paper.

[17] *National Review,* 22 (1971): 685, 739, 776. Cf. ibid., pp. 789, 800. See also *Chicago Tribune,* June 25, 1971, p. 1; note 64, this paper. Indeed, the *New York Times* would probably have been in trouble among journalists if it had been learned that it had had the Pentagon Papers and had *not* published them! Consider the criticism of the press by the *Chicago Tribune,* for the "disposition to protect Senator [Edward M.] Kennedy from his own weaknesses" (June 27, 1972, sec. 1, p. 12). Cf. note 79, this paper. See note 57, this paper.

settle the question of whether publication of it may be enjoined, not even if the designation seems to be both authorized and reasonable.[18] After all, our form of government is such that periodicals are obviously left free, in ordinary constitutional circumstances, to publish materials that may indeed (and all too often do) harm the national interest. Yet the government's case and the concessions made by the newspapers[19] would tend to permit Congress to provide for suppression by injunction of *any* publication that is likely to cause serious damage to the country. That is, the orthodox opinion with respect to these matters does not seem to me to realize that it permits, *in principle,* press censorship in the national interest, irrespective of whether the materials involved have been classified.[20] We see here the fundamental questions under the First Amendment touched upon by this litigation, questions that should indicate why the current prejudice against "absolutes"[21] (and hence in favor of selec-

[18] See, e.g., *Documentary History,* pp. 900–01, 909–10, 947, 1220, 1222. See also *New York Times* v. *United States,* 403 U.S., at 732; notes 2, 20, 30, this paper.

[19] See, e.g., *Documentary History,* pp. 469–70, 474, 1152, 1219, 1224, 1234. See also notes 21 and 47, this paper.

[20] Justice White summed up in this way the government's position: "The responsibility of the Executive for the conduct of the foreign affairs and for the security of the Nation is so basic that the President is entitled to an injunction against publication of a newspaper story whenever he can convince a court that the information to be revealed threatens 'grave and irreparable' injury to the public interest; and the injunction should issue whether or not the material to be published is classified, whether or not publication would be lawful under relevant criminal statutes enacted by Congress, and regardless of the circumstances by which the newspaper came into possession of the information" (*New York Times* v. *United States,* 403 U.S., at 732 [1971]). See notes 47, 59, 62, this paper.

[21] Counsel for the *New York Times* in the New York District Court, June 18, 1971: "I am not claiming, as we said in our brief, that even the prior restraint element in the First Amendment is an absolute. I've spent some years of scholarship, if I may say so, resisting the idea of absolutes and I am not now turning around and embracing it now" (*Documentary History,* p. 474). See also ibid., p. 1224. With respect to absolute prohibitions, cf. Anastaplo, *Constitutionalist,* p. 809; *New Yorker,* August 26, 1972, p. 76. Cf. also the remarks of Senator Henry F. Ashurst (at the time of the consideration in 1917 of the Espionage Act), as quoted by Justice White (403 U.S., at 734, note 4): "... '[F]reedom of the press' means freedom from the restraints of a censor, means the absolute liberty and right to publish whatever you wish; but you take your chances of punishment in the courts of your country for the violation of the laws of libel, slander and treason" (the above quotation is cited from the text of the *Congressional Record,* 55 [1917]:2005).

tive previous restraints) conceals genuine dangers to our form of government.[22]

It seems to me constitutionally improper for the government, in its effort to suppress by injunction the intended publication of secret documents, to rely upon any standards or reasons that would justify as well the suppression of publications based not on secret or classified materials but on what anyone may figure out from unclassified materials to be happening in the United States or abroad. The latter kind of publication, despite its lack of reliance on any classified materials, may be in a particular instance much more damaging to the national interest than the former. Would not "everyone" agree that informative[23] publications based on unclassified materials should be beyond the reach of the law both before and after publication? Still, if the test is that which was evidently agreed to by the government and the newspapers in the Pentagon Papers litigation, why should not Congress be able to act against such publications even though they are not based on classified materials?[24] This is one reason I suggest that the orthodox approach with respect to these matters does not appreciate what it opens the door to.

What, then, one might ask, *is* the purpose of classifying documents if newspapers cannot be prevented by injunction (at the option of the government) from publishing whatever should come into their possession? Classification is justified, as I have already indicated and as I shall develop below, with a view to the way the government (pursuant to law) tries to control the information it

[22] I am reminded, by the government's position and by the press's concessions, of the "clear and present danger" test of unhappy memory. See, in Anastaplo, *Constitutionalist,* the discussions of *Schenck* v. *United States,* 249 U.S. 47 (1919). See also *Documentary History,* pp. 313–14, 639, 1209–10; note 47, this paper. Cf. note 65, this paper.

[23] We need not consider on this occasion the problem of "incitement." See Anastaplo, *Constitutionalist,* e.g., pp. 520–22, 541–43; Alexander Meiklejohn, *Political Freedom* (New York: Harper & Row, 1960), p. 123; Malcolm P. Sharp, "Crosskey, Anastaplo and Meiklejohn on the United States Constitution," *University of Chicago Law School Record,* 20 (Spring 1973):3, 8.

[24] Whether the executive may classify documents and on its own authority secure an injunction raises "separation of powers" issues, which underlie those considered in the case. See Malcolm P. Sharp, "The Classical American Doctrine of 'The Separation of Powers,'" *University of Chicago Law Review,* 2 (1935):385. See also notes 2, 25, 29, 35, 37, this paper.

considers important to the national interest to keep secret, not with a view to what the government may do to recapture information of which it has lost control.[25] For if the government is permitted to recapture or immobilize by injunction certain information of which it has lost control, at the same time that it concedes (as it now does) that some classified documents may be published by the newspapers without judicial interference, it can do so (as I have just argued) only on the basis of legal principles and standards that would undermine and endanger that general freedom of the press upon which our regime so much depends to keep the sovereign public informed about what its government is or should be doing.

Thus I am obliged to submit, in the face of the currently orthodox opinion on this subject, that the government can have no authority, in ordinary constitutional circumstances, to secure even "in the national interest" a previous restraint upon publication of any materials (classified or unclassified) which happen to be in the possession of the press. This submission seems to me not only to be doctrinally sound (echoing as it does the genuine orthodoxy of Milton's *Areopagitica*) but also to be in accord with contemporary journalistic practices.[26]

iii

We need not assume, in making these observations about the legal merits of the newspapers' position in the Pentagon Papers controversy, that American journalistic practices today are necessarily the best way of ordering things. We need only assume that they are what we have come to expect and to depend upon, partly because of the character of our regime, and that any realistic effort to justify suppression must take these practices (as well as the character of the regime) into account. Lest too much be made of the harm that may be caused by publication of classified material (it *is* obvious that harm can result from such publication as well as from the publication of unclassified material), it should be kept in mind that

[25] See Anastaplo, "Due Process of Law—An Introduction," *University of Detroit Law Journal,* 42 (1964): 195, 215–16. See also James L. High, *A Treatise on the Law of Injunctions,* 4th ed. (Chicago: Callaghan, 1905), p. 29 ("Criminal acts not enjoined").

[26] See Anastaplo, "Due Process of Law," pp. 195, 205–08.

leaks of classified documents and of high-level military decisions were expected and experienced throughout the Vietnam war. Indeed, such leaks are frequently promoted and exploited by our government (especially by high officials in the Pentagon) for political as well as for military (including propaganda) purposes.[27]

There have been, it should be remembered, more important revelations about the conduct of the war published in newspapers in recent years than anything found in the Pentagon Papers, revelations that did not have their news value dramatized either by massive publication or by the Attorney General's efforts.[28] There was probably little in the Pentagon Papers that the Viet Cong and the North Vietnamese did not already long know. Indeed, it is evident in these papers that all too often the primary "security" concern of our government was not to keep information (say, about air strikes or about offensives) away from the enemy (for the enemy had already experienced them and may have sometimes known of them in advance), but away from the public and even from Congress.[29]

[27] See, e.g., *Documentary History,* pp. 396f, 414f, 416f, 424f. See also *Chicago Tribune,* June 25, 1972, sec.1A, p. 17, reporting the testimony of a former ambassador to India that "he [had] routinely leaked classified government documents to the press": "I found it easier to bring my views to bear on the President by way of the *Washington Post* and its New Delhi correspondent than by way of the State Department."

The judges of the Court of Appeals (as well as the trial judge) in the District of Columbia were even more skeptical about the government's Pentagon Papers case than their counterparts in New York: Washington courts *should* be more immediately aware of "how things are done" in government. See notes 8, 15, 58, and 64, this paper.

[28] See, e.g., *Documentary History,* p. 1141n. See the documents reproduced at the pages of *Documentary History* cited in note 27, this paper; also, "Hanoi Seen Fighting for 2 Years," *Chicago Tribune,* September 13, 1972, p. 20 ("The substance of the reports was made available to the *New York Times* today by highly placed intelligence officials").

Something should be said, at least in passing, about the usefulness today of potential enemies' knowing a good deal about each other's capabilities, intentions, and even modes of solving problems: ours has become a world in which surprise and the erratic should be minimized, lest things get completely (and permanently) out of hand. Cf. note 87, this paper. Cf. also note 56, this paper.

[29] Congressman Les Aspin observed, "If members of Congress were asking the Pentagon to disclose current and actual operations [to be?] taken, then this information might be useful to the enemy and be withheld in the interests of national security. All we are asking is information on a biweekly or monthly basis delineating the sortie and tonnage rates in each theater of

It seems common knowledge in Washington that most government documents (some experts have testified to as many as 95 percent of those that are restricted) should not be classified.[30] It seems that the use of the "secret" classification is often exploited either to prevent political embarrassment or to make a document or the official classifying it seem worthy of serious attention. Is it not obvious that the best way to improve security, and to enlist the necessary cooperation of publishers in such an effort (for publishers *will,* for good as well as for bad motives on the part of suppliers, be supplied classified documents from time to time), is scrupulously to reserve the "secret" classification for appropriate documents?

It is also said (to continue this review of arguments about the possible adverse effects on security as a result of the publication of the Pentagon Papers) that the prospect of more such revelations inhibits our private negotiations with foreign governments. Once again, one has to examine cases and circumstances. Curiously enough, the Pentagon Papers suggest that it was secrecy, rather than exposure, that often inhibited negotiations during the past decade. That is, one sees again and again that our government pretended in public during the course of the Vietnam war that it was open to negotiations even while it worked in private to prevent them.[31]

The relative lack of conversations with foreign governments in the documents published by the *New York Times* is, we are told, in part due to the fact that the supplier of the material to the news-

---

operations. It is not secret to the people of Indochina that they are being bombed, but apparently the Pentagon hopes to keep it a secret from the American people" (*Congressional Record,* 118 [March 14, 1972]:E2489). See notes 31, 34, and 35, this paper.

Congressman Paul N. McCloskey, Jr., said about the information withheld with respect to the war in Indochina, "The deception is not a matter of protecting secret information from the enemy. The intention is to conceal information from the people of the United States as if it were the enemy" (*New York Times,* June 15, 1971, p. 18).

[30] See, e.g., *Congressional Record,* 117 (December 16, 1971):E13655; ibid. (December 16, 1971):S21833; ibid., 118 (May 4, 1972):E4706. See also *Documentary History,* pp. 519f, 527, 1221.

[31] Cf. note 38, this paper. One wonders what information is routinely kept from our people which all governments in the world know. See, e.g., an article on how *Jane's Fighting Ships* gets its information about the navies of the world, *Congressional Record,* 117 (November 12, 1971):E12166. Cf. also note 14, this paper.

paper retained the four volumes of the Pentagon Papers archives dealing with negotiations. That is to say, *he* also evidently tried to take the interests of the United States into account, as did the publishers who drew upon the materials they did receive.[32] This should point up the fact that the primary concern of the government should not be improper publication, but rather keeping truly sensitive materials from coming, in the first instance, into the possession of someone inimical to the interests of the country. Such a possessor of sensitive materials is not likely to send them to American newspapers for publication, but rather to foreign governments; and this he is likely to do in secret, not giving our government an opportunity either to intervene before he acts or to apprehend him after he acts.

I go one step further concerning our dealings hereafter with foreign governments. Did not the publication of the Pentagon Papers improve rather than damage our standing abroad? That is, did not publication help the American people begin to repair the damage done by our government (because of Vietnam) to our standing, and hence our interests, among civilized people everywhere? Was there any *serious* criticism of the 1971 publication from communities with a form of government similar to ours? I suspect that many

[32] See Ellsberg, *Papers on the War,* p. 44. Cf. *Chicago Sun-Times,* July 2, 1972, p. 64: "Disclosure of one of the most sensational British intelligence operations of modern times came from Washington with publication of the latest volumes of the Pentagon Papers. British authorities are angry with their American friends. Embarrassed, too, that their bugging of a Soviet leader [during a London visit] has exposed them to Moscow attack. . . . The British government expressed concern to the United States in the summer of 1971 when the first batch of Pentagon Papers was published. British worries were related to the use of various secret messages that had passed between London and Washington about Vietnam. The new disclosures plainly have deepened that concern, although no government minister or Foreign Office spokesmen would comment publicly." The article (from London) also observes, "It is, of course, possible that most important statesmen assume their conversations and activities are monitored anyway. But British authorities see a distinction between an assumption and something that has been confirmed." I suspect that "British authorities" considered this most recent episode useful as an opportunity to "get back" at the Americans, "remembering bitterly how lapses in their own security system were assailed by Americans. . . ." However that may be, certain publications *can* be irresponsible, even when not illegal. See note 11, this paper.

governments were relieved to learn that a country as powerful as ours had begun to pay greater respect than theretofore to what an informed world opinion thinks about the way we use our power.

It is said as well by critics of the press that publication of operational documents inhibits discussion among the President's advisers. One is tempted to reply, "Well and good, let's have more such inhibition. That is, let's have it understood that it *can* become known (within a short time, if political in-fighting among such advisers gets serious) what considerations are taken into account in the making of public policy. Perhaps this will make our leaders take old-fashioned morality more seriously and "realistic" power politics less seriously than they have heretofore."[33] But even such a reply does not appreciate how brutal the maneuvering and hence the disclosures around the presidency can be—so brutal or so altruistic that it often does not matter to the disclosing agent that the government might try either to secure an injunction to halt a known impending publication or to punish after publication the parties involved.

In any event, we the people simply cannot tolerate a dispensation under which vital public information about what goes on in government councils is limited (as would be the case with a tame press) to what the dominant faction in government chooses to disclose.[34] Here, too, the character of our regime virtually requires

[33] On modern freedom of speech, Machiavellianism, and the morality of public opinion, see Anastaplo, "Preliminary Reflections on the Pentagon Papers," *University of Chicago Magazine,* January–February 1972, pp. 7–9 (*Congressional Record,* 118 [July 24, 1972]:S11563); this passage is also available in *The Journal: Forum for Contemporary History,* June–July 1972, p. 33). See also Anastaplo, *Constitutionalist,* p. 779.

On the "moral indifference" of our 1972 bombing of North Vietnam, see *Life,* August 25, 1972, p. 12 ("... we aren't deliberately bombing Hanoi or Haiphong as Dresden, London, Hamburg or Tokyo were bombed. But we have been laying waste a land where our own survival is not at stake"). It is a commentary upon the ambivalent moral sense of the American people both that such an editorial had to be written and that it could appear in a popular magazine. See notes 14, 41, 62, 65, 79, and 104, this paper; see also note 46 for my article on this subject in the *Chicago Tribune.* Cf. Ellsberg, *Papers on the War,* p. 294 (on bomb damage comparisons).

[34] Senator Stuart Symington observed, upon the publication of the Pentagon Papers, "What the press is really doing here is a job the legislature should have done for itself" (*New York Times,* July 1, 1971, p. 16). See also Justice Douglas (dissenting), *Gravel* v. *United States,* 92 Sup. Ct. 2614, 2633

the practices to which we are accustomed, practices that offer important advantages along with the occasional risks they pose.[35]

iv

What, then, should the press *not* be "legally" entitled to print? That is, what should be subject to previous restraint upon application by the government? Most orthodox students of this subject would agree —from even this I dissent—that tactical information and decisions should be, if the government wishes, kept secret (*with the use of injunctions*) until the immediate *military* advantage of keeping them secret passes.[36] Such a rule (even these orthodox students might con-

---

(1972); *Congressional Record,* 118 (August 16, 1972):S13612; ibid. (August 18, 1972):E7657; notes 38 and 53, this paper.

See Plutarch, *Life of Timoleon* (on the dangers to democracy posed by "citadels," where tyranny can take hold). (Compare private property as a useful refuge, in Anastaplo, *Constitutionalist,* p. 213.)

[35] The risk of improper disclosure, as well as the pressure toward it, may be reduced if Congress is kept properly informed. Congressional committees had tried several times to get copies of the Pentagon Papers, if only on a classified basis, before they were published in the press. See *Documentary History,* pp. 543–44, 567f, 578; Justice Douglas (dissenting), *Gravel* v. *United States,* 92 Sup. Ct. 2614, note 5; Ellsberg, *Papers on the War,* p. 45; notes 2, 24, 29, 53, this paper.

In order to preserve its influence, Congress should discipline those of its members who so abuse their privileges as to place all congressional prerogatives under a cloud. A responsible Congress is certainly to be preferred to irresponsible journalism. Does not the former make the latter less likely?

See Senator Symington's complaint about what is kept from Congress (but not from "potential adversaries") with respect to the deployment of nuclear weapons (*Congressional Record,* 118 [August 4, 1972]:S12832). He made this complaint even though he was at the time the only member of the Senate sitting on three congressional committees concerned with atomic energy. Congressman William S. Moorhead entitled a speech of his, "Will Somebody Please Tell the Congress What the Administration Is Doing? Because We Cannot Find Out On Our Own" (ibid. [July 25, 1972]:E7056). See also ibid. (July 27, 1972):H6968; ibid. (July 31, 1972):E7189. Cf. Joseph Kraft, "Senators Hide During Crucial Time in S.E. Asia," *Chicago Daily News,* May 15, 1972, p. 16; Dean Acheson, *The Korean War* (New York: Norton, 1971), pp. 26, 29–34, 110–11, 146.

For an argument *against* bipartisanship in foreign policy, see Kendall, *Contra Mundum,* p. 128 (on the need for the "native good sense of the American electorate" with respect to foreign affairs).

[36] See notes 19, 20, 21, 22, this paper. See also note 54, this paper.

cede) should not preclude public debate on national policy, certainly not when there is no state of war declared.[37] Should there not be a presumption against keeping secret either what the enemy already knows or discussions of the overall purpose of what our government is doing?[38]

There does remain the problem of morale, but suppression of publications with a view to morale (which recalls the Eighteenth-century offense of "seditious libel") presupposes there cannot be any substantial question legitimately open to the community about the purpose of what the government is doing and for which maintenance of morale is needed.[39] The responsible public servant should be taught not to try to conceal from the community either that which is safely subject to public debate or that which is so decisive in determining public policy as to require public examination and ratification. The responsible servant of the public, whether in the government or in the press, knows that the attempt to keep the wrong things secret (or the appearance of having tried to do so) can corrode public opinion, corrupt the country's leadership, and permanently damage the political morale of a people. (The re-

[37] Was not a contrary rule in force during the Vietnamese hostilities? We were told much more about daily operations (perhaps too much) than about the decisive policy deliberations by which the daily operations were directed.

The need to rely upon a declaration of war recognizes the constitutional role (and restraining power) of Congress. Cf. "Symposium—Legality of United States Participation in the Viet Nam Conflict," *Yale Law Journal,* 75 (1966):1085; *Congressional Record,* 116 (May 13, 1970):S7117; ibid. (May 21, 1970:S7591).

[38] See note 29, this paper. Obviously, a certain kind of serious deliberation is possible only in private. An example is the Constitutional Convention of 1787. But there was expected to be, and there was, an extensive debate afterward in public.

The men close to a President are, ultimately, too much "his men" to be able to bring to a debate, in closed meetings, what men in Congress and in the press, who have independent political and public bases, can bring. See Ellsberg, *Papers on the War,* pp. 34–35.

[39] It should again be noticed that if the government may suppress with a view to morale, the government's power would extend far beyond control of secret documents: even, for example, the routine listing of food or stock market prices in the press can affect morale adversely. See, however, Parts IV and V of this paper, on the legitimate concern of the community for the character of its citizens.

sponsible servant of the public, whether in office or out, should also know how to talk about delicate matters when they do need to be aired publicly.)

Thus our concern for security and for breaches in security always brings us back to the question of the kind of regime ours is or should be. What is the effect on the public, on the competence and morality of our people and its Congress, if it does not have, and believe itself to have, a pretty good idea of what is going on? Lord Halifax included among his "Maxims of State" (in 1692) the observation "That the People will ever suspect the remedies for the diseases of the state where they are *wholly* excluded from seeing how they are prepared."[40] And the President of the United States said (in 1972), in ordering more liberal procedures to be used in classifying information, "Fundamental to our way of life is the belief that when information which properly belongs to the public is systematically withheld by those in power, the people soon become ignorant of their own affairs, distrustful of those who manage them, and—eventually—incapable of determining their own destinies."[41]

The more complicated (or diseased) our community becomes, the less the kind of secrecy sought by our government with respect to Vietnam is likely to be useful. Secrecy is more apt to hurt us than disclosure is apt to help any potential enemy. Even our economic difficulties of the 1970s, for example, can be traced back to the unwillingness of the Johnson administration in the middle 1960s to tell Congress what it planned to do about the war. The refusal of the administration to face up publicly to what it was doing and what it was likely to do meant that our vast expenditures for Vietnam could not be financed properly. Such secrecy is also apt to hurt us when it raises fundamental doubts for a generation, espe-

[40] Halifax, *Complete Works*, ed. J. P. Kenyon (Baltimore: Penguin Books, 1969), p. 149 (emphasis added).

[41] See *Chicago Sun-Times*, March 11, 1972, p. 23. My inclination, I believe it salutary to add, is to presume whenever possible the good faith (but less so the good sense) of government efforts. But see Tom Braden's column, *Chicago Sun-Times*, September 1, 1972, p. 52: "... the President's great success in this war has been so to arrange troop withdrawals and the draft that Americans can continue to pulverize a tiny country without having to think about it." See also Clayton Fritchey's column, *Chicago Tribune*, September 17, 1972, sec. 1A, p. 5; notes 14, 33, 79, this paper.

cially among the more articulate young, about the good faith of any government in the United States.

Still, it is realistic to recognize explicitly and to help the young recognize, even as we attempt to confine legitimate government secrecy to the narrowest possible extent, that any regime in which public opinion is as critical as it is in ours does have serious limitations.[42] It is no doubt better to be ruled by wise men than it is to be dependent upon what the public may happen to believe from time to time. Wise men can safely determine, for example, what it is salutary to reveal to the public. But, unfortunately, there are far fewer wise men among us than there are men who believe themselves, or are believed by others, to be wise. It must be recognized as well that it is rare when the genuinely wise man (who must be distinguished from the ideologue) is permitted to rule, even if he should be willing to do so. Indeed, it is a mark of practical wisdom for us to recognize that we must often settle for far less than the best possible regime.[43] And, considering the dreadful alternatives we have been offered this century, constitutional government, especially when tempered by a sense of its own limitations, by a people's sense of natural justice, and by tradition, may be the best kind of regime available in our time.

Justice Black, in his concurring opinion in the Pentagon Papers litigation, observed that "paramount among the responsibilities of

[42] One problem with public opinion is reflected in the fact that publication of the Pentagon Papers *did* matter: there was very little in them that was new; but much that should have been generally known (and was already available in the press) was brought together in a dramatic manner. See, on responsible rhetoric, Plato, *Crito, Gorgias;* Anastaplo, *Constitutionalist,* pp. 500, 735–36. See also Part V, sec. ii, notes 14, 33, 41, 62, 78, 79, 92, this paper, as well as the text after note 56 (on the occasional need for "veils") and the text at note 68, this paper.

[43] See Part VI, this paper. We must also settle for far less than complete information. Indeed, the men who are regarded to be in a position to have superior information all too often fail to see what is apparent to moderate men watching (that is, truly examining) from the sidelines. What, for example, *was* the disastrous First World War all about? What justified putting Europe into that almost fatal state of shock which may only now be beginning to wear off? See, e.g., Colin Simpson, "Luisitania: A Great Liner with Too Many Secrets," *Life,* October 13, 1972, p. 59; Sidney B. Fay, *The Origins of the World War* (New York: Free Press, 1966), II, 547f; Anastaplo, *Constitutionalist,* pp. 784–85.

a free press is the duty to prevent any part of the Government from deceiving the people and sending them off to distant lands to die of foreign fevers and foreign shot and shell."[44] There is something archaic about his "foreign fevers and foreign shot and shell." It was appropriate, in the course of unprecedented litigation that touched upon questions about the very nature of our regime, that one of the oldest justices ever to sit on the Supreme Court of the United States should have, in his last official pronouncement, instinctively reached back, in language as well as in thought, to the very foundations of this republic.

V

I believe it salutary that it be generally believed that both the Supreme Court and the press have begun in recent years to redeem American honor and to restore the faith of Americans in their institutions, especially at a time when many have become resigned to mindless violence.[45] It is important for our civic health that the United States diligently expose its own misdeeds and that it be generally understood that it will continue to do so. Thus it is important to notice that although the three dozen analysts who originally prepared the Pentagon Papers were selected by Department of Defense officials, they were nevertheless willing and able to *begin* a serious assessment of the mistakes of our government in Vietnam. It is also important to notice that the district court judge in New York who ruled for the *New York Times* had just been appointed to his post by the administration which was bringing before him its unsuccessful suit for injunctive relief.

One can see both in the press and in the courts, when its mem-

[44] *New York Times* v. *United States,* 403 U.S., at 717 (1971).

[45] See the dissenting opinion of Judge J. Skelly Wright, in the Court of Appeals for the District of Columbia, in response to the government's efforts to stop publication of the Pentagon Papers by the *Washington Post:* "As if the long and sordid war in Southeast Asia had not already done enough harm to our people, it now is used to cut out the heart of our free institutions and system of government" (*United States* v. *Washington Post,* 444 F. 2d. 1322, at 1325 [1971]).

It is significant, I believe, that there has been so little public disapproval of the Supreme Court's decision in this litigation.

bers are served by and drawn from a high-minded bar, the institutionalization of a respect for reason and for ethical judgment in public affairs. On that occasion, the Supreme Court ratified, in effect, what the press had done. And it did so at a time when the public was prepared to be assured that its mounting ethical concerns about the war were in fact justified.[46] I suspect that the fact that the Court did not forbid the *Times* and the *Post* to continue publishing the Pentagon Papers may be far more important in this case than what the Court said in acting as it did. In fact, much of what the Court said (after a hurried argument and on the basis of an inadequate record) seems to me dubious, as was its refusal to repudiate categorically the use of temporary restraining orders in such circumstances.

What the Supreme Court did hold depended on two propositions: first, that there has always been a presumption in American constitutional law against any restraint upon a publisher prior to publication, except in the case of immediately impending irreparable harm[47] to the security of the United States; second, that the government did not show on this occasion that there *was* "irreparable harm" threatening the country as a result of the intended publication of the Pentagon Papers. (The analysis that follows accepts for the moment what I have already questioned, that there *are* circumstances in which the government may properly suppress by injunction a publication that is likely to cause serious damage to the country.)

It should be evident, in the light of the comments I have made about the security aspects of this matter, why the government could not measure up to the "heavy burden of showing justification for

[46] See notes 33, 41, and 45, this paper. See also Anastaplo, "Vietnam, Insubordination, and Self-Government," *Chicago Tribune,* June 25, 1972, sec. 1A, p. 1; reprinted in the *Congressional Record,* 118 (October 5, 1972): E8414; ibid. (October 10, 1972):E8480. Cf. ibid. (July 27, 1972):E7130; ibid. (October 16, 1972):E8754.

[47] A variety of formulations, with respect to the quantity and immediacy of this harm, was used in the course of the litigation. See *Documentary History,* pp. xiii, 3, 19, 25, 642, 665, 685, 883, 932, 933, 952, 963, 1116, 1123–24, 1146–47, 1150, 1152, 1162, 1166, 1219, 1222–27, 1234. See also notes 19, 20, 22, this paper.

the imposition of such a restraint" as it had asked for.[48] The sort of evidence which might have been persuasive to the Supreme Court, but which the government could not provide, would have described an impending publication, in time of war, of information about troop movements, weapon development, and strategic planning, or perhaps an impending publication of materials that would seriously interfere with negotiations vital to the very survival of the country.[49]

The three justices who dissented in the Pentagon Papers case did *not* claim that the government had made the required showing, but argued instead that the government should have been given a further opportunity to show what it could in the federal district courts. (In fact, the Supreme Court was, on certain fundamental issues, unanimous.) Complaints were registered in the dissenting opinions about the lack of sufficient time to make the kind of record needed for proper consideration of the issues in the case.

There *is* something to the complaints of undue haste.[50] Thus it was pointed out in a dissenting opinion that the *Times* was pressing for an immediate disposition of the case, in the name of its readers' "right to know," when it itself had held back the documents and its story for months. But on the other hand, is it relevant how long a publisher has been contemplating publication? When he moves, he is constitutionally entitled to be able to publish immediately, unless there is a clear legal prohibition.

Still, it should be said that *if* the government's argument is accepted to the extent it was accepted by the newspapers (to the effect that injunctions may indeed be secured to prevent "irreparable harm" to the country), then the government should have been given more time to make its case at the trial court level, even to change if necessary its original allegations and to introduce new evidence as it became more familiar with the voluminous record.

[48] The quotation is from *Organization for a Better Austin* v. *Keefe,* 402 U.S. 415, 419 (1971). It is quoted in the *per curiam* opinion of the Supreme Court, *New York Times* v. *United States,* 403 U.S. 714 (1971). See also *Near* v. *Minnesota,* 283 U.S. 697 (1931).

[49] See, e.g., *Documentary History,* pp. 334, 340, 369, 616, 618–20, 633, 639, 667, 836, 926–29, 1064, 1067, 1070, 1106, 1173–74, 1206. Cf. ibid., pp. 1214–15. See also notes 19, 21, 22, and the text at note 36, this paper.

[50] See Anastaplo, *Constitutionalist,* p. 632f. Cf. *Documentary History,* p. 640.

In such circumstances, it is unrealistic to expect everyday rules of civil procedure and of evidence to be scrupulously observed.[51]

But there would have been no case at all if the *Times* had published in one issue everything it had.[52] Nor would there have been a case requiring immediate appeal to the Supreme Court, after accelerated hearings in the trial and intermediate appellate courts, if the government had limited itself to what it clearly had a legal right to try at leisure (assuming the existence of a relevant statute), a criminal prosecution of those persons improperly possessing or communicating classified documents.[53]

That is to say, the government has in such circumstances a remedy, even if there should be (as I have argued) an absolute prohibition upon previous restraints of the kind sought in the courts on this occasion. In fact, it has several remedies, including recourse to the power (in the event of certain truly critical emergencies, to say nothing of an impending "nuclear holocaust") of declaring martial law or of suspending the writ of *habeas corpus*. Such emergency measures would permit, for example, effective control for the moment of any publisher regarded as likely to attempt to publish anything (classified or not classified) the government believes should

[51] See, e.g., *Documentary History,* pp. 973, 975, 998, 1002–03. Is the hurrying which is virtually intrinsic to such litigation still another argument against previous restraint?

[52] It had considered doing this, we have been told. It is possible that commercial considerations for resorting to serial publication were not irrelevant. See notes 74, 75, 80, 90, 106, this paper, as well as the text at notes 73 and 74, this paper.

[53] Does "communicating" include "publishing"? Congress has always been reluctant to make disclosure of official secrets criminal, since it has always depended very much on leaks to keep it informed of what "the government" is doing. See notes 34 and 35, this paper. On the relevant statutes (especially with respect to "publishing"), see Justice Douglas (concurring), *New York Times* v. *United States,* 403 U.S., at 720–22 (1971).

"The crimes that [Daniel] Ellsberg and [Anthony] Russo are charged with in Los Angeles all relate to a much earlier period between March 1969 and September 1970 when they allegedly photocopied the documents for unauthorized use. Specifically, Ellsberg or Russo or both were indicted on fifteen counts of three different offenses: stealing and mishandling government property, improperly receiving and communicating documents relating to the national defense (a crime under the Espionage Act) and conspiring to defraud the U.S. by obstructing its controls over classified documents" *Newsweek,* June 26, 1972, p. 29). See notes 54, 55, 63, 64, this paper.

not be published under the circumstances. Thus extraordinary remedies are available which permit our people and its government to set aside temporarily our traditional constitutional privileges and practices. But such remedies are of so obvious a magnitude that no sensible people will permit them to be invoked except in the most extraordinary circumstances.[54]

Nor does an absolute prohibition upon previous restraints mean that the government cannot take, in circumstances far less serious than the most critical emergencies, vigorous measures to try to prevent newspapers from acquiring government documents that, once they have them, they cannot be prevented *at law* from publishing. To illustrate, the government can make it evident that it will

[54] On emergency measures, see Anastaplo, *Constitutionalist,* e.g., pp. 48, 209–13, 467–79, 480–81, 598, 612–13, 626–27, 712–13, 814 ("habeas corpus"); David Hume, *An Inquiry Concerning the Principles of Morals* (Indianapolis: Library of Liberal Arts, Bobbs-Merrill, 1957), pp. 26–27; Plutarch, *Lives* (New York: Modern Library, Random House, n.d.), p. 124. Cf. ibid., p. 132.

The "nuclear holocaust" language is from Justice Brennan's concurring opinion, *New York Times* v. *United States,* 403 U.S., at 726 (1971).

Congressman William S. Moorhead has charged that "secret government contingency plans would allow President Nixon to impose national censorship during a limited war such as the Vietnam conflict. . . . Morhead said he acquired a copy of the plan as a result of an investigation by his House Foreign Operations and Government Information subcommittee. He said it conflicted with testimony from the Office of Emergency Preparedness, which, he said, 'implied that all of their plans were pointed toward a censorship system for use only in the event of a nuclear attack upon the United States' " (*Chicago Sun-Times,* October 23, 1972, p. 28).

However that may be, there certainly is no sense of emergency at this time in the country at large. Thus, Malcolm P. Sharp and I could, in the course of an extended television discussion with Daniel Ellsberg (in Chicago, in September 1972), predict that he would never spend a single day in jail on his then pending indictment. "Dr. Anastaplo said that when he offered Mr. Ellsberg 3 to 1 odds that he will never spend a day in jail, Mr. Ellsberg seemed astonished. Mr. Ellsberg said he had been hearing much darker opinions elsewhere. ['This is the first time anyone has said this to me,' he observed. 'I wish my wife could hear it.'] Dr. Anastaplo then explained to him that he was able to see a less gloomy future for Mr. Ellsberg because 'we in the Midwest are far more moderate than you people on the East and West Coasts.' " *Rosary College Rapporter,* September 20, 1972, p. 3. "Some people who did not experience the '50s find it hard to comprehend how much that period differed from the present." Walter Schneir, "The Second Frame-up of Julius and Ethel Rosenberg," *Ramparts,* August 1973, pp. 41, 49.

(*pursuant to legislation*) discipline all who transmit documents they are not supposed to transmit; the government can from time to time discipline those responsible for such unauthorized transmission (without being obliged to show "irreparable harm");[55] the government can guard carefully the documents it is most concerned about; the government can be careful also about the people to whom it entrusts such documents.[56] In addition, the government can attempt

[55] Cf. *Documentary History,* pp. 1221, 1222, 1234 (concessions of the Solicitor General about the difficulty of subsequent criminal prosecution if the Supreme Court permitted publication in *New York Times* v. *United States.* Cf. also the defense made in the Los Angeles criminal prosecution following upon the Pentagon Papers distribution (as summarized by *Newsweek,* June 26, 1972, p. 32; see note 53, this paper): "The stolen property charge is invalid, they say, because what was taken was not physical material (the original documents were returned after copying) but information. Espionage Act violations cannot be proved, they contend, because the prosecution cannot show [the defendants] acted with 'intent' to damage the interests of the United States (the prosecution argues that there is no need to prove intent under the sections of the act it has cited). And classified information is so commonly leaked by government officials themselves, the defense maintains, that any illegality attached to the practice has long since been eroded." It should be added that highly selective prosecution, as with the charge in *United States* v. *Berrigan* (D.C., Penna., 1972) of smuggling letters out of a prison, raises serious due process questions. See note 63, this paper. See also Clayton Fritchey's column, *Chicago Tribune,* July 18, 1972, sec. 1, p. 16. Cf. note 64, this paper.

The most obvious discipline for unauthorized transmittal of documents remains dismissal from government service. See, on the dismissal of insubordinates, an account of the relief of General Douglas MacArthur in Acheson, *Korean War.* (On the other hand, the serious mistake of the United States government in the Korean war—a kind of insubordination under its United Nations mandate—may have been its failure to stop at the thirty-eighth parallel once the initial invasion had been repulsed.)

[56] Do we want people in the government, who have been scrupulously examined for their patriotism, *never* to reveal to the public any matters that affect the national interest when they believe that interest to be seriously threatened by continued secrecy? Do we want to prosecute such men, even when they are mistaken in their judgment? On the other hand, do we want to prosecute the men in government whose misjudgments may have been responsible for 50,000 American dead (and perhaps hundreds of thousands of Vietnamese dead) in Indochina? Or are such decisions (whether to reveal secrets or to conduct a war) based on political judgments that are not subject to proper disposition in the criminal courts?

Should not a distinction be drawn between, on the one hand, these actions and, on the other hand, ordinary espionage or deliberate massacres of civilians or the refusal of officers to obey orders limiting their warmaking? Consider the irresponsibility of the Air Force in entrusting supposedly vital

to "persuade" newspapers not to publish certain documents that do happen to come into their possession. Such persuasion (which can take various forms, some of which it may be better to leave veiled) depends, in part, on the government's being able to show publishers that it is serious and knows what it is doing, that its classification system is reasonable, and that it is dealing in good faith with both the press and the public.

When the state of affairs becomes such that one respectable publisher after another refuses to respect a government's requests and decrees that there be no publication, is not that in itself a good reason for getting to the root of the apparent loss of confidence in the government? We should be reminded by these observations of the most important measure available to a besieged government, and that is to redress the long-standing grievances that (in a healthy community) usually lie at the heart of such open defiance of government and such generally endorsed repudiation of the Vietnam war as we saw in the Pentagon Papers episode.[57]

---

secret documents to a sergeant "whose mind had been clouded by twenty years of chronic alcoholism" (*Chicago Tribune,* August 12, 1972, sec. 1, p. 3, reporting a three-year prison sentence upon conviction for "attempting to smuggle crucial defense secrets to Soviet agents"). "The Russians allegedly promised to free three American prisoners of war in North Vietnam in exchange for the material" (*Chicago Sun-Times,* August 10, 1972, p. 57). See notes 28 and 46, this paper.

Consider also General MacArthur's unauthorized press releases, which contributed to his dismissal (Acheson, *Korean War,* pp. 76–77, 80, 94, 101–03, 105f, 113). Cf. note 12, this paper. But see note 65, this paper.

I should add that it does not seem to me to serve a useful purpose, or to be strictly fair, to keep in prison any longer the *misguided* burglars of the Watergate headquarters of the Democratic National Committee. See note 2, this paper.

[57] See Anastaplo, "The Declaration of Independence," *St. Louis University Law Journal,* 9 (1965): 390. See also notes 33, 41 and 45, this paper.

For discussions of the recent Frank Committee Report on the British "Official Secrets Act," see [*London*] *Observer,* October 1, 1972, pp. 1, 12; October 15, 1972, p. 2: "Mr. [Anthony Wedgwood] Benn said he believed that if various groups with special interests could achieve better access to the Press and broadcasting 'many of the frustrations in our society could be eliminated.' He called for less secrecy from the top. '[T]he Official Secrets Act . . . makes it an offence to reveal anything that happens in government. . . . [W]e must look to those who either run the mass media or have access to it—and I think one of the remaining roles of the politician may be that he commands attention because he has been elected—to see that public atten-

vi

It can be argued that the *New York Times* did "freedom of the press" a disservice by not publishing in one issue all that it intended to publish from the Pentagon Papers archives, thereby preventing the Attorney General from even attempting to secure an injunction and from establishing the dubious precedents that may survive the litigation. True, the Supreme Court ruled that the injunctions in this case could not be continued—but no majority of the Court said that they should never have been issued even on a temporary basis. I believe it would have been healthier, as well as a sounder reading of the Constitution, if the Court had lifted the remaining restraining orders immediately upon reading the lower courts' opinions after each case had been filed on its docket. It would have been sufficient, under the circumstances, simply to have affirmed the final substantive rulings of the district court in each case. It would have been even better to have singled out for approval the initial ruling by the district court in Washington.[58]

Instead, it may seem to have been established by what the Court did (and did not do) that a temporary injunction may properly be secured merely upon an allegation by the government of grave danger to national security.[59] In a sense, such a remedy can be said

---

tion is brought to discontent as soon as possible after the event occurs.' " Cf. the American "Freedom of Information Act," 5 U.S.C. 552 (*Congressional Record,* 118 [October 16, 1972]:E8792). Cf. also note 17, this paper; *Congressional Record,* 119 (April 2, 1973):S6329.

[58] That initial ruling (by Judge Gesell, on June 18, 1971) may be found in *Documentary History,* p. 652 (*New York Times,* June 19, 1971, p. 10).

Justices Black, Douglas, Brennan, and Marshall would have had the Court rule for the newspapers on June 25, 1971. See *New York Times* v. *United States, United States* v. *Washington Post,* 403 U.S. 714–15, 942, 943 (1971).

[59] After the announcement of the Supreme Court's decision, counsel for the *New York Times* said "that the ruling placed the press in a 'stronger position.' He maintained that no Federal District Judge would henceforth temporarily restrain a newspaper on the Justice Department's complaint that 'this is what they have printed and we don't like it' and that a direct threat of irreparable harm would have to be alleged" (*New York Times,* July 1, 1971, p. 1). Cf. notes 20 and 62, this paper. Thus I consider a setback what counsel considered a gain, just as with respect to television (see Part V, sections v–vi, this paper) I would consider a gain what most Americans would consider a setback.

to have always been available for the government, for it did secure it the first time it was moved to seek it. But it may have been better for us not have had such a "first time." It took a massive, even unprecedented stimulus to prod the government into an attempt this first time. Far less may suffice next time, now that the wall has been breached. It remains to be seen whether we will remember this litigation primarily for what it confirmed about the extent of freedom of the press or primarily for what it suggested about previously unsuspected powers in the government to abridge (if only temporarily on this occasion) that freedom. To suggest that the government has powers from which, in practice, it cannot really benefit makes it likely that we will lose sight of the rationale for the powers the government does have and from which it can benefit.[60]

The relevant constitutional doctrine, concerned as it is primarily with the ability of citizens to discuss freely and fully all matters necessary for making political judgments, is itself reflected in the everyday practice that is so revealing about the character of our regime. Suppose, for example, that the government had succeeded in preserving its injunctions, if only until extended hearings had been conducted in the district courts. Precisely what would such hearings, or even the entering of permanent injunctions thereafter, have meant both in these circumstances and as precedents? It appears that nothing could have prevented publication of the Pentagon Papers by *some* newspapers in the United States.

That is, the permanent injunctions sought by the government against the *New York Times* and the *Washington Post* would not have applied to other newspapers even in this country until the government had moved specifically against them as well (as it had already moved against the *Boston Globe* and the *St. Louis Post-Dispatch*). But the government would have had no legal basis for thus moving until such other newspapers had published, or had indicated they were about to publish, articles based on the same or similar top-secret archives. A "victory" by the government in the *Times* and *Post* cases would have meant that the enterprising editor

[60] The powers the government does have for ordinary circumstances permit it to rely upon such measures as those of which I have provided a half-dozen illustrations (in Part III, sec. v). Cf. note 54, this paper.

on another newspaper with access to the same material, if *he* desired to publish without government interference, should have brought out in one issue everything he intended to publish. This he could have done, it should be noticed, without the special liability (psychological as well as legal) which would follow upon deliberate defiance of an injunction.[61]

It should also be noticed in this connection that no sensible judge wants to issue an impotent decree. The Supreme Court obviously realized that it would not do much good to maintain restraints upon the *Times* and the *Post,* in order to give the government time to make whatever case it could, when newspapers all over the country were appearing almost daily with their own gleanings from the "secret" documents under review. There is something to be said for having court orders conform to what people are going to do anyway.

Thus, one result of all this litigation may be to induce dedicated (as well as irresponsible) publishers to print immediately hereafter all that they have which they believe the government might be disposed to challenge in court (unless they decide that they or the community might benefit from the publicity attendant upon an attempted suppression).[62] By printing immediately everything that

[61] See Kalven, "Even When a Nation Is at War—," p. 34, note 156. See also note 12, this paper.

[62] After the announcement of the Supreme Court's decision, the Solicitor General said, "Maybe the newspapers will show a little restraint in the future" (*New York Times,* July 1, 1971, p. 1). Cf. notes 55, 59, 64, this paper.

Popular interest in the Pentagon Papers fell sharply once the legal effort to suppress them had failed. (See note 42, this paper.) It is not difficult to understand why government officials should have been moved to feel (by so massive a leak) that they "ought to do something." A more sophisticated, politically astute Attorney General would probably have conducted himself otherwise. See notes 12 and 65, this paper.

Consider, on the nature of popular interest and of public opinion, an observation by Mike Royko about the "silent majority": "Whose fault is it if people prefer being silent to speaking up? Who says they have to endlessly watch pro football, instead of a few political debates? Who says they have to take greater pride in knowing some stranger's batting average than in keeping up with the way their congressman votes? . . . For a couple of decades one of the fastest growing industries has been leisure-time activities. People have jumped from one time-killer to another. But many have found that fun and games aren't enough. They have found that they can't identify with

they intend to publish, and taking their chances on criminal prosecution thereafter,[63] publishers avoid the inconvenience and sometimes considerable expense of even a temporary injunction, contingencies that they will be advised to assess hereafter.

It should now be apparent why it is that everyday practice, as well as the constitutional doctrine that reflects and ratifies such practice, makes previous restraint an illusory remedy for the government to rely upon. When a newspaper has unauthorized possession of any material, the first the government usually knows of it is when it is published—and then no injunction is useful. *This does not mean, of course, that the conscientious publisher should not, in certain instances, consult with responsible government officials before he uses the material that comes to hand.* He is not bound to publish whatever he cannot be legally prevented from publishing. Will, however, the memory of government efforts with respect to the Pentagon Papers tend to discourage publishers from consulting government officials before publication (as, it seems to me, it would be sometimes patriotic for publishers to do)? Should not the government now say something to counter such a tendency, something disavowing recourse to injunctions when consulted voluntarily by publishers? That is, should we not try to restore that traditional relation between the press and the government which the Pentagon Papers litigation has to some extent disturbed?[64]

---

a quarterback who peddles shaving lotion. Now, they are finding that politics gives them something they can actually do, and feel they are a part of something. They can have fun, and thrills, and a greater sense of identity out of politics than out of all the store-bought pursuits. For this they are being called elitists" (*Chicago Daily News,* July 14, 1972, p. 3). See notes 33, 75, 78, 92, and 104, this paper.

[63] In such criminal prosecution, the question of the defendants' intent to harm the country may become vital; a jury trial is available; and the burden of proof remains the government's. All this assumes, of course, that there *is* a constitutional statute governing what may be published. See notes 53, 54, 55, 57, this paper.

[64] See Meg Greenfield, "Some Reflections on the Pentagon Papers," *Washington Post,* June 30, 1971. The *New York Times* reporter who was primarily responsible (from the newspaper side) for the publication of the Pentagon Papers has reported that "he has suffered no significant loss of rapport with his Washington contacts in government as a result of the disclosures.... 'The military weren't shocked at all. I can't say that the publishing of the Pentagon Papers has changed any relations with a single

It also should be now apparent from what I have said that (whatever the illusions and dangers of certain precedents) there cannot be among us an effective system of previous restraints upon publication through the use of specific injunctions. Previous restraint requires, except in rare circumstances calling for suspension of some constitutional processes, a comprehensive system of censorship that ensures that all prospective publication must be reviewed by the government. That seems hardly likely in the foreseeable future.

What should the press do with the virtually unlimited right it has been shown to have (at least in everyday practice) to publish what it chooses to publish without previous restraint? Perhaps all one can say here is that the press should try to act responsibly—and that we the people should speak up when we believe it has not done so. Certainly, it is delusive and hence self-defeating, considering our traditions and constitutional circumstances, to expect either in-

---

high-ranked source' " (*Chicago Sun-Times,* February 24, 1972, p. 24). See notes 15, 27, 28, this paper.

It seems to me too early to be certain about the effects of the three cases decided by the Supreme Court on June 29, 1972, in which newspaper reporters had been subpoenaed to divulge before grand juries the nature and sources of information that they had gained in confidence. My guess is that the Court's support of the grand juries on this occasion will not make much difference in the long run: not only can reporters often take care not to learn who their informants are, but the jailing of reporters will usually be politically impossible (whatever the courts may be willing to say). Consider also the *Chicago Tribune* editorial of July 8, 1972, in protest against the Court's decisions: "As for the suggestion that newspapers are more interested in printing stories about crime than in doing anything about it, it is so naive as to be astonishing. The type of crime most often involved in the confidences we're talking about is corruption in government. Who would ever stop it if it were not exposed in the press? How would the press be able to expose it without the help of confidential informants who were willing to tell what they knew to reporters whom they trusted?... Any reputable newspaper's purpose in exposing corruption is precisely to see that something *is* done about it." Consider, as well, *Chicago Tribune,* October 18, 1972, pp. 1, 16. "The Chicago Tribune has announced a contribution of $1000, in support of Peter Bridges, the Newark newspaperman who has gone to jail for contempt of court rather than disclose information given to him in confidence." Cf. note 12, this paper. But see note 65, this paper.

Nor did it seem to me likely that even a conviction in the Los Angeles case described in notes 53 and 55 of this paper would have made much difference in the flow of classified documents to newspapers. See the text after note 33, this paper. See also, note 54, this paper.

junctions or criminal sanctions to compel the press to conduct itself other than it always has.

But the education, as distinguished from the intimidation, of the press is always in order.[65]

IV

I have referred to "the character of our regime" and to the necessary "ability of citizens to discuss freely and fully all matters necessary for making political judgments." What is required to create and preserve a public that is fit for the conduct of a republican form of government?

Some means of general communication among us is, of course, required. The size of the country has long precluded the possibility

[65] We should not exaggerate, even as we recognize and provide against, the risks a free community runs in permitting its press to publish freely. Private citizens, whether publishers or publishers' informants, have far to go even to begin to match, either in scope or in effect, the deadly misjudgments of the past decade with respect to Vietnam by the government of the United States. See, e.g., *Congressional Record,* 118 (September 14, 1972): E7896 (on the human and other costs of the Vietnam war).

Nor should we exaggerate the risks *to* the press, because of the precedents of the Pentagon Papers litigation. We *are* left with the fact that the *New York Times* and the *Washington Post* could publish what they chose from a virtually complete forty-seven-volume set of "top secret" documents *known* to be in their possession and relating to a war still in progress. This suggests that virtually anything can now be published without previous restraint. Cf. Ronald F. Bunn, "The *Spiegel* Affair and the West German Press," in *Media Sociology: A Reader,* ed. Jeremy Tunstall (Urbana: University of Illinois Press, 1970), p. 439; *Schenck* v. *United States,* 249 U.S. 49 (1919) (note 22, this paper).

Has the Pentagon Papers episode contributed to the embittered toleration of official lawlessness reflected in the statement by the Republican leader quoted in note 12 of this paper? (Cf. notes 15 and 79, this paper.) A week later, however, a presidential aide was reported by a broadcaster to have said about alleged Republican surveillance and sabotage of Democratic party activities, "Don't expect the President to admit anything before the election, but a lot of people in the White House are appalled at how far things got out of hand." The acting director of the Federal Bureau of Investigation was reported, in the same broadcast, to have cautioned the President that the F.B.I. "had established more serious direct links to the White House than the President might know about." See *Chicago Tribune,* October 24, 1972, p. 3. In short, the war has been brought home to the American people. See notes 33 and 45, this paper. See also Robert Novak and Rowland Evans, "The President's Alger Hiss Case?," *Chicago Sun-Times,* October 21, 1972, p. 36. Cf. note 94, this paper. (For a preliminary assessment of these revelations, see note 116, this paper.)

of exclusive reliance on speeches promulgated only by natural means. Artificial means of communication seem inevitable, and this the press has traditionally provided the American people.

The right of the people to know, of which we hear much today, includes the duty to think. And this has, as a precondition, the opportunity to learn as well as the ability to discern what it is necessary to learn. Information and opinions about vital matters of public concern are needed among us on a day-to-day basis.

Even more important than day-to-day concerns, however, and indeed central to this paper, are the perennial questions of what kind of people is presupposed by our institutions (institutions that include the absolute prohibition, at least in practice, of previous restraints on the press), and of what produces and preserves such a people. Thus, is not a people of a certain character—not merely a people with certain information and political opinions and morale—presupposed by our institutions? Of course, there could be the prior question of whether we want the institutions we do happen to have. That is, are there better ones available? On this occasion, however, we must set aside this somewhat theoretical question (however engaging it might be) and proceed on the patriotic assumption that our traditional institutions *are* to be preserved and utilized.

Serving our traditional institutions, and indeed shaped by and shaping them, has been the press. Whatever its faults—and they have always been serious—it has been something to which we have accommodated ourselves and upon which we have relied for generations. The press is, then, essentially old-fashioned, having developed in this country along with our institutions and the character of our people. For the most part, the possible mistakes in editorial judgment to which I have referred in Part III affect national security interests; they do not threaten directly the character of the regime itself. I now propose to argue that in considering what we should do about the mass media, our primary concern should not be with the unauthorized revelation of secrets (that is, information about military weapons or strategic policy or diplomatic negotiations), but rather with the promulgation among us of influences and images that shape (that is, reshape) the character of our people.

I have argued that, for most practical purposes, there has been since 1791 no effective legal limitation upon the information made available to the public about the performance of its governments, once the press has managed to secure such information. It seems to me too late in the constitutional day to change this dispensation: too much depends upon it; we are accustomed to it; good-intentioned men, both in the press and in the government, have learned how to deal with this considerable freedom from previous restraint of the press.

Vital to a people's self-governance are its experience and ability in recognizing, assessing, and choosing (if not even forming) its leaders and policies. This means that the character of our people cannot be left to chance or to private influences or to the vagaries of a "free trade in ideas." That is, we should be concerned to preserve in our people a character that permits it to use responsibly the extensive freedom of speech and of the press traditionally (and constitutionally) available to it.

Before we turn to a consideration of what the mass media (and particularly television, which is distinctively of the mass media) do to the character of a people such as ours, we should note one immediate effect that television has on our political institutions. The modern mass media tend more toward centralization of power, while the old-fashioned press tended to be more localizing in its efforts and effects. The local is apt to be both more provincial and healthier; certainly, it is to be encouraged in this day and age.[66] When we go "national" today—whether in the media or in politics

[66] Because of the role television has taken nationwide, radio is now more diverse and more locally oriented than it used to be. See notes 86 and 92, this paper. Television, I shall argue, is centralizing, and yet subversive of community. In fact, by undermining local attachments, it repudiates the natural sense of community a people may still have. See Anastaplo, *Constitutionalist,* particularly chap. 7, for arguments on behalf of states' rights; see also Anastaplo, "Is U.S. Prosecution of Local Politicians Healthy?" *Chicago Tribune,* April 22, 1973, sec. 2, p. 3; notes 100 and 109, this paper. Cf. Crosskey, *Politics and the Constitution,* pp. 30–31, 35–36, 39–41, 47, 50f, 284, 287–88, 319–20, 359, 363n, 394, 428, 511–15, 518–20, 541, 561, 629–31, 635f, 662, 669f, 754f, 818f, 934–37, 994f, 1000f, 1049f, 1083f, 1161f, 1322. Cf. also Marshall McLuhan, *Understanding Media: The Extensions of Man* (New York: McGraw-Hill, 1964), p. 310 ("One of the most extraordinary developments since TV in England has been the upsurge of regional dialects"); note 87, this paper.

The "free trade" quotation in the text is from Justice Holmes's dissenting opinion in *Abrams* v. *United States,* 250 U.S. 616, 630 (1919).

—everything tends to become somewhat more gross and less discriminating: that is, a facile simplification is rewarded and hence promoted. Is there then a tendency toward homogeneity of taste and opinion as well as a general lowering of effective moral, political, and intellectual standards?

Industrialization with its marvelous technology can be said to be responsible for such developments. With such developments come also the sense of helplessness and of rootlessness to which modern man is peculiarly subject. In modern circumstances one has less the impression of being "one's own man," of being able to do things for oneself. One is forced into a passive role, not the role of the alert observer but that of the pampered slave.

Television is, of course, distinctively dependent upon the technology of modern industrialization. (It is so new that there has not yet developed—one must wonder whether there *can* develop—the carefully thought-out system of checks and balances there is among us in practice with respect to the press.) Do we not all recognize that television has had profound effects on our way of life? Should we not ask, then: What are the effects of television? Have those effects been good? What *is* the nature of the medium? What is there about television (and hence the mass media) which is different from everything previously relied upon or accounted for by our institutions? What, if anything, can now be done about television?[67]

V

i

The press, I have suggested, is (despite its efforts to imitate television and to modernize itself) still essentially old-fashioned. It is (partly

[67] We shall return below to the problem of the social effects of television after we consider the effects of television on individuals. On addiction to the radio, to the cinema, and to the modern press and best seller, see Q. D. Leavis, *Fiction and the Reading Public* (London: Chatto & Windus, 1932), pp. 55–58.

If we do not care enough to do *something* about television's massive effects on us, it will be hard to take seriously the other things that affect American character today. But see Anastaplo, *Constitutionalist,* pp. 252–53, 729–30, on the significance of what Cicero said in a letter to a friend: "Cato means well: but he does hurt sometimes to the State; for he talks as if he were in the republic of Plato and not in the dregs of Romulus." See also notes 4, 78, and 112, this paper.

because of things intrinsic to it) still moved somewhat by a sense of natural justice, as is the public opinion that it serves.[68]

The press continues to provide us with the serious searching out and recording of the news of the day, whereas television is in this respect essentially parasitic. I believe it significant that the newscaster on television is rarely the man who has investigated the story being broadcast. Rather, he is usually part of a "show" that draws primarily on what newspapermen have gathered and put on the wire. Thus there is no necessary connection between the influence (or "image") of television "personalities" and their competence.[69] These television personalities wield tremendous influence, but such influence is both ephemeral and beyond their comprehension and hence their control.

Television may help keep the press "honest" by presenting events that will be subsequently described on the printed page. But, one must wonder, at what level is such honesty promoted? What level suffices to satisfy the television viewer? What can be adequately described by television?

[68] See notes 14, 33, 41 and 107, this paper. Cf. note 42, this paper. Vice-President Agnew put this challenge to the television industry: "You have our children almost from the time they are able to sit in front of a TV set. Help us to make them good citizens. And while you're doing that, let's enlist a few more adults in a national effort to improve ourselves and our environment. Your power to do this is unprecedented in America's history" (Louis Reichman and Barry Wishart, eds., *Issues 4: Critical Questions for the 70's* (Beverly Hills: Glencoe Press, 1972), p. 156. Cf. Christopher S. Wren, "How to Find the Live Ones on Children's TV," *Saturday Review,* September 16, 1972, p. 53.

[69] Does not competence tend to encourage a sense of responsibility, as well as to equip one to *be* responsible? Does the public somehow sense the fundamental irresponsibility of the mass media? See notes 79 and 94, this paper. (Consider also *Chicago Daily News,* September 9–10, 1972, "Panorama," p. 23: "Since CBS telecast 'The Selling of the Pentagon' on February 23, 1971, the networks have done little investigative reporting. And since public television broadcast both the Nader Report and 'The Banks and the Poor' in the 1970–71 season, PTV has become more fearful and the voice of the Administration and the establishment." See note 116, this paper.)

On the relation of virtue and knowledge, see Plato's *Apology* and *Republic.* See also Aristotle, *Nicomachaean Ethics,* I, vi. Consider the introduction of the Third Murderer by a suspicious Macbeth, perhaps contributing thereby to the botching of the Banquo assassination. Consider also note 14, this paper. Cf. Ellsberg, *Papers on the War,* p. 306.

ii

To speak, as I have, of "public opinion" is to recognize in "public" a body that acts, which is somehow keyed to political concerns; it is also to recognize in "opinion" something that does depend ultimately upon notions of right and wrong and hence upon reason. This is quite different from the passive "audiences" upon which television depends and which it creates.

The television industry, in its distinctive modernity, is particularly representative of the mass media and their infatuation with appearances. The term itself, "mass media," aptly records what happens when modern electronic technology is applied to communications: the decisive factor becomes the necessarily "mass" character of passive and pacified audiences (made up of countless private—that is, isolated—parties), and the emphasis (as seen in the term "media") upon the industry as little more than conduits. Does not a people lose its moral (and hence political) sense when it becomes the "masses"? One may even be obliged to consider whether some previous restraint of the press might not become necessary if the people should, because of the debilitating effects of the mass media, become so childish as to be unable to govern themselves.

Both the massive character of the audience and the conduit character of the media very much affect the content and the effect of broadcasts, even though the principal concern of broadcasters may not be with either content or effect but with the constant compulsion upon them to attract large audiences and with the pressing need to keep supplying something to ever changing (and yet "always there") audiences. To regard a people as a "mass" is to say, and perhaps to make it likely, that it will become something that is moved primarily by "force and accident," by arousals of passion rather than by appeals to reason.[70]

[70] "Force and accident" is from *Federalist* no. 1. See the text at note 116, this paper. See also note 92, this paper.

Two observations throw further light on the nature of the term "mass." "In a large measure the technical characteristics of the media dictate the conditions of its use and the content of the communications. The word 'mass' itself implies some of these. It is a detestable word for a deplorable phenomenon. For the nearest likeness in its day the *New Testament* uses the word 'multitude,' signifying a multiplicity of individuals. The word 'mass'

We should not be surprised to hear the effect of television on audiences spoken of as an "impact" that can be "surveyed" and "marketed." The intrinsic quality of particular programs becomes irrelevant—television executives will sometimes admit what their conduct always exhibits—if the surveys do not "measure up."

iii

The effects of television are pervasive and are felt both directly and indirectly: directly through what almost six hours a day *of exposure* (not necessarily of viewing) do to the souls of our people;[71] indirectly

---

implies singularity and shapelessness. The individual is obliterated in the collectivity..." (C. O. Rhodes, *Mass Communications and the Spirit of Man* [London: Lindsey Press, 1959], p. 10). "He [the Pro-Rector of the University of Salzburg] did not like the term 'mass media.' 'Mass' implied dampness, dullness and density. It was a disdain of humanity and a depreciation of the individual. He preferred the title 'media of public opinion.' Public life was essential for these media..." (*Symposium on Human Rights and Mass Communications,* p. 71). See also Anastaplo, *Constitutionalist,* p. 499; notes 5 and 75, this paper. See *Congressional Record,* 118 (May 1, 1972): S7002 for the abundant use of "masses" by a worldly-wise yet curiously naive conservative columnist who is charmingly unaware of Marxist influences upon him. See also notes 91 and 94, this paper.

We should keep in mind, in our concern for the community, that there *are* pitfalls to be avoided. Consider, for example, the sentiments inspired by the Hitler movement among young Germans in the early 1930s: "We were taken seriously—taken seriously in a quite remarkable way—and that aroused our enthusiasm. We felt we belonged to a large, well-organized body that honored and embraced everyone, from the ten year old to the grown man. We sensed that there was a role for us in the historic process, in a movement that was transforming the masses into a *Volk*..." (quoted in Beate Ruhm von Oppen, *Student Rebellion and the Nazis* [Annapolis: St. John's College, 1972], p. 47). See notes 99 and 105, this paper.

[71] This is said to be the national average of sets *turned on.* The amount of time spent by Americans with television has been described in various ways: "The year-round per family average of daily television viewing is now estimated at five and a half hours, rising to six and a half hours in midwinter; the estimate for grade-school children is twenty hours a week" (W. H. Ferry and Harry S. Ashmore, *Mass Communications* [Santa Barbara: Center for the Study of Democratic Institutions, 1966], p. 30). "There are sixty million homes in the United States and over 95% of them are equipped with a television set. (More than 25% have two or more sets.) In the average home that set is turned on some five hours and forty-five minutes a day. The average male viewer, between his second and sixty-fifth year, will watch television for over 3000 entire days—roughly nine full years of his life"

through the adjustments the press and others consider themselves obliged to make to compete with the television industry in capturing people's attention and thus being able to stay in business.

It should be noticed that much of the time devoted to television must be taken from other activities, such as reading or writing or conversation or courting or playing. What had been the effect on us heretofore of such activities? What is the effect of their radical curtailment? It is unrealistic to assume that such revolutionary changes as we have undergone have no significant effect on the souls of people.[72]

Commercial considerations are obviously much more important for television than for the press, whatever may be said about the influence of advertisers upon publishers. Television was born during a more commercial age than was printing; the press evolved more naturally as an extension of thinking and writing rather than as an

---

(Bernard Rosenberg and David M. White, eds., *Mass Culture Revisited* [New York: Van Nostrand Reinhold, 1971], pp. 169–70). "According to one study, children will have spent two to three thousand hours watching TV before they enter the first grade. The trend, in this regard, is toward a nation of viewers, not of readers" (James J. Kilpatrick, *Congressional Record,* 118 [June 30, 1972]:E6605). "... before a child reaches school, from the ages of two through five, he spends an estimated one-fourth to one-half of his waking hours in front of a television set" (*Issues 4,* ed. Reichman and Wishart, p. 156). "In the current crop of young Americans, the first television generation in history, each has spent an average of three hours and 40 minutes a day before a television set. It's a generation whose members have logged—by one estimate—an average of 22,000 hours watching TV by the time they were 18 years of age, more time than they spent studying or reading or talking with their parents" (ibid., p. 158). " 'Television viewing alone occupies nearly one-fourth of the waking hours of the average American' according to a Report of a Congressional Committee" (Ralph L. Stavins, ed., *Television Today: The End of Communication and the Death of Community* [Washington, D.C.: Institute for Policy Studies, 1969], p. 6).

[72] A former chairman of the Federal Communications Commission told a college graduating class, "If you approximate the average, you have already spent more time with television than you spent with a teacher, a minister, a priest or rabbi—and, in many cases, more than you spent with your family" (*Chicago Tribune,* June 17, 1972, sec. 1, p. 8). Another observer noted, "It is the first time in history that a piece of furniture, without a soul of its own, has become a member of the family" (*Congressional Record,* 118 [June 6, 1972]:E6009). (Does not the automobile still have a similar exalted status? See notes 101 and 106, this paper.)

agency for advertising and selling.[73] The commercial aspects of the press simply cannot assert themselves as much as the commercial aspects of television do. Thus one can easily ignore the advertisements in a newspaper. But no one doubts the considerable effect that sponsors have in the United States upon the content of television programs and upon audiences.[74] The commercial aspects of television, which are so important in so many critiques of the industry, are not, however, my primary concern on this occasion.[75]

[73] But we should not forget the concern expressed by responsible churchmen, whether in Roman Catholic Europe or in Puritan New England, about the expansion of literacy among common folk. Consider also the history and purpose of the kind of licensing against which John Milton directed his *Areopagitica,* as well as the threat once perceived in the translation of the Bible into popular tongues. Cf. Martin Luther, *Works* (Philadelphia: Fortress Press, 1972, 1967), vol. 49, pp. 34, 44, 147 ("He who adds to someone's knowledge also adds to his pain"); vol. 54, pp. 42–43, 72, 135–36, 171, 183–84, 210–13, 235–36, 243, 274–75, 358–59, 373, 400–1, 408, 423–24. See notes 92 and 98, this paper.

[74] On the historic relation between American television and commercialism, see *Congressional Record,* 118 (May 10, 1972):E4948. Congressman John M. Murphy has observed, "The networks are infatuated with violence for two reasons. The portrayal of violence is one of the easiest ways to attract an audience and most important of all, it sells soap. As long as we in Congress give them the option of 'doing better' or making money, I am afraid they will choose the latter course" (*Congressional Record,* 118 [June 12, 1972]:H5504). See also Mike Royko, "A Black Day in Movieland," *Chicago Daily News,* October 17, 1972, p. 3; *Congressional Record,* 119 (April 2, 1973):H2351.

Cf. John Whale, *The Half-Shut Eye* (London: Macmillan, 1969), p. 14: "Although advertisers on Independent Television in Britain simply buy time in between programmes which are entirely devised by the broadcasting company, ITV news programmes look remarkably like American ones. So do news programmes on the British Broadcasting Corporation's channels, which at present carry no advertising. It is true that ITV still has to draw an audience, to keep its advertising rates up; and so does the BBC, if it is to be allowed an occasional increase in the license fee demanded of all viewers which finances it. . . . The curbs on television's coverage of news and politics are more subtle and extensive than can be explained simply in terms of human greed." See notes 81 and 106, this paper.

[75] Commercial considerations do lead producers to try to provide what they believe audiences want. This can have the effect of accentuating the bad tendencies intrinsic to television. Thus, since television thrives on "action," there is frequent recourse to the coarsening violence of which so much is heard. See, e.g., Tunstall, ed., *Media Sociology,* pp. 314, 526; Joseph T. Klapper, *The Effects of Mass Communication* (New York: Free Press, Macmillan, 1960), p. 135f; *Congressional Record,* 118 (May 22, 1972):E5580; ibid. (June 12, 1972):H5503. "In addition to gun control and compensation

Nor does the specific content of television broadcasting concern me here—for this could perhaps be corrected by a people determined to do so—but rather the very form of it and the consequent effects of the displacement by television of the other means by which souls have been engaged heretofore. The remarkable success of television since the Second World War in sweeping all before it should make us wonder what there is about it that makes it so

---

of gun victims, Mayor Daley suggested [to a House of Representatives committee] that television 'be obligated to carry commercial warnings of the danger of handguns and the need to control them. This would be fitting since so much of TV entertainment is devoted to violence,' he said" (*Chicago Sun-Times*, June 29, 1972, p. 5).

On the significance of the decline in the relative popularity of baseball, see McLuhan, *Understanding Media*, p. 326. See also Bill Veeck's column, *Chicago Sun-Times*, July 9, 1972, p. 145: "Football (as yet untouched by its much-publicized over-exposure) comes across on television with speed, action and violence—the essence of the game intact. The excellence of football's physical telecasting, camera coverage, closeups, instant and slow-motion replays, point up the inadequacy of baseball on TV. Somehow the leisurely pace of baseball comes over (maybe rightly) as dullness rather than slow-moving charm. Football uses TV; baseball is its victim. . . . While both baseball and football have slipped in popularity since 1969, baseball's fall from grace has been more dramatic, rapid and severe. Whether the slide reflects a switch from spectator to participation sports is not clear." (On baseball, see Anastaplo, *Constitutionalist*, p. 660.)

"Force" (and thus violence?) may be required to move "masses." (See notes 5 and 70, this paper.) Does not television mean that more radical politics is likely than with the press (not necessarily because of any explicit advocacy on television, but because of what television may do to the human soul)? Thus the money-making desire may contribute, eventually, to the radicalization of our political (or at least our social) life. See notes 1, 83, 89, this paper. See also notes 62, 74, 102, and 106, this paper.

One effect of film (and even more so television) on the human soul (but not the most profound effect) is indicated in an observation by Achmed Sukarno of Indonesia: "The motion picture industry has provided a window on the world, and the colonized nations have looked through that window and have seen the things of which they have been deprived. It is perhaps not generally realized that a refrigerator can be a revolutionary symbol—to a people who have no refrigerators. A motor car owned by a worker in one country can be a symbol of revolt to a people deprived of even the necessities of life. . . . [Hollywood] helped to build up the sense of deprivation of man's birthright, and that sense of deprivation has played a large part in the national revolutions of postwar Asia" Marshall McLuhan and Quentin Fiore, *The Medium Is the Massage* (New York: Random House, 1967), p. 131. Cf. Joseph Cropsey, "The Right of Foreign Aid," in *Why Foreign Aid?* ed. Robert A. Goldwin (Chicago: Rand McNally, 1962).

attractive.[76] What is the effect of having such a window to the world? What comes through, what is held back, by the filter of the television camera?[77]

[76] From 100,000 television sets in the United States at the beginning of 1948, the total increased more than one million during 1948, "and thereafter in a rapidly rising curve" (Wilbur Schramm, ed., *Mass Communications* [Urbana: University of Illinois Press, 1960], p. 6). See note 71, this paper. On book and newspaper publication, see *Scientific American,* September 1972, pp. 38–41.

It has been suggested that "every revolutionary change in the means of communication is followed by a change in the entire structure of society" (Gilbert Seldes, *The New Mass Media: Challenge to a Free Society* [Washington, D.C.: Public Affairs Press, 1968], p. 9). See also McLuhan and Fiore, *Medium Is the Massage,* p. 8.

Consider, on the attractiveness of television in itself, Aristotle, *Nicomachaean Ethics,* 1171b31 ("... lovers find their greatest delight in seeing those they love, and prefer the gratification of the sense of sight to that of all the other senses, that sense being the chief seat and source of love ..."); Shakespeare, *Troilus and Cressida,* III, iii ("the eye itself, that most pure spirit of sense"; "things in motion sooner catch the eye than what not stirs"); Klapper, *The Effects of Mass Communication,* pp. 111–12.

See the Gyges episode in Herodotus' *History,* bk. 1: the sensible man know that rules (heard things) must restrain desires (things seen to be touchable) if communities are to protect men in the enjoyment of their own. (Is there not here the true origin of the wars between the Greeks and the Asians?) See also Sigmund Freud, *Civilization and Its Discontents* (New York: Norton, 1961), p. 46, note 1 (on the relation of "visual stimuli" to "sexual excitation"). Cf. Plato, *Banquet;* Ovid, *Metamorphoses,* 3:247–48; W. H. Auden, "Precious Five" ("True seeing is believing"). Cf., also, Hans Jonas, "The Nobility of Sight: A Study in the Phenomenology of the Senses," in *The Phenomenon of Life* (New York: Harper & Row, 1966), p. 135f; Shakespeare, *Antony and Cleopatra,* I, i, 12–14 ("Take but good note, and you shall see ... the triple pillar of the world transformed into a strumpet's fool. Behold and see.").

William Marcy (Boss) Tweed is reported to have said of Thomas Nast's cartoons, "I don't care a straw for your newspaper articles—my constituents don't know how to read; but they can't help seeing them damned pictures." *Chicago Sun-Times,* Nov. 11, 1972, p. 47. Cf. *Kaplan* v. *California,* 93 Sup. Ct. 2680 (1973).

[77] A former film director for the United States Information Agency has argued, "The camera is a liar. All those lenses, viewfinders, turrets, cranks and buttons have been made to preserve the visible on film or tape or for live transmission. But that assumes the visible is the truth. It's not. The invisible is the greatest truth" (*Congressional Record,* 118 [June 6, 1972]: E6009). Consider the U.P.I. photograph of two men in an Olympic pool at Munich, one of them with his arms upraised, which appeared in the newspapers of September 4, 1972. The *Chicago Sun-Times* (p. 74) had the cutline "Russia's Vladimir Bure is happy with second behind Mark Spitz (right),

It need not be denied that there are good programs from time to time on television, genuinely good things in addition to the many apparently good things to which large audiences are attracted.[78]

---

who earned sixth gold medal in 100 freestyle." The *Chicago Tribune* (p. 1) had for the identical photograph the cutline "Vladimir Bure, of the Soviet Union, raises arms angrily after Mark Spitz won his sixth Olympic gold medal, a record total..." The viewer cannot tell which cutline is correct: that is, the picture needs interpretation, if one is to be able to distinguish joy from anger. Cf. *Chicago Tribune,* September 12, 1972, sec. 1, p. 14, col. 6 (a correction of the *Tribune* cutline).

See Plato, *Republic* 507b–11e; Euripedes, *Hippolytos,* 1004–6; G. E. Lessing, *Laocoön.*

[78] There are good things as well about the *private* automobile—still another form of "mass medium"—but perhaps not so many as to outweigh the disastrous effect it has had upon the community and its social fabric. See notes 95, 101, 107, this paper.

See the opening lines of Aristotle's *Nicomachaean Ethics* and *Politics.* See also David M. White in *Mass Culture Revisited,* ed. Rosenberg and White, pp. 15–16: "I agree that today high culture is accessible, in fact more so than in any previous period of history. So why doesn't the average man avail himself of his ever-increasing leisure to study Bach's two-part inventions or attend lectures on the Postimpressionists at his local museum of fine arts? Why, in other words, does he choose to sit passively in front of the television set night after night? Why are the mass media so seductive of his hard-won leisure hours? Perhaps because the seductee is getting what he has always craved—a partial, palatable answer to the questions all men ask themselves, whether they are philosophers or coal-miners: Who am I, why am I here, what is the meaning of my life vis-à-vis the universe? Tough questions, seldom-come-to-grips-with questions, for most men, long before the mass media served them as an anodyne." Cf. notes 62, 82, 86, 89, 90, 96, 104, 112, this paper. Cf. also Plato, *Ion,* 535e.

Would the American people make far less use of television than they do if they came to recognize it only as a means of entertainment (and entertainment that obviously has no healthful exercise accompanying it)? That is, do we permit ourselves as much "entertainment" as we do through television partly because we can still tell ourselves that television contributes to education, to serious political discourse, and to the answering of "the questions all men ask themselves"? Thus Point 4 of the suggestions collected in Part VI of this paper may truly be central (because of the latent aspirations, as well as the residual respect for the "Puritan work ethic" of the American public) to a practical and yet profound reform of television at this time. See note 42, this paper.

Was not Thomas Becket wrong to believe it "the *greatest* treason" "to do the right deed for the wrong reason" (T. S. Eliot, *Murder in the Cathedral* [New York: Harcourt, Brace, 1935], p. 44)? (Italics added.) In everyday affairs, much is to be said for inducing men to do the right thing even when they do not understand (that is, even when they do not have *the* right reason). See *Federalist* no. 10; Plato, *Republic* 414b sq. Cf. ibid. 619b–e.

Nor need it be denied that television can seem a blessing to old people, to the ill, and to harassed mothers with young children. Other salutary effects can be catalogued: the promotion of an acceptance among us of racial justice because of the displays before national television audiences of attractive athletes, politicians, and actors who happen to be Negroes; the dramatization (sometimes even cathartic in effect) of national ceremonies, such as the inauguration or the funeral of a President; the presentation of intelligent men attempting to discuss serious problems of national concern. It has also been noticed that television does reveal the personalities of public figures, that it "takes the clothes off a man." The audience may well get an impression it might not otherwise have been able to get of what some public figures are like.[79]

[79] This was most dramatically obvious during the Army-McCarthy hearings of 1954: the Senator from Wisconsin exposed and destroyed himself politically before a national television audience and thus prepared the way for his senatorial censure. Cf. note 17, this paper. Cf. also Charles Bartlett's column, *Chicago Sun-Times,* August 4, 1972, p. 46: "In the Eagleton affair, the nation had a taste, more of a taste than it liked, of the media's capacity for inhumanity to man. [Thus, Senator Eagleton was asked on television], as he battled to save his career, why he trembled and perspired. . . . [The new mood of self-examination within the media, induced by Spiro Agnew] has not yet inspired the media to try to reclaim its largely missing attributes: good manners, a modicum of respect for the basic dignity of human beings, even public officials, and an occasional show of compassion. The media has to learn to avoid boorish behavior as it presses to the nub of an issue." For a serious assessment of Senator Eagleton's case, see Tom Braden's column, *Chicago Sun-Times,* August 16, 1972, p. 62. (Republicans who complain about the "malice" toward them of the press [see, e.g., notes 12, 65, and 116, this paper] should remember that it was also the press that developed the Eagleton issue, which proved so damaging to the Democrats in the 1972 campaign. That is, the press is a two-edged sword, which often finds it in its interest to cut *something.* See note 91, this paper, on Oedipus's two-edged talent.)

"If TV tends to 'personalize' politics, it is because it encourages viewers to scrutinize the motives of people who appear on the screen. These viewers focus less on what the *truth* is than on who can be *trusted.* Trusting in their own ability to know who can be trusted, they will accept policies they might otherwise oppose, so long as their advocate seems 'sincere' and 'honest' " (Kurt Lang and Gladys Engel Lang, *Politics and Television* [Chicago: Quadrangle Books, 1968], p. 308). Cf. note 89, this paper.

"Although David Butler considers that television usually shows those who appear on it 'in a fairly true light,' he has also described Harold Wilson (before the devaluation crisis) as: '. . . probably the ablest exploiter of tele-

And yet, are not the "good things" on television always an incidental part of the whole? Are not even the good uses to which television has been put due in large part to chance? The issues that capture public attention and get considerable "play" are all too often contrived or accidental. However adept television may be at exposing some public figures, the professional television personalities are themselves little more than animated masks so far as the viewing audience is concerned. Why this should be so depends, I suspect, on the very nature of the medium.

Among the inevitable effects of television—including effects of the technology itself, which are accentuated by the expense of television and its consequent need for large audiences—are distortion and superficiality. Television cannot help but cater to the worst in us, even when it is trying to do its best.[80] Certain things are made too easy for the audience; other things are made to appear easier than they really are. Shallow illusions are promoted, including the illusion that the viewer can learn enough from capsule presentations (a kind of discourse by headline) to get a serious notion of what is going on in the world and to be able to make responsible judgments and choices.[81] Television seems to liberate even while it really crip-

---

vision the country has yet produced. He can speak straight to camera with unmatched force and clarity conveying statesmanship and sincerity. . . . But the qualities of ingenuity and cunning which so impress those who deal closely with him, friend and foe alike, are totally absent from his television *persona*' " (Jay G. Blumler and Denis McQuail, *Television in Politics: Its Uses and Influence* [Chicago: University of Chicago Press, 1969], p. 117, n. 12). Cf. Anastaplo, *Constitutionalist,* pp. 789–90. See note 115, this paper.

Some would add, as an accomplishment of television, that it "brought home" the Vietnamese war to the American people. But others would question whether this was a good use of the medium. Are we not going to be permitted any war hereafter, simply because we cannot "stand" to watch it in our living rooms? The salutary or the useful (painful and bloody medical operations come to mind) may simply not be "viewable" by laymen. On the other hand, what is out of sight should not be out of mind; see notes 33 and 41, this paper.

[80] These criticisms, I should emphasize, do not depend ultimately upon who is running the television networks or upon whether they are commercial enterprises. See notes 74 and 106, this paper.

[81] For what "discourse by headlines" means in practice, see the television schedule reproduced in Anastaplo, *Constitutionalist,* pp. 555–56. See also Irving Kristol, "The Odd Distortions of TV News," *Wall Street Journal,*

ples—and it does this in so enticing a manner as to drive its competitors either out of the market or into suicidal imitation.

Thus, television creates the illusion that it has informed us and that we have "participated" in something we have witnessed "close up." It emphasizes that one must "get it" at once; one can't tarry to look at what has been broadcast, to take one's time studying what one may not understand. One must get it all *now,* for something else is coming soon. One is discouraged from looking back: everything is before us; recollection and reflection are discouraged or at least made very difficult. Is not all this more appropriate for entertainment than for serious discourse?[82]

November 16, 1972, p. 20; Clifford A. Ridley, "What Ails TV News," *National Observer,* April 21, 1973, p. 23.

We are told that 60 percent of our population now gets its news primarily from television. See notes 71 and 89, this paper. Cf. James Curran, "The Impact of Television on the Audience for National Newspapers," in *Media Sociology,* ed. Tunstall, pp. 104, pp. 107f, 129–30.

The producer of a nightly network news program is quoted as saying, "When I read statistics that show 60 percent of Americans get all or most of their news from television, I shudder. I know what we have to leave out" (Sterling Quinlan, "That Invincible Idiot Box," *Chicago Sun-Times,* June 11, 1972, "Showcase," p. 19). Cf. Timothy Green, *The Universal Eye: The World of Television* (New York: Stein & Day, 1972), p. 33: "The 60 percent of Americans who claim that television is their prime source of news are well served. Most of the major city stations run at least an hour of local or combined local and national news in the early evening and follow this with the half-hour network news at seven. . . ." See notes 74, 99, and 116, this paper.

[82] See Don Druker, "How to Watch Movies," in *University of Chicago Maroon: The Grey City Journal,* May 26, 1972, p. 15: "The important thing is that the film not drag; and thus I find most filmed plays unbearable. . . . Another way of stating the problem is to say that, generally, where dialogue overly dominates, the film suffers. For film is primarily visual. D. W. Griffith once stated: 'Above all, my task is to make you see.' " See notes 76 and 116, this paper.

"So broadcasters work under the obligation of being immediately understood, with no going back; and before an audience of greatly varying education and intelligence. For this reason the broadcaster has to be careful all the time that what he says should be simple; and for the television broadcaster it has to be picturable as well. This is the equipment that television brings to the reporting of politics. Politicians already have an urge to simplify: partly to be understood, partly to be persuasive, partly because they may not fully understand the issue themselves. Television abets them. One of the classic simplifications in British politics was the argument about nuclear

With the emphasis upon the immediate, appearance becomes very important: it is hard to pin things down. Is not almost everything about television ephemeral? If so, are not ephemeral qualities in the soul appealed to and legitimated?[83] The unreality of it all

---

defence. . . ." (Whale, *The Half-Shut Eye,* pp. 22–23). See note 115, this paper.

Cf. *Symposium on Human Rights and Mass Communications,* p. 21: "A newspaper calls for reflection and reasoning. The editor has arranged the layout as he sees it, chosen headlines in keeping with his interpretation of the news, set what seems important to him in heavy type; but the reader reacts as he pleases. He may look up and reflect, mentally correcting the choice of headlines. If an article interests him, he cuts it out, files it or asks people whose opinion he respects what they think of it." Cf. also ibid., pp. 22–23, 24–25; Weaver, *Ideas Have Consequences,* p. 102f; *Congressional Record,* 118 (June 30, 1972):E6605. But see Ezra Pound, *Instigations* (New York: Boni and Liveright, 1920), p. 246.

"Much is written comparing television and the press and their respective influence. The newspaper seems to be principally a medium of information, whereas television is a source of entertainment. . . ." (*Symposium on Human Rights,* p. 24). See also "Entertainment versus Public Issues," in Kalven, "Broadcasting, Public Policy, and the First Amendment," *Journal of Law and Economics,* 10:28f.

Not the least of difficulties in promoting serious discourse through television is that it is hard to retain a record of what has been said on the air: this remarkable harnessing of light generates "instant Dark Ages." Thus I have often the barest recollection of exactly what has been said on the three dozen or so radio and television programs I have been on. Audiences must be even worse off—and it is usually impossible, especially after a few years, to check archives. Indeed, I can sympathize with the *elderly* Russian who asked, upon being told in a Moscow park that Boris Spassky had lost the world chess championship, "How do you know he lost? Where is it written?" (*Chicago Sun-Times,* September 2, 1972, p. 6). Cf. *Congressional Record,* 115 (July 28, 1969):E6294; ibid., 116 (February 16, 1970):E935.

My critique of television, it should be noted, is as well a critique of mere experience: it is a commentary, in effect, on the inferior status of experience (as against ideas). Even so, the experience of the everyday world is more substantial and less misleading than the illusion of experience projected by television. Consider also the emphasis on polls and numbers, almost as a substitute for debates and ideas, found during the 1972 presidential campaign. See note 99, this paper.

[83] "TV makes for myopia. The young people who have experienced a decade of TV have naturally inbibed an urge toward involvement in depth that makes all the remote visualized goals of usual culture seem not only unreal but irrelevant, and not only irrelevant but anemic. It is the total involvement in all-inclusive *nowness* that occurs in young lives via TV's mosaic images. This change of attitude has nothing to do with programming in any way, and would be the same if the programs consisted entirely of the

is intensified by television's reduction of the visible world to a box that is smaller than the size of the human being: this can be both immediately enticing and eventually unpersuasive, if not even psychologically disturbing. The illusion of immediacy is fostered—an illusion that the press finds it more difficult to sustain—and then with the click of a switch the "real world" is gone. Thus reality is distorted, as it is with the unnaturalness in the amount and variety of things shown on television (as well as with the apparent intimate access to things that men are used to having, and keeping, at a distance).[84]

---

highest cultural content. The change in attitude by means of relating themselves to the mosaic TV image would occur in any event. It is, of course, our job not only to understand this change but to exploit it for pedagogical richness" (McLuhan, *Understanding Media,* p. 335). See note 75, this paper.

Television, some might argue, is no more ephemeral or insidious than the theater which was the highly regarded educator of the ancient Greeks. The ancient theater, however, gathered together in one place citizens who knew each other and who shared well-known traditions upon which their plays were based. These plays (in which dialogue, not the visual, was critical) were absorbed in company with others: one could not help but be affected by the responses of others. Playwright and performers knew immediately the responses of their public: an exchange could take place which informed and sustained everyone involved. (On political instruction and the Greek theater, see Laurence Berns, "Aristotle's *Poetics,*" in *Ancients and Moderns,* ed. Joseph Cropsey (New York: Basic Books, 1964). See note 106, this paper.

The movies are halfway between live plays and television. See note 95, this paper. Even so, both movies and television make too much of spectacle, that element of tragedy which can be most readily dispensed with. See Aristotle, *Poetics,* chap. 6. (On "action" and violence, see note 75, this paper.) How often *does* one see a movie that one would bother to read if "the same thing" (but without the spectacle, of course) were "said" in print? Consider how rare it is for a movie to be as good as the book on which it is based. See *Newsweek,* October 30, 1972, p. 108B (on David O. Selznick's resistance to "attempts to movie-ize" good books).

[84] See Anastaplo, *Constitutionalist,* pp. 546–47. See also Kurt Lang and Gladys Lang, "The Unique Perspective of Television and Its Effect," in *Mass Communications,* ed. Schramm, p. 544 (on "MacArthur Day in Chicago"); Green, *Universal Eye,* p. 192: "In Cairo, Egyptian broadcasters were equally frank. 'In Arab nations television is the sure way to rule people,' said one of the directors of the United Arab Republic's television service. 'This is how the people get to know and love their leader. Everywhere I go in the Arab world I tell the rulers, "Learn how to be loved by your people through that marvelous machine." Nasser himself,' he went on to point out, 'was not really known by our people until we had television. Before that they had only *heard* him' —he twigged his ear— 'on radio, but after 1960 everyone *saw* him.' "

The electronic media are voracious and insatiable. Consequently, they promote novelty. And novelty seems to fit in better with youthfulness, with those who are by nature always changing and experimenting. Consequently, a "culture" keyed to or shaped by the mass media is bound to be youth-oriented, an unnatural state of affairs for a community. Thus there is constant change—and a consequent profound dissatisfaction and rootlessness. Fashions become more important and character less. Since the visual is necessarily emphasized, the length of discourse that can be presented on television is much shorter than serious issues require, much less than what would be possible in a meeting hall. And yet most viewers *are* given the impression that television presents enough.[85]

The addictive effect of television is revealing: one turns it on; it stays on for hours. It is much less likely that this can happen, routinely, with reading. Even if one moves through a prosperous American suburb—that is, among those who have the material resources and the education to be able to do what they choose—one can see through almost every living room window the dominating television set turned on all evening as well as much of the day. Are our lives so empty as to be in need of such narcotics? Certainly television reinforces whatever sense of emptiness there may be in modern life.

We also can see the effects of television on the faces of our children. Observe them watching even the commercials with vacuous avidity. It is no wonder that many teenagers become jaded (if not even psychically disturbed), with nothing to challenge them, nothing to excite them but the most bizarre and the most violent. Of course, broadcasters do not do all this deliberately: in fact, just as they are really unknown to their audiences, so their audiences are unknown to them. Contact between broadcaster and audience is not really human, but rather mechanical, artificial, and fleeting. It is remarkable that broadcasters can stand the life they lead. Are they sustained only by what is said about them face-to-face, and now and then on the printed page?

[85] On the curtailment of political speeches, see Whale, *Half-Shut Eye,* pp. 34–35; Anastaplo, *Constitutionalist,* pp. 555, 790.

Far more important in making one an important public figure to be reckoned with is one's public image, not one's moral character or one's competence in dealing with serious problems. See note 17, this paper.

It is sometimes said that the young (and some of the old) today know much more about the world—how big and diverse it is, for example—than people did a generation ago. The mass media no doubt contribute to this sense of liberation: they do open up the world. But, because of the inefficiency of television—consider the amount of material that can be spoken as against what can be read in a given time—one simply cannot get much detail.[86] Our young —even the "educated" young—probably know less than any generation heretofore about what has gone before or about the serious questions to which men have always addressed themselves. Our young spread themselves over much more than did their predecessors, but much more thinly—and hence they cannot begin to know themselves. Yet they readily believe themselves to be more enlightened than their predecessors.[87]

[86] See *Symposium on Human Rights and Mass Communications,* p. 24; Stavins, ed., *Television Today,* pp. 71–73. Making television even more inefficient, especially for the study of serious things, is the fact that it places far too much emphasis upon process and the dramatic, not enough on detail and argument and self-discipline. Radio is, for all its faults, less of a problem in this respect: it need not immobilize the audience (although, it should be noted, some television viewers sometimes manage to do other things as well: in fact, the very inefficiency of television makes it possible to keep track of things with only sporadic attention); radio, because it is not visual, is more demanding and less hypnotic (and more stimulative of the imagination); and, as we shall see to be important, words rather than images are the key to radio's "message." See notes 66, 67, 92, this paper.

The television picture *seems* to add much more than it really does. I followed the 1972 National Democratic Convention on the old television set I reserve for such purposes—that is, a set on which only the sound works. (One effect of television's influence is to make it unprofitable for commercial radio to carry extended accounts from such meetings: one has to have recourse to television for "gavel-to-gavel" coverage.) I found that I could understand without the picture almost all that went on during those long nights. (For the effect of television on the national conventions, see the *New Yorker,* September 16, 1972, p. 114. See also notes 99 and 116, this paper.)

On television, process, and passivity, see McLuhan, *Understanding Media,* pp. 309–11, 328; McLuhan and Fiore, *Medium Is the Massage,* p. 125; Klapper, *Effects of Mass Communication,* pp. 110–11, 234f.

[87] What is the relation of the emergence of the mass media to the hopes of the Enlightenment? (See notes 5 and 96, this paper.) The culmination of the Enlightenment may be seen in the high-minded but politically questionable sentiments of Alexander Solzhenitzyn: "There are no internal affairs left on our crowded earth. And mankind's sole salvation lies in everyone making everything his business" (*Congressional Record,* 118 [October 13,

Television means that it is even more difficult than heretofore for reason to play an important role in assimilating and ordering the information that comes to people every day.[88] The pictures and sounds that dominate contemporary "culture" are not speeches: the stimuli of television may go from the passions of the televiser to the passions of the audience without lingering in the reason of either.

Once the need to speak well is reduced, the common language is likely to degenerate. The politician who once made weekly radio reports to his constituents finds, upon being *obliged* to switch to television because of what is happening all around him, that he cannot continue to be as idea-oriented as he had been on radio: he must move from dealing *somewhat* in ideas to "plugging" almost exclusively his name and picture (that is, his "image"). Thus the practical politician conforms to the demands and limits of the dominant communications medium of the moment—and the next generation is trained (or should we say "conditioned"?) accordingly.

Children, as well as adults, are discouraged by television from becoming practiced in reading.[89] Once television becomes available,

---

1972]:S18147). Cf. ibid., p. S18146, col. 2. See note 66, this paper. Cf. note 28, this paper.

For the effect of television on the young, see McLuhan and Fiore, *Medium Is the Massage,* p. 126; Rosenberg and White, *Mass Culture Revisited,* p. 20. See also notes 71, 75, 78, 102, 106, this paper.

[88] Consider the effects of popular music today, some of which is even recommended as having the capacity of "blowing your mind." Cf. Aristotle, *Nicomachaean Ethics,* 1118a2 sq.

[89] "Adams [a barrister] stared at the empty bookcase in the far corner of the room [in an English working-class house]. Books had disappeared in houses such as the one he was in. Television had swept them into limbo" (Jeffrey Ashford, *Counsel for the Defense* [New York: Harper & Row, 1960], p. 137). See also Leavis, *Fiction and the Reading Public,* p. 56. Cf. note 78, this paper.

Has not British television been drawing, for its celebrated historical and dramatic programs, upon a rich political and cultural heritage nurtured by years of considerable serious reading by those who shaped public opinion? See note 106, this paper.

A reading public is much more likely to be disciplined and moderate than a viewing audience. Perhaps, some might argue, people such as those who now rely so much on television *never* read much anyway. But who shaped them heretofore? Were not the influences upon them radically different before television? The teacher, preacher, and politician have been replaced by television personalities and hence by chance. (With chance more important, radical change is more likely; but such change is not likely to be

reading appears to most people even more laborious, even less attractive than it had been; the attention span is likely to be shortened for activities requiring deliberate effort; discipline is not encouraged for serious work—and this suggests that everyday passions are even more likely to make themselves felt than they have always been.[90] The general deterioration of serious reading ability will eventually lead to deterioration of the ability to write. And does not this mean the impairment of the ability to think seriously?

Despite what is said about television's ability to "take the clothes off a man," a man's television "image" is likely to be quite different from what the man is like. In fact, it may be virtually impossible for a man to be more than an image before the camera. But his written statements may be very much what he is. In fact, they may be essentially what he is, insofar as he is a thinking being.[91]

---

arrived at rationally.) Previously, citizens might have sensed they did not know, and they could conduct themselves accordingly, either by trying to learn or by respecting those who did seem to know. Now, personality is replacing both character and argument as the thing to be valued. See Leavis, *Fiction and the Reading Public,* pp. 82f, 308. See also notes 17, 71, 75, and 79, this paper.

[90] Is this related to the rise among us of obscenity? See Anastaplo, "Obscenity and Common Sense: Toward a Definition of 'Community' and 'Individuality,'" in *Toothing Stones: Rethinking the Political,* ed. Robert E. Meagher (Chicago: Swallow Press, 1972; reprinted, with additions, in *St. Louis University Law Journal,* 16 [1972]:527). See also David Lowenthal, "Obscenity and the Law," *Political Science Reviewer,* 2 (1972):242; note 104, this paper.

Has television made advertising even more important than it already was in American life, cheapening and degrading the word? See Richard M. Weaver, "The Best of Everything," in his *Life Without Prejudice* (Chicago: Regnery, 1965); Leavis, *Fiction and the Reading Public,* p. 274. See also Ron Powers, "A 'Giant Advertising Bludgeon' We Know as Television," *Chicago Sun-Times,* October 24, 1971, "Showcase," p. 22.

[91] Cf. Plato, *Seventh Letter,* 344c–d; *Phaedrus,* 275a–78a. But see Xenophon, *Memorabilia,* I, vi, 14. See also Laurence Sterne, *Tristram Shandy,* II, xi: "Writing, when properly managed (as you may be sure I think mine is), is but a different name for conversation. As no one, who knows what he is about in good company, would venture to talk all;—so no author, who understands the just boundaries of decorum and good-breeding, would presume to think all: The truest respect which you can pay to the reader's understanding, is to halve this matter amicably, and leave him something to imagine, in his turn, as well as yourself. For my own part, I am eternally paying him compliments of this kind, and do all that lies in my

Indeed, it can be said of the mass media that they promote an "education at once universal and superficial." We move inexorably "toward goals which are ill-defined and yet magnetic." We sometimes seem oblivious of "the enormous processes of collectivization which are at work among us."[92]

---

power to keep his imagination as busy as my own." See, e.g., Anastaplo, *Constitutionalist,* pp. 581, 786–87; notes 70, 94, and 99, this paper.

Is it desirable that television (or anything else) "take the clothes off a man"? What kind of public man would permit himself to be routinely "stripped"? Is it not natural for men to attempt to conceal their nakedness (if only behind an "image")? Is not Oedipus's shattering incest the culmination of his sometimes useful talent for solving riddles that baffle ordinary mortals? That is, Sophocles' Oedipus has a (god-given? natural? acquired?) talent, which has contributed to his success in Thebes, for exposing what is hidden to other men—and this, the observer is led to see, almost necessarily leads to his undoing. Or, put another way, Oedipus is good at uncovering things; but he lives long enough to discover that he has uncovered one thing too many. See Genesis 4:1; 19:8; 19:30–38. See also Anastaplo, *Constitutionalist,* pp. 783, 798. Does Oedipus ever appreciate how much a decent community depends for its stability on received—that is, fundamentally unexamined—opinion? See, e.g., notes 76 and 104, this paper.

See Jacob Klein, "Speech, Its Strength and Its Weaknesses," *The College* (St. John's College, Annapolis, Md.), July 1973, p. 1; Anastaplo, *Constitutionalist,* pp. 559–60, 723; Aristotle, *Poetics* 1460a12 (for a suggestion of the relation in language of the natural to the conventional).

[92] The three quotations in the text are from Winston Churchill, *Thoughts and Adventures* (London: Odhams Press, 1949), pp. 194, 195, 196. This 1932 essay ("Mass Effects in Modern Life") includes, on pp. 194–95, these observations: "Public opinion is formed and expressed by machinery. The newspapers do an immense amount of thinking for the average man and woman. In fact they supply them with such a continuous stream of standardized opinion, borne along upon an equally inexhaustible flood of news and sensation, collected from every part of the world every hour of the day, that there is neither the need nor the leisure for personal reflection. . . . We must not forget the enormous circulations at cheap prices of the greatest books of the world, which is a feature of modern life in civilized countries, and nowhere more than in the United States. But this great diffusion of knowledge, information and light reading of all kinds may, while it opens new pleasures to humanity and appreciably raises the general level of intelligence, be destructive of those conditions of personal stress and mental effort to which the masterpieces of the human mind are due." (See notes 73, 104, and 106, this paper.)

This essay by Churchill antedated the development of television, but it applies to television even better than to the press and radio. In fact, television has made radio look better than it is, just as television and radio have made the press look better than it may be. See notes 66 and 95, this paper.

On "public opinion," see pt. V, sec. ii, this paper.

iv

But, it should immediately be added, collectivization is not the same as community, just as ill-defined goals may not truly be goals at all. We turn now from considering primarily the effects of television on human beings to saying something more than could be said in Part IV of this paper about the effects of television on community and on the possibility of community.

Serious association with one another (whether for purposes of entertainment or of education or of worship or of politics or of sports) is undermined by television, especially since viewers and performers (or, as they once were, people and leaders) can make no serious contact with one another. Thus, for example, people who would once have been our political leaders tailor what they say, and eventually what they believe, to what can be "put across" on the television screen. The screen depends upon and encourages the wrong kind of simplification: no matter how complicated the subject presented may really be, it is all too often pretended (perhaps it is sincerely believed) that it can be adequately dealt with, as if magically, in a few minutes.

May not the frequent public protests in this country against the partisanship of the mass media be crude reflections of a deeper, perhaps instinctive concern among us about what is being done to the human soul by the mass media?[93] And yet it is also felt that

[93] It is difficult for us to stand aside and observe the effects among us of television. The effects of television on one's country may be easier to appreciate when most programs come from abroad. Thus the effects of American television on, say, Canada are not only quite evident in that country but also a matter there of continuing public concern. It is not only that entertainment is affected, but the very manner of life is apt to be profoundly affected as well.

On Canada, see Henry Comor, "American TV: What Have You Done to Us?" in *Broadcasting and the Public Interest,* ed. John H. Pennybacker and Waldo W. Braden (New York: Random House, 1969), p. 83; Green, *Universal Eye,* p. 43. On television and Israel, see Green, *Universal Eye,* p. 17; Rosenberg and White, *Mass Culture Revisited,* p. 17. On television surmounting the Berlin Wall, see Green, *Universal Eye,* p. 178; Tunstall, *Media Sociology,* p. 252. On television and the Japanese, see Green, *Universal Eye,* pp. 9–10, 218.

In Greece the recent rapid expansion of both television and tourism, both of which undermine "the old way," can be expected to undermine as well (or at least to moderate the effects of) the colonels' tyranny. On Greece

something like television is needed for an aggregate as large as the United States has become. It is, some might even say, a necessary evil to remedy an even worse one, the divisiveness of bigness.[94]

Television does bring us all together, in a way, but too many at a time and at too low a level. In the process it breaks down smaller communities that, until its coming, had still been viable (despite the onslaughts of the automobile and of the Second World War). Thus the isolation of people (whether the elderly or the infirm or the housewife), which is intensified if not induced by the disruption of our towns and urban neighborhoods, seems to lead to a "need" for television.[95]

---

today, see Anastaplo, *Constitutionalist,* p. 564; *Congressional Record,* 118 (January 24, 1972):S333; ibid. (September 27, 1972):E8149; ibid. (October 17, 1972):E8811; *St. Louis Post-Dispatch,* July 29, 1973, p. 2D (letter to the editor); *Christian Science Monitor,* August 1, 1973, p. 16 (letter to the editor); *New York Times,* December 7, 1973, p. 40 (letter to the editor).

[94] Cf. *Federalist* no. 10; Green, *Universal Eye,* p. 44 (on broadcasting in Canada assuming "great importance as a lifeline holding the nation together").

Mr. Agnew's criticisms of the mass media have not been directed as much to the intrinsic effects of television as to its alleged partisanship. See, e.g., *Congressional Record,* 118 (May 1, 1972):S7002 (notes 70 and 91, this paper). Cf. Peter McGrath, "Why McGovern Can't Win," *Chicago Journalism Review,* July 1972, p. 12. Cf. also Leo Strauss, *Natural Right and History* (Chicago: University of Chicago Press, 1953), p. 35 (on the supposed distinction between facts and values). Is it not a mistaken notion of the meaning of "objectivity" that leads journalists to fail to recognize or to report as salutary or reprehensible that which may indeed be salutary or reprehensible? See notes 69 and 77, this paper. See also notes 65 and 68, this paper.

[95] Television ratifies and intensifies a development that had been evident before (see, e.g., Leavis, *Fiction and the Reading Public;* Weaver, *Ideas Have Consequences*) and which had been reflected in and caused by our high rate of mobility, by our steadily increasing recourse to urban apartment living, and by the consequent general disintegration of the "extended family." It should be remembered, however, that radio *can* supply, but in a somewhat less insidious way, the "need" served by television. See notes 66 and 92, this paper.

Cable television, which promises us dozens of channels to choose among, will not really help matters, except perhaps to help dispel the illusion that television does bind us together in a "global village." (On "the new electronic interdependence," see McLuhan and Fiore, *Medium Is the Massage,* p. 95.) Cf. William F. Buckley, Jr., "Survey of Leisure Activity Bolsters Case for Pay-TV," *Chicago Daily News,* Aug. 16, 1973, p. 10.

The movies, with all their traumatic effects for modern man, do have

Some, however, see the American people, in tens of millions, elevated politically and culturally by the mass media. Such elevation, others reply, is not good for these millions: they cannot become truly enlightened; they are much more likely to become frustrated. Most people, it seems to me, have *not* been elevated; rather, their cultural life (as well as their politics) has become inferior to what it had been, and their thinking less disciplined and more sentimental than it need be. If they are frustrated, it is perhaps because they have acquired a sophistication that their circumstances cannot permit them to enjoy—and the old loyalties and the consequent simple pleasures have been undermined. All the while their precious linguistic inheritance is being cheapened.[96]

The easy intrusion of television into our lives undermines what friendship and influence should really mean. Appearance becomes even more important than it had been. It is my impression that

---

the advantage of requiring audiences to assemble periodically. In the movie house there is a kind of community and hence some effort at sharing: one sees and hears others and is likely to be guided and restrained by their responses. (Consider the man who "laughs at the wrong places.") At least, movie houses take us out of our private caves into some kind of association. See Plato, *Republic,* 514 sq. See also George Wead, "Movies, Art, Popcorn Pleasure," *Chicago Sun-Times,* August 19, 1973, "Midwest Magazine," p. 14; note 83, this paper.

Movie houses are to television reception somewhat as railroad stations are to airports: railroad stations are in and of the city, whereas airports are artificial satellites of the city, a kind of suburb for transients. A comparison may be made as well between our older roads and the new interstate expressways: many more people are on the highways today, but they have (unless they are so fortunate as to suffer a breakdown) less contact with each other or with the people of the regions through which they pass than was formerly the case. (On the bridle of Theages, see Plato, *Republic,* 496a–b.)

[96] For the arguments of articulate apostles of the Enlightenment, see Edward A. Shils, *The Intellectuals and the Power and Other Essays* (Chicago: University of Chicago Press, 1972), p. 248; McLuhan, *Understanding Media,* pp. 314–15, 322–25. But see Leo Strauss, "What Is Liberal Education?," in his *Liberalism Ancient and Modern* (New York: Basic Books, 1968); Willa Muir, *Living with Ballads* (London: Hogarth Press, 1965). See also notes 5, 78, 87, 115, this paper; Leavis, *Fiction and the Reading Public,* p. 235: ". . . the general reading public of the twentieth century is no longer in touch with the best literature of its own day or of the past. . . . It is almost impossible for the novel which is an aesthetic experience to become popular, and, on the other hand, popular fiction cannot now contain, even unwittingly, the qualities which have made the work of Defoe, Dickens, and Smollett something more than popular fiction."

television fits better with an emphasis upon presidential rather than congressional or state politics.[97] A kind of rule by television plebiscite seems to be evolving among us, a rule that would be peculiarly responsive to the volatile mass taste that television promotes and serves.[98] The constitutional tendency of television—of the way of life that permits and is in turn shaped by television—is to unleash desires and expectations that undermine the moderation of tradition, the restraints both of diversity and of a genuine respect for quality, and the requirements and advantages of federalism.

We can sum up this social indictment of television in the following words: Each of us is constantly addressed by television apart from the others, and yet none of us is ever really spoken to. The ability to read, and hence to think and to join in serious common discourse, suffers. Every kind of association is filtered through the camera and stripped of its humanity. The community is depreciated while a hollow privacy is emphasized; communal tastes are reduced to the lowest common denominator and catered to. Spectacle replaces theater; feeling replaces thought; image replaces character. The world of television—the world shaped by television—is an

[97] "[H]is proven vote-getting power is less important to a would-be Prime Minister [in Great Britain] than to a presidential aspirant [in the United States]. Instead, political advancement depends very much on an individual's standing with his parliamentary colleagues. Some observers believe, however, that the arrival of television on the political scene has helped to change the situation. They consider that the office of the Prime Minister is steadily evolving towards the presidential model, and that television enables a confident user of the medium to base his authority on a favorable public image. It is also suggested that in general television is strengthening the influence of personality factors in British politics...." (Blumler and McQuail, *Television in Politics,* p. xv). Cf. note 115, this paper.

[98] See Whale, *Half-Shut Eye,* p. 42. Cf. David Riesman and Reuel Denney, "Do the Mass Media 'Escape' from Politics?," in *Reader in Public Opinion and Communication,* ed. Bernard Berelson and Morris Janowitz (Glencoe, Ill.: Free Press, 1950), p. 327.

Contributing to whatever heightened volatility there may be in American life today is what is happening to what had been a fairly stable set of religious opinions among us. The media have, it seems to me, helped take the awe out of modern religious life. See note 73, this paper. See also Rhodes, *Mass Communications and the Spirit of Man,* pp. 29–30; Anastaplo, *Constitutionalist,* pp. 611–12; Joseph Cropsey, "The Human Vision of Rousseau: Reflections on *Emile*" (1973 Annual Meeting of the American Political Science Association); Laurence Berns, "Gratitude, Nature, and Piety in *King Lear,*" *Interpretation,* 3 (1972):27.

empty one, starved and frenetic, dreamlike and debilitating. It can be expected to culminate eventually in mediocrity and perhaps even in tyranny.[99]

[99] See Anastaplo, *Constitutionalist,* p. 815, for discussions of Martin Heidegger. See also note 70, this paper. Consider as well Friedrich Nietzsche's "last man" and his "blinking" (*Thus Spake Zarathustra,* Prologue, v).

But whatever may happen eventually to us, we already have the transformation of our political life implied in the report that a candidate for the presidency (in this case Senator McGovern) was cheered by "clerks and secretaries [in Hartford, Connecticut] as though he were a movie celebrity" (*Chicago Sun-Times,* October 31, 1972, pp. 1, 5). Cf. "Show Biz in Politics," *Newsweek,* September 25, 1972, p. 34.

Theodore H. White observed of the 1972 presidential campaign, "It is being done in terms of visual things. Fine for TV, but it robs the campaign of intellectual coherence and people say, 'What is McGovern all about?' Campaigning now is less strenuous physically, but more difficult intellectually. How do you break through on the American mind? Ideas are lacking right now. It is an almost desolate intellectual wasteland in which we are conducting this campaign" (*Chicago Sun-Times,* October 13, 1972, p. 52). See notes 82 and 115, this paper.

Richard M. Nixon has said of his 1960 presidential campaign, "Some object that when two candidates confront each other on television, one may have an unfair advantage—if only because some people look better on television than others do. I certainly can sympathize with this objection. I will never forget my frustration after my first debate with Senator Kennedy, when I learned how arbitrary factors of this sort had affected the result. I had left the studio confident that I had driven across my arguments and successfully met my opponent's. Polls later indicated that a majority of those who heard us on radio or read the debate in the newspapers felt that Nixon had outscored Kennedy. But of those who saw the debate on television, a solid majority felt Kennedy had won. What irritated me was that while I had put all my emphasis on content, the thing that influenced the television audience was my appearance. I suppose I should have anticipated that I might look worn and washed-out on camera. Laid up for two weeks with a serious knee infection, I had left the hospital four or five days before my doctor wanted me to and embarked on two weeks of intensive campaigning. . . . I was so intent on the battle that I never stopped to think about how I looked. I have always detested makeup [and so did not use it on this occasion]. . . . After the program, as the unfavorable reports on my appearance began to come in, I changed my attitude. TV experts explained that makeup for television is not the same thing as makeup for the stage. Its purpose is not to make a person look better than he really does but to correct for unnatural effects produced by the TV cameras. So for the other debates we got the best TV makeup people we could find. . . ." (Richard M. Nixon, "L.B.J. Should Debate on TV," *Saturday Evening Post,* June 27, 1964; reprinted in *Congressional Record,* 118 [September 27, 1972]:H8830). Cf. Tom Littlewood, "Nixon Campaign: Masterpiece of Public Relations," *Chicago Sun-Times,* October 22, 1972, p. 8.

V

It is indeed curious that such innovations—another recent one with remarkable unanticipated consequences (both good and bad) has been air conditioning—should be permitted among us without serious authoritative consideration of what they may do to our way of life. But then, we are all too often inclined to take our way of life for granted, as if there should be no conditions for its existence or, for that matter, any transcendent standards and purposes to which it is dedicated. Perhaps we see the only thing necessary to our way of life to be an openness to constant change and hence experimentation.[100]

Human beings may, by their nature, seek newfangledness.[101] We do seem to have an "unbounded passion for variety."[102] Is there

[100] But one should not speak even of "experimentation," for that is to assume a permanent standard by which experiments are to be guided and to be assessed. Self-gratification seems to be emphasized unduly. Is this not the most likely way most people will interpret "pursuit of happiness"? Compare the state of opinion when "the common good" is spoken of instead.

As for taking our way of life for granted: the *Federalist* also virtually ignores the problem of educating the citizen body. Thus Leo Paul de Alvarez writes, in his review of Willmoore Kendall's *Contra Mundum*, "Where, for example, *The Federalist* says almost nothing about virtue in the sense of shaping men's character into a certain habit of soul, Kendall makes the shaping of character central to the American experience. And again, where *The Federalist* deliberately seeks to weaken the influence of local communities upon the people, Kendall emphasizes the importance of local communities as the main agents in the formation of the character of the people" (*National Review*, August 24, 1971, p. 936). See also note 66, this paper.

[101] Geoffrey Chaucer, *The Canterbury Tales* (Baltimore: Penguin Books, 1959), p. 421. See also Leavis, *Fiction and the Reading Public*, p. 39: "Cf. the shrinking of social life in one generation caused by the changes that have replaced the axiom, 'No nice girl dances more than twice in one evening with the same man,' by the regular dancing-partner, evenings at home round the piano when friends dropped in to sing and dance, providing their own entertainment, by evenings at the dance-hall and the cinema, neighbourly informal visiting, by whist-drives and bridge-parties and telephone calls, and the close contacts of religious interests by Sundays out in the car. The car has replaced the piano as the sign of social status."

[102] Edward Gibbon, *The Decline and Fall of the Roman Empire* (New York: Modern Library, Random House, n.d.), I, 74.

The not unnatural "passion for variety" (see Plato, *Phaedo* 60A–C) seems to be exploited in the much-praised children's program *Sesame Street*. This seems to be one reason why the mistake is made of presenting learning

not, in such openness to novelty, a constant challenge to piety, to what should be worthy of reverence? Certainly there is a challenge to the established way with respect to both opinions and conduct. When a feverish taste for novelty is legitimated among a people, even a good community can become suspect merely because it has been so well-constituted as to survive and become old.[103]

I do not believe that most of the harmful effects of television can be avoided so long as we have it.[104] Some of television's more

---

as episodic and "fun," rather than as something that often requires painful effort and prolonged application in order to achieve worthwhile results. A certain facility may be promoted by such programs, even as they cater to the limited attention span for which television is in part responsible. Indeed, television generally discourages extended and consecutive thinking, displaying a rapid succession of scenes that have no causal connection with one another, thereby distorting our rational sense and perhaps endangering our psychic health. (See note 106, this paper.) Such a hit-and-run, as well as hit-and-miss, approach may make us even more susceptible to fads and to transient passions than democrats have always tended to be. See Anastaplo, *Constitutionalist,* p. 779; also Plato, *Gorgias,* 501e sq.; note 75, this paper.

[103] See the opening of Plato's *Euthyphro.* Compare a government policy, such as that among the Japanese prior to the nineteenth century, against "the making or designing of new things" (Akira Kukimoto, *Summary of Japanese Patent Law* [Tokyo: Japanese Group of AIPPI, 1971], pp. 3–4). Compare also the civic screening of inventions in Francis Bacon's *New Atlantis.*

See also Ovid, *Metaporphoses,* I, 89f ("Golden was that first age, which, with no one to compel, without a law, of its own will, kept faith and did the right. . . . Nor yet had the pine-tree, felled on its native mountains, descended thence into the watery plain to visit other lands; men knew no shores except their own").

[104] Our carelessness and even thoughtlessness with respect to these matters are dramatically evident today in the fashionable attitude toward obscenity. It seems to be generally assumed, at least among intellectuals, that we need not consider seriously what contributes to or what makes difficult the development and preservation of the good citizen and the good community. See Anastaplo, *Constitutionalist,* pp. 735–36; tributes by Leo Paul de Alvarez and others to Mertha Fulkerson, *Congressional Record,* 117 (December 14, 1971):H12556; note 90, this paper.

Cf. Tom Littlewood, "Nixon Gives Advice to Taxpayers," *Chicago Sun-Times,* October 22, 1972, p. 28: "President Nixon told the people Saturday to stop feeling guilty about wanting to keep as much of their paychecks as they can instead of paying for more social-improvement programs that are directed at a minority of the public. . . . Rejecting the notion of 'a leadership class,' Mr. Nixon said 'the advantage of a superior education should result in a deep respect for, and never contempt for, the value judgments of the average person.' He explained that he would take unpopular

obvious abuses can perhaps be ameliorated from time to time. But the intrinsic character of this electronic possession is such as to have profound effects on fundamental relations among us—between man and man, between community and human being, between lover and beloved.[105] In short, television is, in both its means and its inevitable consequences, simply unnatural and remarkably corrupting.[106]

---

stands when necessary, but never on matters involving how people 'should live their lives . . . involving the values of the people themselves.' " See notes 33, 62, 78, and 92, this paper.

See also, on widespread sensuality and its social effects, J. A. Symonds, *Studies of the Greek Poets,* 3rd ed. (London: Adam & Charles Black, 1902), 1:290–91. "[T]his was the flower-time of the Aeolians, their brief and brilliant spring. But the fruit it bore was bitter and rotten. Lesbos became a byword for corruption"; Catullus, *Poems,* no. 51.

[105] Even the small towns of the country are affected by this development, with the television industry exporting to them both the tired sophistication and the desperate aimlessness of our large and lonely cities. "[A London actor] says television separates people and is a factor in spreading loneliness, which he says is Britain's 'greatest single illness' " (*Chicago Tribune,* July 5, 1972, sec. 2A, p. 1). Cf. Michael Young and Peter Willmott, *Family and Kinship in East London* (Baltimore: Penguin Books, 1962); note 70, this paper.

[106] Being *un*natural, it has, strictly speaking, no ends? Does the money-making "art" govern? Even public-spirited broadcast networks, such as the BBC, must draw large audiences to justify politically the costs of television. (See notes 52, 74, and 75, this paper.) At what level, then, must one operate to secure large audiences consistently? Notice that the BBC must set limits upon the amount of American programming that it will use: if the British public should get what it "wants," BBC programs would deteriorate quickly enough. "The 'battle of the ratings'—using various systems of measuring the audience—is as violent in Britain as it is here" (Seldes, *New Mass Media,* p. 83). See Hugh Greene, "The Future of Broadcasting in Britain," *New Statesman,* October 20, 1972, p. 549.

For a challenge to most of the criticisms of the effects of television on children, see Hilde Himmelweit, "Television and the Child," in Bernard Berelson and Morris Janowitz, *Reader in Public Opinion and Communication,* 2nd ed. (New York: Free Press, Macmillan, 1966), p. 418. Cf. Eugene David Glynn, "Television and the American Character: A Psychiatrist Looks at Television," in *Television's Impact on American Culture,* ed. William Y. Elliott (East Lansing: Michigan State University Press, 1956), pp. 175, 180: "How lulling television can be has been widely observed. Most homes soon give in to the temptation of using television to keep the children quiet and out of mischief. It does this, but in a way much different from playing games. Marriage after marriage is preserved by keeping it drugged on television: television is used quite consistently to prevent quarreling from breaking out by keeping people apart. This points up a somewhat less obvious side

It is obvious—or at least it has long seemed obvious to me—that the television industry should be abolished completely in this country, that nothing short of this can remove its crippling influence from American life. If this is indeed a society open to experimentation, then let us deliberately experiment for at least a decade with the remedy of complete suppression of television.

If television should be abolished, we would be obliged to go out again into our streets (if only to attend more movies). Local entertainment, local gatherings (religious as well as secular), and even genuine popular culture might become more important again. Even more important, the intrinsically harmful influence of television would no longer have to be contended with.

Is it not revealing that something so harmful as television should have become so entrenched so soon? It is like certain weeds that happen to be blown in by the wind. Its abolition today is, of course, virtually unthinkable; and yet we did not really have it at all a generation ago, however natural it may now seem to most of us.

---

of watching television: its schizoid-fostering aspects. Television seems to be a social activity, an activity performed by many people together. Actually, though, it smothers contact, really inhibiting interpersonal exchange. A group watching television is frequently a group of isolated people, not in real exchange at all. . . . The complaint is common enough today that social visiting has lost its social, conversational, engaged side." Cf. also note 83, this paper. See Klapper, *Effects of Mass Communication,* p. 206f.

I have observed, no matter what time of day I have visited the psychiatric wards of hospitals, that the television set is always on. "It is," one patient explained to me, "almost like another person whom we cannot do without." See note 72, this paper.

Is not the best in us, as well as the worst, suppressed (or at least muted) by television? See note 92, this paper. Consider the implications of the following observation: "*Your Show of Shows* [with Sid Caesar, Imogene Coca, Carl Reiner and Howard Morris] belongs to the fabled Golden Age of Television. . . . Funny and inventive as [it] was, it struck an ominous note for the future of television comedy. The savage appetite of the medium for fresh material and the agonizing strain that the program put upon even these four gifted comics meant that, no matter how fresh and original *Your Show of Shows* was, it couldn't last long. Just the routines selected for [a recent retrospective] film might have carried any one of the stars through a lifetime of performing on the vaudeville or nightclub circuit; as it was, the creative strain finally proved too much and the show went off the air in 1954." Don Druker, "The Golden Age of Television," *Chicago Reader,* April 2c, 1973, p. 5. Consider also Edmund Wilson, *Upstate* (New York: Farrar, Straus and Geroux, 1971), pp. 385–86.

If we moved against television, we would reassert ourselves as a community even as we acted together on behalf of communal interests. That is, we would show we care about what affects us, thereby again becoming a community. We would show as well that we recognize that mere desires should not govern our lives, that temperance is vital to enduring happiness.

But, it may be objected, if we should abolish television, that would open the door to further infringements of our liberty: there might be attempted public interference thereafter with other activities among us which also aim at self-expression and self-gratification. This objection is not groundless. Would we not be obliged to consider, upon the abolition of television, what else needs to be remedied? After all, modern industrial society was far from perfect before television took root among us.[107]

vi

Thus I believe it salutary to argue that there should be, in ordinary constitutional circumstances, both an absolute prohibition against previous legal restraints of the press and an absolute previous restraint (that is, total abolition) of the television industry. We want the press a certain way because of the nature of our regime—and the considerations that lead to an advocacy of extensive guarantees for the press may lead as well to an advocacy of complete suppression of television.

I see in the abolition of television no serious First Amendment problem.[108] Rather than abridge the "freedom of speech" guaranteed

[107] The press *is* a problem. See, e.g., the Churchill essay quoted in note 92, this paper. See also note 78, this paper.

We might experiment, for instance, with the abolition of all private motorized traffic (including snowmobiles and motor boats) north of Sturgeon Bay in Door County, Wisconsin. (See the Mertha Fulkerson tributes cited in note 104, this paper.) Cf. Edmund Wilson, *Upstate,* p. 377f.

"That is, we are obliged to return again and again to what may be for us on this occasion the key question: 'What *is* it legitimate for the community to be concerned about?' " Anastaplo, "Obscenity and Common Sense," *St. Louis University Law Journal,* 16:552, note 25. See note 4, this paper.

[108] There would be serious First Amendment problems, however, if the government should try to determine the political content of what is shown on television. President De Gaulle's control and use of television, to say nothing of the Russians', would raise quite serious First Amendment questions

by the First Amendment, the abolition of television (and hence a radical reform of the mass media) would enlarge freedom of speech among us.[109] Television interferes, I have argued, with serious general education in a country such as ours: it affects the ability to read, and hence the ability to think and the very status of thought among us, playing up as it does to the passions. Thus abolition of television would probably contribute *among us* to the preservation of self-government and hence genuine freedom.[110]

Such abolition, it should be noticed, need not bring with it the problems of widespread attempted evasions, with all their attendant evils, which we have known from time to time with respect to prohibitions upon alcohol and narcotics and obscenity. (That is, abolition should be fairly easy to effect *once the community decides to do it.*) Nor must we accommodate to television as we must to the presence in the world of atomic weapons. We may be obliged to make efforts to neutralize the possession by others of atomic weaponry, for we can be critically affected by their behavior. But this is not the case with television: if people in other countries are corrupted by television, that is no reason why we should be also.

It should be noticed that the major cost of the abolition of television would be borne not by the broadcasters but by those who would benefit most of all from such abolition, the millions of

---

in this country. See Marvin Barrett, ed., *Survey of Broadcast Journalism 1970–1971: A State of Siege* (New York: Grosset & Dunlap, 1971), p. 32. On De Gaulle and television, see Whale, *Half-Shut Eye,* pp. 129–31; Green, *Universal Eye,* p. 116. On Castro and television, see ibid., pp. 54–55; *Symposium on Human Rights and Mass Communications,* p. 75. "While American television is primarily in the business of selling goods, Russian television's concern is promoting socialist achievement" (Green, *Universal Eye,* p. 155). See also *Congressional Record,* 118 (September 12, 1972):E7843; ibid. (October 10, 1972):S17288; note 3, this paper.

[109] If a serious constitutional problem should be thought to exist, then a constitutional amendment could empower Congress *and* the states to abolish television. ("Local option" with respect to these matters is technically feasible and would be healthy. See note 66, this paper.) But we hardly need to concern ourselves with such constitutional problems on this occasion. See note 4, this paper.

[110] I stress "among us" since it would be doctrinaire to insist that television may not have a salutary, even civilizing, effect on certain peoples. Neither freedom nor virtue is a "product of every clime." See note 10, this paper.

owners of private television receivers: the aggregate cost of private receivers is far larger than that of all the capital invested by broadcasters.[111] If the largest single source of television revenue (that is, cigarette advertising) can properly be eliminated in what is thought to be the public interest, then there is no reason in principle why all television advertising cannot be eliminated in the public interest or, to go one step further, all television.

Or are we to assume that there is such a thing as physical health, but no such thing as moral character and social health, as legitimate for the community to protect and to promote?

VI

We are, of course, no more likely to abolish television (and to purge the public and the press of its corrupting influences) than we are to curtail radically the private use of the automobile.[112]

[111] Stavins, ed., *Television Today,* p. 56 ("The value of the sets outstanding in the nation's homes exceeds the costs of station-owners' plant and equipment by a factor of at least 20 to 1"); Ferry and Ashmore, *Mass Communications,* p. 30 ("Viewers have a total investment of $27,500,000,000 in their receiving sets, and the networks and stations have invested $800,000,000 in transmitting equipment").

Broadcasters *could* be compensated for their loss if television should be abolished; or the curtailment of television could be phased, permitting broadcasters to recoup most of their investment in the process. The high rate of return available to broadcasters should permit any period of phased curtailment to be fairly short. (A British advocate of commercial television has admitted, "A television license is a license to print money" [Green, *Universal Eye,* p. 84].) In addition, the talented and sensitive men enmeshed in the toils of the television industry would be released for less questionable endeavors; that is, they too would be benefited by abolition of this new slavery. See Plato, *Republic,* 516c–d.

[112] After all, the desires of man are old. See Plato, *Republic,* 419. It is difficult for a people, once they become aware of the *availability* of infinite diversions, to disavow recourse to the "variety of attempts to intensify and enjoy the motions of the soul." See Anastaplo, "Obscenity and Common Sense," p. 555.

Still, there is some value in the espousal of lost causes and impossible loyalties. See Weaver, *Life Without Prejudice,* p. 138. See also Tacitus, *Dialogue on Oratory,* 39 ("What I am going to say will perhaps seem trivial or absurd, but I shall say it anyway, even if only that it may be laughed at"); Charles Dickens, *Christmas Carol* (London: King Penguin Books, 1946), p. 137 ("Some people laughed to see the alteration in [Scrooge], but he let them laugh, and little heeded them; for he was wise enough to know that nothing ever happened on this globe, for good, at which some people did not have their fill of laughter at the outset . . ."); notes 4 and 67, this paper. See also, Plato, *Gorgias,* 494a sq.

I recognize that I have been talking, in effect, about the constant need to review the consequences of our technological development. Is television an essentially derivative manifestation of this overall development? Do I attack merely a symptom? Perhaps such an attack can be so put as to illuminate the underlying problems, thereby provoking serious discussion of what we are (and are not) doing and why. To ask as I have for the abolition of television may do no more than to remind ourselves, in a pedagogically useful manner, that the common good should take precedence over private gratification.

One can see in the role of television among us a powerful industry in the thoughtless (and virtually inevitable) service of the passions. *Mutual exploitation as well as unthinking toleration becomes the order of the day.* It is not incidental that spectacular rewards or influence seems to some to be available through television. This makes it even more difficult for us as a people to do what is necessary to conserve what we can of the old way, to resume humane, local, and deliberate control of what instructs and entertains us and hence forms our character and our institutions.

All this may be no more than to say that the way of life brought forth on this continent two centuries ago is in the course of profound alteration, that we have become unable to understand and control what is happening to us. That is, all this should remind us of the vulnerability of reason in the conduct of human affairs, of how difficult it is for any people truly to govern itself.

To govern oneself does mean that one must accommodate oneself to circumstances, that one must make do with what happens to be available, and that one must be prepared to settle for less than the very best. What *can* be done about television, short of the total abolition I have advocated? Various reforms, which reflect some of the criticisms I have made in this paper, can be attempted. I collect here (as illustrative of how one may begin to think about reforms) a half-dozen suggestions:

1. There should be a curtailment in the amount of television available daily. It would be good *not* to have continuous television, but only a couple of hours of transmission at a time, followed by an extended intermission during which there is no local transmission

at all. It would also be good to have certain evenings of the week, and perhaps most of (if not all) of Sunday, completely free from television (as well as from most other commercial activity). In any event, the total number of hours of transmission each week should be markedly reduced.

2. The commercial influence upon television in this country should be reduced. It would be good to experiment with the means by which British commercial television has ensured that there be no identification of advertisers with particular programs.

3. What is the relation between television's pervasive commercialism and its national programming? Whatever it may be, there is much to be said for encouraging local programming, thereby emphasizing the importance of the local (that is, the real?) community. (We should expect, with more local programming, a decline in the professional quality of programs, at least until local talent begins to assert itself.)

4. The immediate effect of television on our political life should be eliminated if we are to be left free and equipped to assess such things as television upon that way of life. Should not television be explicitly reserved for entertainment purposes, leaving the discussion of politics to more appropriate forums? It would probably be good to permit no political activity at all on television. Perhaps, indeed, all news broadcasts (except for emergency announcements) should be eliminated or should be confined to extended readings from newspaper columns.

5. If there is to be politics on television, the emphasis should be on lengthy talks and extended civic proceedings. It would probably be prudent to reconsider the "fairness doctrine," for that may provide an overly zealous administration in Washington too great an opportunity to control the political discourse of the country. Insofar as television *is* permitted to provide a forum for political discourse, it is good for us that it should be able to rely on First Amendment privileges.

6. The nonpolitical content of television, with a view to the effects on viewers of such things as the portrayals of violence and the legitimation of greed, should be periodically assessed by public counselors who recognize that the virtues, vices, and accomplish-

ments of human beings are not without causes.[113] In addition, there should be on television considerable instruction in reading and a number of hours each week during which the picture is accompanied only by well-written subtitles and good music, not by talk. It should be routinely emphasized on the screen that the viewer must supplement by extended reading and discussion what he sees on television, if he is to understand the matters under consideration.

7. It should go without saying that any family (or neighborhood) which "deprives" itself of television is likely to be better off than those families (or neighborhoods) addicted to it.[114] Indeed, it may even become generally apparent someday—perhaps even in time to make a difference—that the many who are saddled with television are being exploited by the few who profit from it and that the exploited are so deluded as to "choose" this form of self-enslavement. It may then become generally apparent, that is, that any community respectful of its integrity or concerned about the underprivileged should abolish television root and branch.[115]

[113] See Plato, *Meno; Republic,* 427a–c. See also Aristotle, *Nicomachaean Ethics* (conclusion).

[114] Compare the suit prosecuted in Chicago by "officials of two north suburbs [who] said they will try to halt construction of the Sears Tower [the world's tallest skyscraper] on grounds that the alleged television interference it will create will hurt property values. . . . 'Such interference [one of them said] will greatly reduce the desirability of these suburbs as a place to live' " (*Chicago Daily News,* March 24, 1972, p. 8). But see Plato's *Apology* on the desirability of keeping one's neighbors from corruption. See also Herodotus, *History,* 1:134; note 93, this paper.

[115] "No home in America is so poor it does not have television. In fact, the poorer the home, the more time the children watch television" (*Chicago Tribune,* June 17, 1972, sec. 1, p. 8). See note 71, this paper.

In this critique of television I have challenged the implications of such typical observations as the three that follow: "As an official of a broadcast network said recently, television is 'the only mass entertainment and information medium that does not disfranchise the rural and urban poor' " (*Scientific American,* September 1972, p. 155). "I feel this—and I feel it passionately—people who deny themselves television deny themselves participation in life today. They are horse and buggy; they are atrophied; they are self-exiled from the world" (Rosenberg and White, eds., *Mass Culture Revisited,* p. 212). "Television is potentially one of our greatest windows on the world. It is one of the best ways in which we could expand our horizons, bring a sense of reality to faraway events, make a more informed judgment on public figures, share the lectures and demonstrations of our great universities, see the kind of opera, ballet, drama, museums, and concert artists

VII

How long will our present decline take to reach bottom? In the United States it could take generations, since we do have considerable political capital to draw upon. But the present generation of Americans may be the last one with a genuine opportunity to return the country to the "old way": there are still many among us who have been raised without the influence of television. Thus it can truly be said that "the crisis at which we are arrived may with propriety be regarded as the era in which that decision is to be

---

formerly available only to a few fortunate people, most of them in great cities. If television isn't being used that way, what a great social waste it is! What a loss we are suffering! And whose fault is it? Basically it is the fault of the people who don't watch it [because they consider it 'just trash'] and don't do anything about improving it" (Schramm, ed., *Mass Communications,* pp. 651–52). See also James Reston, "A Tribute to Television," *New York Times,* February 26, 1973. Cf. notes 89, 96, and 107, this paper.

I have been told by a former member of the Federal Communications Commission that mine is the first serious argument for the abolition of television which has come to his attention. (See note 4, this paper.) The trend, however, *is* in the other direction. Consider, for example, an editorial in the (London) *Observer,* October 22, 1972, p. 12: "The decision of the House of Commons to bar television cameras from its debates is lamentably shortsighted. Of course, they would have been 'intrusive' and liable to make people feel hot and uncomfortable under the glare. Certainly, extracts from debates would have needed careful editing, to avoid both boredom and giving undue attention to the more exhibitionist MPs. And the House's valuable intimacy of debate might well have been disturbed by those who fancied themselves as platform orators. It is also true that TV is often used merely to trivialise and entertain. All these objections have something in them, but they are really beside the point: which is that television, like it or not, is here to stay and is an important part of modern life. MPs deceive themselves if they think they can dismiss it without paying the price of growing isolation. Already many young people think Parliament out of date or irrelevant; they will now be confirmed in their view, and their number will increase.... Can nothing be done to dispel MPs' suspicions and save the Commons from its self-destructive decision?" But see notes 79, 82, 97, and 99, this paper.

However that may be, we have had the rule in our family, on the occasions when we have had a television set in the house (because of the misplaced generosity of well-meaning friends), that a short written report had to be prepared by each child for each program watched. (Children soon realize that most programs are not "worth the effort.") It should be added that families usually do not realize how much television they do watch. Nor do they usually realize how much valuable reading aloud to a child is casually sacrificed when television invades the home.

made," the decision whether "accident and force," rather than "reflection and choice," are to shape our lives. People shaped by television—by that most influential of the mass media—are, I have argued, destined thereafter "to depend for their political constitutions on accident and force."[116]

It *is* instructive that we do not (perhaps, by now, cannot) see the risks we are running, and that we will not do anything serious (partly because of immediate pleasures and profits, partly because of profound confusion about causes and effects and about the nature itself of cause and effect in moral and political matters) to attempt to return ourselves to a more austere and healthy way of life, a life more conducive to a republican form of government and to the full development of the human soul. It would also be instructive if the reader, in attempting to assess the argument I have presented here, should be induced to investigate and to make explicit what we take for granted as to *how* a particular way of life is established and perpetuated.[117]

[116] Or at least, it should be added, more so than their predecessors. The last four quotations in the text are from *Federalist* no. 1.

A recent comparison of the press and television, with respect to the alleged political "surveillance and sabotage" referred to in note 12, reinforces the observations made in this paper: "Other newsmen besides the [Washington] *Post*'s have been working the story hard. . . . [The *New York*] *Times*'s redoubled effort brought it some illuminating exclusives, as did similar enterprise by *Newsweek, Time, The Los Angeles Times,* and *The Washington Star-News.* The TV networks have been considerably less productive. 'It's not the kind of story we do best,' conceded the NBC Washington Chief. . . . 'It's not visual and it's also very complicated' " (*Newsweek,* October 30, 1972, pp. 76–77). But, it should be added, the further revelations recorded in note 65 of this paper did originate on a network news program. (It should also be added, however, that these further revelations did not seem at first glance to be as well documented as those produced by the press.) See also notes 69, 79, 81, 82, and 86, this paper. The *Newsweek* story concluded, "As the latest Louis Harris poll showed, most voters seemingly do not care much about [this affair]. But the story was far from over. 'As sure as God made apples,' predicted a *Washington Post* editor, 'this story will be with us after Election Day.' "

"Sen. George McGovern would edge President Nixon by 51 percent to 49 percent if last year's presidential election were held today, according to a nationwide poll conducted [by Oliver Quayle & Co.] for NBC News" *Chicago Sun-Times,* August 5, 1973, p. 6. See note 2, this paper.

[117] See Anastaplo, "Natural Right and the American Lawyer: An Appreciation of Professor Fuller," *Wisconsin Law Review,* 1965, p. 322; "Law and Morality: On Lord Devlin, Plato's *Meno,* and Jacob Klein," ibid., 1967,

It should be evident, from what I have said about the curtailment of television, that the case I have made in this paper for an absolute prohibition upon previous restraints of the press cannot rest simply upon a sentimental desire to see freedom "maximized." Rather, we are obliged to consider (if we are truly to govern ourselves) what among us promotes and serves human perfection, the common good, and hence a rational liberty. Such considerations can lead citizens to the reasoned conclusion that some activities in a community such as ours should be given free rein while others should be vigorously held in check.

---

p. 231; "Human Being and Citizen: A Beginning to the Study of Plato's *Apology of Socrates*," in *Ancients and Moderns,* ed. Cropsey.

A letter of mine to the editor of the *University of Chicago Maroon* (February 16, 1973, p. 7) suggests the modest contributions one can try to make, on the most local level, to the perpetuation of a civilized way of life. That letter, entitled "Epistle to the Barbarians," read,

"Several instances of mindless misconduct which I witnessed on the [University of Chicago] campus this weekend merit comment in a student newspaper.

"One evening I came upon a student shamelessly trying to remove an electric clock from a wall in Cobb Hall. The following evening I was seated in Bond Chapel where I could hear, in addition to a fine performance by the Collegium Musicum, the insistent thumping of the beat by one member of the audience and the repeated coughing by several others. Indeed, a chap in front of me managed to cough at least a dozen times during the concert.

"The casualness with which all this was done makes me suspect that these offenders—the would-be thief, the walruses and the thumper—may not know better. Perhaps no one has ever told them how to behave. Or perhaps they may even believe they are entitled to express themselves as they happen to please. They may not realize that such self-expression is no more than childish self-indulgence. Nor may they realize that self-discipline is vital to civilization and to development of a self worth taking seriously and 'expressing.'

"Of course, barbarians are not likely to read letters to the editor. But perhaps their acquaintances do—and can explain to them what we both have a right and a duty to expect of one another as of an academic community. Consider as an alternative, the fate of Mycalessus described by Thucydides (VII, 29)."

For an application to the "Watergate" and Presidential impeachment issues of the argument for moderation made throughout this paper, see Anastaplo, "Impeachment: Playing with Fire?", *University of Chicago Maroon,* November 30, 1973, p. 2 (reprinted in the *Chicago Sun-Times,* December 9, 1973, sec. 1A p. 3; also in *Congressional Record,* 119 [November 29, 1973]:E7595, *ibid.* [December 1, 1973]:E7672, *ibid.* [December 22, 1973]:E8185). The Republican Congressman who placed this article in the

Unless we are prepared to curtail the mass media and to restore the local press to its rightful place as the principal forum for general discourse among our citizens, we should expect to have hereafter only the masses rather than a community of citizens to reckon with. Indeed, there would then not even be any "we" to make judgments and to act. For "we" (as in "We the People") presupposes a public, not audiences, as fundamental to community and to the body politic.

Record of December 22, 1973, observed, "Mr. Anastaplo's approach . . . is by no means one favorable to the incumbant President. His thesis is that we may be going too far, that we may be 'playing with fire' on the impeachment issue because in his opinion it is not good for the country. Since Mr. Anastaplo's views present a somewhat different perspective on Presidential impeachment than the majority of those being offered, I insert the article for the benefit of my colleagues."

Moderation does not mean, however, that one should always "do nothing." See, e.g., Anastaplo, "The Case for Supporting Israel," *Chicago Sun-Times,* October 21, 1973, sec. 1A, p. 1 (reprinted in *Congressional Record,* 119 [November 5, 1973]: E7040). See also Anastaplo, "American Constitutionalism and the Virtue of Prudence: Philadelphia, Paris, Washington, Gettysburg," in *Abraham Lincoln, The Gettysburg Address and American Constitutionalism,* Leo Paul de Alvarez, editor (Irving: University of Dallas Press, 1974).

Cf. Plato, *Republic,* 344d.